WILDLIFE'S QUIET WAR

THE ADVENTURES OF TERRY GROSZ, U.S. FISH AND WILDLIFE SERVICE AGENT

TERRY GROSZ

WOLFPACK PUBLISHING

Print Edition

© Copyright 2018 Terry Grosz

Wolfpack Publishing
6032 Wheat Penny Avenue
Las Vegas, NV 89122

All rights reserved. No part of this book may be reproduced by any means without the prior written consent of the publisher, other than brief quotes for reviews.

ISBN: 978-1-62918-388-6

Library of Congress Control Number: 2018951316

Contents

Chapter One
Tule Fog "Catch Me If You Can" 1

Counting by Their Calls 25

An Adventure with a Tundra Swan 51

The "Pied Piper" 71

The Burly Bunch from Burlingame 92

Chapter Two
The First Animals Off Noah's Ark 121

The San Joaquin Valley's Baited Killing Fields 128

The Weed Field 132

The Burned Wheat Field 146

The Motel 6 Parking Lot Surprise 152

Trapping Dove and Outlaws in Bear Valley, Colusa County 157

Dove, Safflower and Wine Grapes 170

Chapter Three
A U.S. Game Management Agent's "Stew".....195

"Pow! Pow!".. 201

"Splash-Splash" 209

"Ka-Boom!".. 217

A Feather and a Fingerprint...................... 228

A Boatload of Decoys................................. 239

Closed-Season Pheasants by the Gob 247

The Illegal Taking
and Loss of a Great "Critter" 256

Chapter Four
The Stillwater Marshes of Nevada 263

Native American Rights? 270

One Chukar Feather
in the Wrong Place.. 281

"Them is Ring-Necks" and a
Local Politician Falls from Grace 292

"Johnnie Law" and Six Tundra Swans..... 320

Late Shooters and Lightning Storms 336

Chapter Five
Duck Club Funnies One "Red Hot" Duck Blind 369

    Scratch One Set of False Teeth 384

    Beaten Up by a Swan 398

    A "Dump" and a Dump 411

    "Quick, Hide in the Blackberry Bushes!" 427

    "Did You Fall In, Sir?" 450

    Ambushed from "Behind" 472

    Webbed Feet and "Grits" on the "Little Ol' Pea Picker's" Duck Club 491

Excerpt From Wildlife Dies Without Making a Sound, Vol. I: Chapter One

    Tule Lake 523

    Indian Tom Lake 530

About the Author 547

DEDICATION

This book is dedicated to Peter Grevie: loving father, adored husband, grandfather, friend to all, reformed duck "dragger," reformed commercial market hunter, conservative American patriot, deputy sheriff for Colusa County, lover of the world of wildlife, and my dear friend. Pete passed away in June of 2010.

Wherever you are, my friend, may your marshes be full of mallards and Northern pintail. May your duck calls be as on the money as is your shooting eye. When you arrive "home" that evening after the "duck hunt in the sky" with a limit of ducks, may it be to a roast duck dinner, mashed potatoes, thick gravy, fresh garden peas, hot sourdough biscuits, and an apple pie just out of the oven.

Later that evening as you sit out on the eternal porch at sunset with a drink in hand, may you hear the clarion call of Canada geese as you await the arrival of the rest of your dear friends from their earthly world far, far away...

Rest in peace, My Dear Friend.

Wildlife's Quiet War

TERRY GROSZ

Chapter One

**TULE FOG
"CATCH ME IF YOU CAN"**

DURING MANY WINTERS in the Northern Sacramento Valley there always occurred a unique duck and goose-killing weather-assisted phenomenon. That phenomenon was a very dense, ground-hugging fog. That fog sometimes lasted for weeks on end and is locally known as the "tule fog." I am not sure what causes the tule fog meteorologically to occur but with its occurrence the killing of ducks and geese by sportsmen and outlaws hits high gear. Hits high gear because the dense fog makes the flying ducks and geese virtually blind to the dangers awaiting below in the form of the gunning sportsmen. That is, except for the lordly Canada goose. When that species is moving around in the tule fog, they are as quiet as a bunch of mice pissing on a ball of cotton. All the other species of geese are frantically calling in the tule fog because they are so damned lost, and in the process, giving away their locations. And in so doing, many times ultimately "giving away" their lives as well. But not the Canada geese because for some reason they recognize the danger inherent in Mother Nature's dense gray blanket and what lethality many times lies below, especially if one is discovered within gunning range. They slip in and are gone before you even knew they were in country or can raise your shotgun for a killing shot. For some reason, that is just one of Mother Nature's flukes of nature. A fluke welcome to the lordly Canada goose but not so much to the lowly hunter trying to bag such a magnificent and many times difficult and wary bird to lure within gunning range.

In short, many times the fog is so thick that the ducks and geese have one hell of a time finding their ways around. That includes finding places to eat as well as safe places to land and rest. To those experienced in such natural occurrences, a large harvested rice field, skillful use of a good duck or goose call, and a pocketful of shot shells are all one needs in "greeting" such a "soon to be a critter in the pot" phenomenon. That killing opportunity went double for many of the Sacramento Valley's local outlaws possessing a gleam in their eyes, evil thoughts on their minds, and a wicked desire in their hearts to clean out Mother Nature's duck and goose pantry during such a climatological phenomenon.

When the Northern Sacramento Valley tule fogs were in their usual numerous and top dense forms, all one had to do for a good waterfowl shoot was to walk out into an open harvested rice field and listen. Soon one could hear the sounds of numerous lost ducks and geese flying by and many times calling in the dense fog. If one listened carefully, he could also hear the birds' wings hitting one another as they flew around in confused, dense flocks overhead. When the experienced shooter heard those sounds, he would give a couple of quick calls on his duck or goose call. Then listening carefully, he would be rewarded with the sounds of birds' wings hitting each other as they frantically turned around in mid-air towards the sounds of that guiding clarion call on the ground. Carefully listening, the shooter could hear the whistling wings of the flock of birds coming by once again. Only that time, the confused birds would be much lower and flying more slowly looking for the caller on the ground. The smart shooter would wait until the sounds of the near-at-hand birds had barely passed his position. Then would give a couple of quick calls once again. Instantly, the caller would be rewarded with the sounds of flying ducks or geese once again adjusting their flights and quickly turning around. In the process, all followed once again with the giveaway sounds of slapping, colliding wings from the confused flyers now almost overhead.

When that happened, the shooter needed to be ready because within moments he would be swarmed with low-flying ducks and geese looking for the caller on the ground. In short, he was swarmed by close-at-hand, confused birds trying to find a place to land where they last heard the shooter using his call. Then killing began big time because the birds would be fog-blinded, flying slowly, densely packed and in very close gunning range. And with that, based on the inclination of the shooter, the killing or overkilling began. Those sounds of fast and furious shooting during such foggy conditions would be the needed clues for the nearby law enforcement officer, if he was worth his salt and using his ears, to begin the "hunt" for his fellow man.

With the advent of the tule fog, the badge carrier would find his days filled with hard, long work hours trying to corral those taking advantage of the confused and easily killed birds.

Two reasons for the hard work and long hours were paramount. First, the fog concealed the gunner and, if he was so inclined to slaughter, he had the cover and opportunity to do so. Secondly, the confused birds made killing large over limits easier by their closeness, slower speeds, and their overall eagerness to land in order to get the hell out of the dense, vision- robbing fog.

However in my particular case, I had a third very personal reason for the extra hours worked. Every time the heavy tule fogs rolled in, without fail, I would usually get teasing phone calls from the same "voice." Those phone calls would go something like this when I answered the phone. "Is this Terry Grosz? If so, I will be out and about this fine duck-killing day in the fog. Catch me if you can,"...click. And with those challenging, maddening words, the phone would go deader than a car-hit great horned owl. That was usually when I had more damn ducks and geese in the valley than there were Democrat defense attorneys in hell. And my caller had been doing so with his challenging phone calls ever since I had arrived in the valley as a game warden in 1967 and continuing into later years after I became a United States Game Management Agent. Those maddening phone calls seemed to me to be coming ever since the Great Auk had marched into the silence of history (To my unwashed readers, the Great Auk was a penguin-like bird whose numbers were the first to be shot into extinction by American hunters. The last known pair were killed on their breeding grounds off the Atlantic Coast in 1844!).

Later, as the local U.S. Game Management Agent assigned to a Sacramento Valley county that didn't "cotton" to conservation officer types because of many of the locals' past illegal market hunting histories, both my wife and I began getting challenging calls incessantly when the tule fogs rolled into the valley from my unknown challenging outlaw (before caller I.D.). Or even worse, my wife would get calls from the same "voice" saying, "Mrs. Grosz, you need to come down to the Sheriff's Office. Your husband has just been shot in the face with a shotgun and we need you to come in and identify the body... " click.

When such phone challenges, as I called them, rolled my way, I would gear up and head back out into the wildlife field of battle. To my readers, you must remember several things. Things that my local outlaws always seemed to forget. First, it is not nice to mess with Mother Nature or her minions. Second, I knew the Northern Sacramento Valley like the back of my hand. And for the most part, I knew where my ducks and geese would more or less be congregated. With that information and the weather factored in, I would head for my historical hot spots in the hope of catching my "challenging caller" in action. And you could bet your bottom Carson City Morgan silver dollar, if I did manage to cross my caller's path, he would get some "challenging" action as well...

Well, one fine tule fog day, just as sure as Mrs. God makes great gooseberry jam, elder berry jelly, and beer biscuits for Her Fella, I got my usual "catch me if you can" call. This call I was used to, not only due to the now commonly occurring, foggy winter weather events, but now because of the familiar sameness of the tone and tenor of my caller's voice as well. A voice that was so distinctive to my way of thinking after hearing it so many times, that all I needed was to hear it spoken to me face to face. When that happened, you could bet your bottom dollar my caller would be treated with the utmost kindness, patience, loving care, and professionalism...

The only problem I had, well, I had more than one even though I knew my district, was one of time and space. I had a federal law enforcement district that encompassed many thousands of square miles of the Northern Sacramento Valley's wonderful rice farming grounds. This area was commonly used extensively by just about every "waterfowler" for hunting the excellent-tasting, rice-fed species of waterfowl during the winter months. Especially so when the tule fogs arrived. I also had more than three hundred operating private and commercial duck clubs in addition to all my local, unattached field gunners. Just try to find one chap and his familiar voice in that stack of rice straw, goose droppings, tule roots, and spent shotgun shells, if you will. Then throw into that "soup" the covering effects of the dense fog and the great waterfowl hunting going on just about anywhere a duck or goose could drop their feathered behinds. With all those factors, one ultimately had a hat full of hornets even if he was a skilled conservation officer, if you get my drift. Bottom line, the officer held a hand of aces and eights (hopefully you readers know your Deadwood, South Dakota, Wild Bill Hickok history in the late 1800s and what such a hand held for him...), and the wildlife outlaw, a straight flush. But, God was the dealer in such a "card game" and after all, He did in fact create all the critters who had little or no voice, didn't He?

To give all you readers a taste of just how bad the fog could get for the birds, how about this. Several times during my years in the Northern Sacramento Valley, I observed ducks and geese trying to land in the lighted, wet city streets at night thinking it was water. They were that confused by the tule fog... Or they landed on the flat tops of buildings holding a little rainwater from the latest rainstorm thinking it was more than it really was. Or, when driving down the highway, one could only see three white stripes ahead in the road at a time!

When those great wet fogs rolled in, I would average apprehending anywhere from thirty to forty shooters a week with over limits of ducks and geese and for other collateral violations! Just imagine how many more illegal waterfowl shooters throughout the vast Northern Sacramento Valley I missed! Then multiply that by the usual number of tule fogs that rolled into the valley in the winter months annually. Suffice to say, Custer had better odds when it came to knocking the Indians out from their saddles with his single shot, trap-door 45- 70s, during his little skirmish in 1876 in Montana. Truth be known, it seems history has revealed that less than forty Indian warriors were ever killed by Custer's men...! Kind of gives you readers an idea as to the odds I faced even knowing the area as well as I did.

As I was saying before I got carried away, that fine morning so long ago after receiving my usual "catch me if you can" phone call, I loaded up my faithful Labrador retriever, Shadow, into the back of my truck after only three hours of sleep between the two of us, kissed my bride goodbye, and disappeared into the swirling foggy mists. Knowing that just about anywhere I went that morning, I would have "some business" to attend to because I had so many wintering ducks and geese in the valley (over a million!), along with a bushel basket full of lads with itchy trigger fingers who couldn't count for sour owl droppings, off I went with a happy heart.

For starters, I headed west down Highway 20 towards a small local town named Williams. About the time I approached Lone Star Road, my guardian angels were doing "flip-flops." That was their way of telling me some "catching" was in the wind, eh, fog, if I minded my P's and Q's in that historic specific gunning area. With those "warnings in the wind," I turned south on Lone Star Road. Arriving at the junction of Meyers and Lone Star Roads, I stopped, got out of my truck, and listened. By then the tule fog was so thick, I couldn't see more than thirty yards in any direction. But I could still hear, and being blessed with a set of ears like that of a great horned owl or a kit fox, I put them to good use.

Off to my east I heard just one shot. Thinking nothing more about that one shot, I continued standing there in the road bathed in the swirling foggy mists listening because I always had a policy of "moving to the sound of the guns" when "hunting humans." The more guns I heard, the faster I moved! I figured that way I would always be in the middle of anything hitting the fan, if you get my drift. As it turned out, that morning's fog was so thick and wet, any sounds of shooting seemed very distant and almost soft-sounding in nature. True to form, I heard little of interest in that neck of the woods up to that point in time.

Just as I was getting back into my truck so I could "cast my net elsewhere for some little fishes," like the Good Book says, I heard my "one-shot" shooter again. This time from the sound of it, he had changed positions, moving slightly to the northwest.

Then my instincts and guardian angels clamoring around inside my being got the better of me. Why only one shot in such fog with so many birds aloft? I asked myself. Having hunted in such conditions, I never had less than a mess of ducks or geese responding to my calling at any given time. To my way of thinking, only shooting one shot at a time under such potentially great hunting conditions now began piquing my interest. Perhaps "One-Shot" was a serious killer and didn't want to bring any attention to himself, I thought. Self, I thought, maybe we need to fathom that shooter out and examine his intentions more closely. Especially if this "one-shot shooter" is using that technique to throw any "human-hunting law dogs" in his vicinity off his trail.

Picking up and moving east, I stopped just shy of Ohm Road, bailed out, walked a short distance from my vehicle, and listened once again. Listening carefully, I could tell the air was full of birds by all the calling and "wing slapping" I was hearing. Then just north of me towards the Colusa National Wildlife Refuge, I heard my one-shot chap have at it once again. Moments later, an alarmed mess of ducks swished loudly over my head in the fog numbering at least a hundred. I will bet you that is the flock my chap had just shot, I thought, now starting to get really interested in my "one shot at a time" shooter.

To my readers, I had always found over the years that a lone shooter was a proven good bet for a pinch. Be it hunting without a license, no duck stamp, an over limit, or some other sort of chicanery, "singletons" as I called them, when checked, usually were "money in the bank." And my one-shot shooting chap could very well fall into that category with the tule fog, tons of birds, and all, I now surmised.

Hiding my truck among a mess of idle parked farm equipment, I gathered up Dog and took a look at the compass I always carried. With that, I took a bearing on the echolocation of my shooter's last shot. Hopping a small ditch alongside the road, Dog and I headed northwest into the swirling mists. Coming to my first rice check in the field, I paused and listened for the longest time. True to form, the air was filled with nearby ducks and lesser snow geese trying to find a rice field in which to land and feed. They knew from their "onboard natural compasses" and instincts, there was a rice field below them. But damned if they could chance a forty-mile-an-hour flight downward without knowing where the ground was. To do otherwise meant a smashed bill full of rice mud and possible broken bones at the airspeed they routinely traveled.

Boom went my shooter and, from the sound of the fog- dampened shot, it came from the northwest once again! Only this time it sounded like it was about 150 yards distant from where I now stood. Once again within moments of the shot, the air was filled with the whistling wings and ghostly, fog shrouded sights of alarmed and fleeing ducks and geese. With that, Dog and I again moved northward towards our shooter heading for the next rice check in the field and the cover it offered in the process.

Arriving, I took a long look into the fog with my binoculars with no discernible human discovery results. Then stepping off the rice check, I surprisingly found myself standing amidst a dozen freshly killed ducks hidden in the tall water grass heretofore unseen! Kneeling down, I felt the birds' bodies under their wings for body temperature. All of them were still warm to the touch indicating they had been freshly killed. Looking all around, my eyes discovered only gently misting fog droplets raining off my eyelashes for my "look-see" efforts. Then I noticed a pair of footprints leading from the base of the rice check off into the fog and the middle of the freshly harvested, muddy rice field. Figuring that sign was as good as any other clue I had, Dog and I carefully began cold-tracking our footprint maker and hopefully our "one-shot" shooter.

Arriving at the next rice check, Dog and I stopped and listened once again. Then Shadow pitched off the rice check and stuck her nose into the tall water grasses a few yards distant. Up she came with a deader-than-a-hammer Northern pintail drake! Taking the duck from her, I felt its body for warmth under its wings. It, too, had been freshly killed, and as I looked northward into the dense fog, Shadow was quickly at my side once again. This time, she was carrying an American wigeon (medium-sized duck)! Realizing she had found another cache of ducks, I dug into the adjacent water grasses as well. Thirteen ducks later, I had a pile of freshly killed ducks lying at my feet on that rice check as well.

Boom went my shooter once again, only that time he was not a hundred yards distant! Damn, I thought. I have a real killer on my hands! He is out in the middle of nowhere, firing only one shot at a time, and stashing his ducks as he walks along, hiding the evidence in the rice check's grasses. That way he doesn't have to carry the weight of the dead birds and if checked by a law dog, he will be lacking any incriminating evidence of wrongdoing.

It was at that point I began to get pretty darned excited. This case had all the trappings of a very good and experienced local outlaw doing what he did best. And it was always more fun to catch the locals breaking the laws of the land then the run-of-the-mill-dummies. Fun, because many of the better local outlaws needed "catching" anyway, and two, they would subsequently spread the word that the long arm of the law was aggressively out and about among the illegal duck-killing fraternity after being caught themselves. With that kind of word being out and about, it had a chilling effect on many of my locals, especially when it came to pulling their triggers more than they should have. Well, at least for a short period of time, until their necks "swelled" once again with the primal urge to kill rising up from within their miserable carcasses, that is.

Realizing to carry forth wandering about any further might just spook off my man, especially if he saw me before I saw him, I went to ground. Dog and I laid alongside the grassy rice check next to the latest stash of discovered ducks, listened, and waited. I figured it was just a matter of time before my man would return, backtracking himself in the soft mud to fetch his ducks. When he did, I would "fetch" my duck-killin' chap in fine style with his hands deep inside Mother Nature's "duck" cookie jar. Moving a little further down the rice check to a denser stand of water grass to better hide my rather beautiful and magnificent-sized, "pitcher's mound"-like carcass, Dog and I continued "lurking in the bushes."

For the next two hours, Dog and I shivered in the dampness accompanying the rolling, dripping wet fog. Then I noticed the fog was thinning out and beginning to lift somewhat. Lying there hidden on the edge of the rice check, I glassed the area all around me because my one-shot chap had been moving every-which-way around the two sections of land, on which Dog and I currently occupied as indicated by the sounds of his shooting.

With the rising fog, I was finally able to better get my bearings. I discovered I was in the middle of the same rice check in which I had discovered the first pile of ducks! How I got turned around was beyond me, but sure as God made the world's best blackberries for my wife's homemade pies, there I was in all my goofy glory. I guess in all my enthusiasm to catch my suspected shooter, I hadn't bothered to pay heed to my "inboard" compass. Hell, I had been just as lost as many of my overflying ducks had been. To compound the situation even further, my shooter was now nowhere to be seen!

Fortunately, I was still well-hidden and had parked my undercover truck in among a mess of idled rice harvesters and bank out wagons (bank out wagons-a wheeled transport vehicle with a big open tank in the rear, used to transfer the rice grains from the harvesters in the field to a waiting truck and trailer) in an adjacent field. As such, it fit right in and no one, unless they were really looking, would spot my "wheels." That was a good thing, I thought. Because if my shooter or his "drop-off" had discovered my presence, they would be long gone and the ducks would stay in the field until they rotted or were eaten by the local quadrupeds (skunks, foxes, feral hogs, coyotes, racoons, rats, feral house cats).

Dog and I stayed on our rice check until just about dark when the fog began flooding back rather heavily into the valley once again. By then both Dog and yours truly were so hungry we were about ready to eat a couple of the evidence ducks raw. But still no one showed. I was just beginning to wonder if maybe I had been spotted in the field earlier and my "one-shooter" had split the area for good.

Then, a lone black Chevy pickup slowly drove down Meyers Road from the west. Moments later, it sped up, continuing on its way "like nobody's business." Twenty minutes later, the same lone black pickup came slowly driving back down the road. By now it was so dark and foggy, I couldn't make out the driver or any other distinguishing features on the now-suspect vehicle. Finally the pickup slowed and then stopped in the middle of the road. Shortly thereafter, it once again sped off towards Ohm Road. There it turned and sped off to the south. What the heck? I thought. I was sure no one had seen me and yet the truck sure acted peculiarly.

Then out from a small ditch running along the south side of Meyers Road leapt a lone figure sprinting into my field! Running until he reached the first rice check, my runner disappeared behind its mounded earth. Then for the next hour until I no longer could see, I observed nothing moving! Now it was darker than the inside of a dead cow. The sun had long since set according to my watch, and the fog had rolled into the area like a heavy wet woolen blanket. Not a sound could be heard and certainly not much could be seen. But I was still sitting on my mess of freshly killed ducks and that was a given until hell froze over. Plus, I had a highly trained dog who had been chasing duck-killing knotheads for several years now. And, it was hard to beat a good set of dog's ears and their sense of smell when it came to work of the moment.

Then Shadow rose from where she had been snoring most of the afternoon and passed the most God-awful smelling gas imaginable. Sitting back down on her haunches with what had to be a doggy grin, she stared hard towards our pile of ducks not twenty feet away in the dark. Damn, I thought, I certainly hope a skunk hasn't discovered our cache of ducks and is making himself a meal. It was then that I heard the sounds of someone softly walking in our muddy rice field and stubble coming my way! Boy, if those welcome sounds didn't get my cold blood flowing! With that, I waited until the sounds of his boots crunching on rice stubble stopped and I could hear the faint rustling of my pile of close-at-hand evidence ducks being picked up in the tall grasses a few feet distant. Shadow was quietly sitting at my feet and hardly moved but I could tell she was alert as was a mink who was close to a mouse.

Quietly standing, I turned on my flashlight in the direction of the stash of ducks. In the process, I had gathered myself up for the anticipated "jack rabbit" run that was sure to follow from my suspect once the light came on announcing the presence of another close-at-hand human being. To an outlaw's way of thinking, that light source meant nothing nice was in the offing because no one in his right mind would be out in the damp, cold rice field that time of the night unless it was the "law" or an "outlaw." And since he was the outlaw, that could only leave one less-than-favorable prospect of that remaining combination to my visitor's way of surprised thinking.

It was almost as if Bob Brown (not his real name, because his kids still live in the area and I won't embarrass them) from the Town of Williams knew I would be there. Immediately he threw into my face a double duck strap loaded full of ducks previously collected from his other stash points in the field. Then turning on a dime, off he sped into the fog with Dog and me hot on his trail after I had shed his duck straps of thrown ducks.

"Take 'em, Shadow," I yelled as I hit my full stride and got "up on my pursuit step." In an instant, Shadow had a hold of the right sleeve on his hunting jacket. Just about the time my dog arrived so did I in all my John Wayne, "She Wore A Yellow Ribbon", magnificence. When I did, I was sure glad for the soft mud in the rice field because the three of us made one hell of a high-speed, skidding dent in the muck when we collided!

"You got me! You got me!" he yelled as I dug my right shoulder into his back with a flying tackle reminiscent of my earlier college football days as a defensive lineman.

"Let him go, Shadow," I yelled. Shadow let him go but stood over him as if figuring maybe another bite was still needed for all the trouble he had caused in my dog's missing her usual dinner. By then, especially after the crunching tackle, Bob had given up "lock, stock and barrel.'

Recognizing who he was, I said, "You knothead. What the hell did you run for?" I asked as I rose from the mud along with my capture (Even though I was a large man, I was fast for my size. In my younger college days, weighing in at over 265 pounds, I could run a hundred- yard dash in full football gear in eleven seconds. Plus, up until that time, I had never lost a foot race in the valley when chasing my outlaws and had such a reputation.). In so doing, I noticed I sported a generous gob of rice field muddy slop all over my beautiful body. Unfortunately that mud was accompanied by the smell of rotting crawdads and carp that had died in the field when it had been drained prior to harvesting. Now I smelled just as badly as had Shadow when she passed gas earlier back on the rice check.

"You damn well know why, Terry. It is not a good thing being caught by you guys, especially you out here in the valley in the eyes of the local folks," he quietly replied as he got over the surprise, scare and subsequent "dainty" tackle of his capture.

Then it hit me. That voice! I was sure it was the "catch me if you can" voice I had heard numerous times on my phone over the years as a game warden and now as a U.S. Game Management Agent!

"Bob, did you call me this morning at my

home and challenge me to 'catch me if you can?'" I asked. When I asked, I made sure my flashlight light was square on his face so I could see his reaction to what had to be my surprising question.

"No! Hell no, Terry!" he replied, but not very convincingly to my way of thinking, as his eyes instantly looked downward and away from my face.

&

"Look at me, Bob. Are you sure? Because it sure as hell sounded like you this morning and in times past," I challenged once again, "now that I think of it."

"No, I am not that stupid, Terry. I know your reputation for running someone down who has broken the law. Especially if he challenges you like Harry Dart did over an illegal deer"—a case that took me over a year to make after Harry Dart, one of my local outlaws, challenged me by saying I was too damn dumb to catch him.—"That sure as hell wasn't me," he continued, with his not-so-convincing denials and downcast, looking away to the left, eyes (to the serious investigator, a move many times denoting a guilty answer).

However, I was pretty damn sure I had my man with the "catch me if you can" voice on the telephone when the tule fog rolled into the Sacramento Valley. Still looking hard at my capture for a few more moments, I finally let the questioning go. I may have been built like a pitcher's mound but I wasn't that dumb. He was my "man" alright and inside, even though cold and hungry as I was, I felt elated and pretty damn-well satisfied., especially since he had called me with the "catch me if you can" challenge just that morning and now I had him.

After the two of us had picked up all his stashed ducks he had thrown earlier, we walked back to my vehicle. There we cleaned the ducks so they would not spoil. All 54 of them to be exact! Like I said earlier, singletons were always a good bet for doing something wrong when it came to the world of wildlife. And that present capture was nothing more than pure validation of that maxim.

Then I asked rather pointedly, "Bob, who dropped you off?"

"You know I can't tell you that," he replied. "If I did that, my name would be mud in this here valley as a snitch from now on," he continued with worry building in his voice.

I knew what he was saying was true, but I had to ask anyway. Bob also knew if he gave up the name of his drop-off driver, that chap would be getting a citation for aiding and abetting in Bob's little duck-killing venture, just as sure as God made outstanding golden sunsets.

I gave Bob a ride home and there sitting in his folks' driveway sat a similar black Chevy pickup like I had seen dropping him off earlier in the evening. I later discovered it belonged to his cousin from Sacramento and since I had nothing further to go on regarding that piece of the puzzle, that chap skated around the long arm of the law for his aiding and abetting adventure. However, I was dead sure that was the same chap who had dropped Bob off to do his duck-retrieving walk-about in the rice field after the fog had lifted somewhat and the shooting opportunities had vanished with it. Which by so doing, being dropped off that is, allowed Bob to not give away his presence in the field with a suspiciously parked vehicle alongside the roadway, especially to the potential prying eyes of a wildlife law dog on the hunt.

Bob later forfeited bail to the tune of $500.00 in Federal Court in Sacramento. That was the maximum monetary fine in those days under the Migratory Bird Treaty Act. I gave all Bob's ducks to the Colusa County Sheriff's Office so they could be fed to the prisoners and help reduce some of the county's costs associated with their food care. From the looks on the prisoners' faces as they picked all those fat rice-fed ducks, the new menu item was a much anticipated and happy coming event.

That was also the last time I ever checked Bob in the field hunting ducks or geese when the fogs rolled into the valley. You know, after that episode, I never again got another "catch me if you can" phone call from a mystery voice when the tule fog rolled into the Northern Sacramento Valley either. Gee, I wonder why?

COUNTING BY THEIR CALLS

Rolling out from bed at four in the morning, I quietly showered in the shower at the far end of my ranch style home and dressed so as not to awake my two "fireball" sons. In the meantime, Donna, my long-suffering bride, rustled around in our kitchen making me one of her world famous "last-him-all-day" breakfasts. For you chow hound/non-game warden type readers, that breakfast consisted of a pound of fried side pork (an old-time favorite of both me and my dad), fried spuds, four eggs sunny side up, several slices of Donna's world's best homemade bread, a quart of buttermilk (when it was real buttermilk with the big chunks of orange butterfat therein, not the weak-kneed, thin, tasteless gruel they call buttermilk today...), and a generous slice of my bride's "fantabulous" carrot cake. It was a great breakfast in those days and one guaranteed to allow me to run through an 18-hour day without any further grits like "fat through a goose" without a backward hungry glance. But a guaranteed cholesterol killer for this old and getting ready to die carcass of mine during this day and age at the time these words are being written. Damn, it's hell getting old! I don't recommend it for you reader-game warden types or anyone else who routinely beats the hell out of your bodies for that matter.

Kissing my bride good-bye, I loaded Dog into my three-quarter-ton Dodge truck, warmed it up and sailed out into another day's adventures in the world of wildlife law enforcement. Another day's adventures in a typically thick Northern Sacramento Valley winter tule fog that is. Traveling north on the Princeton Highway, I soon turned onto the Maxwell Highway and headed due west. Stopping near the junction of the Maxwell and Four-Mile Roads, I bailed out into the wet foggy soup and quietly listened for the telltale sounds of feeding or resting concentrations of waterfowl. Nearby to my north, Delevan National Wildlife Refuge was a veritable buzz of hundreds of thousands of resting and waking waterfowl all eager for another day of feasting in nearby Colusa, Butte, Glenn, Sutter, Yolo, and Sacramento Counties' recently harvested rice fields. Soon it began getting lighter in the thick fog, and then behind me I heard the roaring sounds of thousands of frantically beating wings lifting off from the refuge in the morning's waterfowl world of wildlife daily "liftoff."

Turning, I observed a huge undulating flock of blackbirds numbering in the tens of thousands emerging from the thick fog as they left their historic tree roosts on the refuge as well. They, too, were heading south for their morning's feeding grounds. Then it happened! In the dense fog as they flew across the Maxwell Highway, the front of the flock flew into the unseen high voltage transmission lines paralleling the highway. In an instant, there was a bright flash of brilliant green light as the birds in the damp fog flew into the killing range of the transmission line's electrical field! Then that bright electrical flash instantly ran back the length of the horde of "bumper-to-bumper" blackbirds in an explosive, crackling arc, and out of sight into the fog on the refuge! How far that aerial electrocution went I didn't know. But I would bet it went the full length of that densely packed flock of blackbirds because of the moisture in the air and the closeness of the birds once they entered the electrical field. Within moments, the air was instantly filled with thousands of brightly falling, sparkling green "diamonds" of dead electrocuted blackbirds! Never in my life had I seen such a mass killing phenomenon! Seconds later, the air was filled with the acrid stench of burned feathers. Amazed at what I had just witnessed, I got back into my truck and drove to the scene of the blackbird electrocutions along the highway and stared in surprise at the road's densely covered and still smoking, bird carcass littered surface. It was carpeted with thousands of dead, charred, still smoking blackbirds! Man, you talk about a mess! It became an even bigger mess later in the day after dozens of vehicles had run over the squishy carpet of bird bodies... However, there were some benefits to those mass electrocutions. The area's yellow-billed magpies and crows sure enjoyed their cooked dinners of filet of blackbird scattered across the highway and refuge lands for the next several day as I am sure did the skunks, foxes, raccoons, feral house cats, and resident Norway rats.

Standing there all agog, the close-at-hand thumping of several shotguns further to my north brought me back from the mass blackbird electrocutions event to reality and my mission at hand for the day. Turning away from the smoking blackbird scene, I listened intently for anymore of those tell-tale sounds of shots being fired. By now, huge numbers of ducks and geese were noisily leaving the refuge as they grouped their ways in the dense fog to their feeding grounds. Their wing-slapping collisions and confused calls in the dense fog, once they left the comforts of the refuge's watered areas, were more than plain to the ear. Soon the thumping of shotguns could be faintly heard again to the north and west. That time I got a rough fix on the shooting sounds' locations. As near as I could tell, the shooting was taking place on the north end of the Newhall Farms' recently harvested rice lands.

That made sense, I thought as I bailed back into my truck. Newhall Farms was one huge mass of freshly harvested rice fields. Being that close and adjacent to the Delevan National Wildlife Refuge made it a natural choice for the masses of hungry waterfowl now leaving that area's confines as they winged their ways to "breakfast." That way the migrating birds didn't have to burn up much precious energy in such a short flight to their chosen field of breakfast "grits." Plus, the birds' "onboard radars" told them the rice fields were near-at-hand, hence their massive flyovers to the adjacent farm properties on the western side of the refuge.

Finally swinging into the Gunner's Field properties just to my north off Four-Mile Road, I turned off my truck's engine, got out, and listened once again. The tule fog was full of milling and confused birds and, if the shooters now directly to my west were so inclined, it would be just a matter of time before they shot once again. Overhead flew thousands of lesser snow geese, easily identified by their characteristic, noisy calls. They were heading due west and I figured they would soon be over my mystery shooters.

Moments later, nothing happened as suspected in the way of shooting as the snow geese milled back and forth over the Newhall Farms' recently harvested rice grounds shrouded in dense fog. That's strange, I thought. Why aren't my chaps shooting? They sure as all get-out have a mess of fine shooting overhead with all the snow geese that are close-at-hand in the air, I thought in puzzlement.

Then overhead, not more than thirty yards off the ground, passed a huge flock of Pacific white-fronted geese identified by their unique trilling calls. Off to the west they also flew and soon I heard a rattle of shots being fired from at least three shotguns. Then it dawned on me! My shooters had to be experienced gunners. They had earlier passed up shooting the lesser snow geese because of their poorer eating qualities. But when the excellent culinary delights, primarily seed-eating white-fronts had swung into gun range, that species got hammered. Damn, I thought. These chaps are experienced in what they are doing. They can recognize the difference in calls between the snow geese and white-fronts in the dense fog. With that differentiation, they were selectively gunning the white-fronts! And since the white-fronts are the better-eating geese, it is those they are selectively shooting when their shapes dimly appeared in the dense fog.

Therein could be a problem, raced through my mind. One could kill six snow geese per person per day in those days. However, the limit on the better-eating white-fronts, or what were considered "dark geese" in those days, was only three per day per person. If one was so inclined to just shoot the better-eating geese in this heavy fog, he would soon have an over limit rather quickly. Especially if he selectively shot and could hit his last part over the fence, I grimly thought.

Leaving my truck parked at the edge of the Gunner's Field property, I let Dog out, and into the foggy nearby Newhall Farms' rice fields we hustled by shank's mare. Stopping and taking a compass bearing on the last shots fired by my shooters, we hotfooted it in that direction.

Overhead the air whirred with the sounds of wings and calls of thousands of ducks and geese as I soon broke out into a sweat laboring across the muddy rice fields. Damn, Terry, I thought. One needs to be lighter than a feather and not as heavy across the "axe handle" as yours truly, if he is to go charging across these danged sticky and muddy rice fields with any degree of speed. Maybe that monster breakfast I had consumed with relish earlier was partially to blame, eh? Perhaps if I hadn't eaten that second piece of my bride's carrot cake...

Overhead flew hundreds more lesser snow

geese and, welcoming the stop and rest I now took, I listened once again. Sure as hell, there were no shots fired by my mystery shooters as that species of goose presented themselves in a swirling mass of tempting targets dead ahead in the fog. Then the swishing sounds of hundreds of ducks which I identified as Northern pintail by their beautiful fluting calls could be heard sailing overhead in the thick fog. With the appearance of that excellent-eating species, my shooters once again opened up. Then I really became interested in my three shooters. It was more than obvious that they were good and experienced at this waterfowl-shooting "thing" in the thick fog. It had become readily apparent when the poorer-eating birds were in country no shots were fired. However, when the better-eating ducks and geese appeared, they banged away like the Yankees did at the Rebels during George Pickett's charge at Gettysburg in 1863. In that dense fog if my shooters could hit their hind ends with both hands, there would be no tomorrow for many of the species that had sailed into their deadly shotguns range. It would be just as deadly as it was for many of the Johnny Rebs on their field of battle at Gettysburg that fateful day in the history of this great country of ours.

Another mess of white-fronts drifted overhead in the dense fog calling loudly for any of their buddies who might now be feeding on the rice ground. Shortly thereafter, a thunderous salvo of shots rent the foggy morning air. I was now close enough so that I could clearly hear the whumps of the heavily bodied geese violently meeting Mother Earth for the last time after being shot out of the air. But I still couldn't see my close-at-hand shooters in the dense fog. However, I was now in the ballpark and within striking distance. Especially if after a barrage of shots the "ground-whumping" of "identified by their calls" goose bodies amounted to any kind of hearing-evidence in the "over limit" department.

Then the evil being who protects all manner of outlaws now sharply intervened! I came to a deep, flooded ditch and, after much frantic searching, couldn't find any place to safely cross unless I wanted to take a swim! Taking a fully-clothed swim during that time of the winter was not really high on my "bucket list" of to- do things. More Pacific white-fronts thundered by and after the shooting had ceased, I clearly heard nine mud-smacking whumps when the dead geese hit the ground. To my way of thinking, that put my shooters over their limits of that species of goose! Way over! Now I was really in a tizzy. I couldn't find any easy way to cross that damn ditch without walking quite a distance in each direction to a known farm equipment crossing.

And dang it, my shooters were just out of "grabbing" range on the other side, still hidden by the dense fog!

Realizing I was in a quandary, I took off trotting back from the direction I had just come towards the closest known farm equipment crossing. Covering about two hundred yards in that direction, I came to a narrow point in the ditch at which I thought I could safely cross. Wrong! Thinking I had solid ground on which to leap upon on the far side of the ditch, I took a chance. Getting up a head of steam, I leaped with all my might like the slightly oversized "gazelle" I was. Alright you readers who know me, a rather stout-sized gazelle, ok? However, the landing spot I had selected was not as solid as I had hoped. In fact, it was nothing short of being pure grass-covered, "lure the stupid federal agent into jumping on top of me" goo! When my dainty three-hundred-plus pounds landed at a high rate of speed, I went right up to my armpits in the icy cold, muddy slop! Dog, who had jumped along with me, found herself in slop up to her chin as well. For the next twenty minutes my shooters banged away at every flock of mallards, Northern pintail and Pacific white-fronts that came by. Me, I struggled like all get-out to rid myself of my stuck-in-the-damn-sucking-mud, up to my armpits position. Finally pulling free and "swimming" my way to shore in the muck, I found solid footing. Scrambling up the far ditch bank, I paused just long enough to clean the mud from the barrel and cylinder of my .44 magnum which had been immersed in the muck as well. Clean it to the point of taking nearby water grass stems to clean the mud out from inside the barrel and cylinders in case I had to shoot some damn dingbat! And at that point in time, I think I would have shot just about anyone for any damn silly infraction of the waterfowl regulations based on my stupid decision at trying my hand at winter mud-jumping-over-a-ditch... The rest of my beautiful carcass could wait, but not the business end of my making a living and staying alive, I thought, as I dug out the last of the clinging mud from the internal workings of my handgun.

Now fuming over my lost opportunity at stopping my shooters from killing gross over limits and having taken a cold damn beautification mud bath in the process, I picked up my closing pace. If nothing else, my jogging rid myself of much of the embarrassing chunks of mud, goose shit and tule roots stubbornly clinging to my magnificent carcass after my dip into the slop. Not all, mind you, but just enough so if asked, I could swear it was part of my natural camouflage to avoid further embarrassing questions that were sure to come once I confronted my shooters...

By now my shooters had stopped shooting. The air was still full of confused birds looking for a place to land, but my chaps had now gone to ground and stopped shooting for some reason. Taking that as an indication that they may now be leaving or gathering up their gear, I went into my sneak mode. Yeah, dang some of you doubting readers. A mud-covered guy my size can sneak and pretty damn quickly if need be. I may not have been a good ditch jumper but a great sneaker I was... However in this immediate circumstance, I now took my time stalking. In the process, I "put on" my best set of mud-covered ears in order not to miss what might be going on with my "still out of sight" shooters. Soon, I was so close to my shooters that I could hear them quietly talking and smell nicotine from the cigarettes they were now smoking. However, I still could not see my chaps in the dense fog. But I was now almost within grabbing range if they decided to jack rabbit on me. And if that were the case, I always chased the largest bodied of my culprits. By so doing, I could always catch the slowest runner of the bunch and thereby gain some satisfaction after my morning's unplanned beautification mud bath treatment. By the way, that beautification treatment did not work...

Stopping and kneeling down to catch our breath, Dog and I held our ground for a few short moments. Then here came more white-fronts and boy, did my chaps let loose a bucket load of lead shot (steel shot was not required or even commercially available in those days). Based on the flock's uniquely trilling calls prior to the shooting, once again I clearly heard seven more whumps of white- fronted goose bodies hitting the soft rice field mud. Now I figured just as sure as the Japanese are still illegally killing whales under the guise of research in the Antarctic, my chaps had major over limits of that species of goose. With that, Dog and I sprang into action like a pair of cheetahs. Well, maybe a couple of mud-coated, slower-moving cheetahs...

Now quickly walking towards the hushed voices of my shooters, I soon came onto about a dozen goose decoys scattered about randomly in the field. At the end of the decoy set near a rice check stood three chaps whom I recognized as some of my local outlaws living in the Delevan area. Soon as those "brave heroes of the day" saw my beautiful hulk emerging from the fog, they ducked down behind the rice check like they had just seen a tiger shark. Now, I know you lads are in the muck as deeply as I was earlier, I thought, based on the exhibition of such furtive movements on their parts, my identification of the geese being shot by their unique calls in the fog, and the numerous whumps I had heard hitting the ground throughout my ditch-jumping interrupted approach.

"Morning, lads. Nice foggy morning," I said as I walked through their decoys. As I did, I picked up two freshly killed white-fronts. "How is the hunting going, lads?" I asked in the most innocent and sweetest of "said the spider to the fly" tones. Finally three heads popped up from behind the rice check after realizing they were had.

The looks on their collective faces told me they would rather be eating Limburger cheese than seeing my beautiful carcass emerging from the fog. Kind of like the same looks on the faces of the Japanese carrier captains when they recognized those were unhampered American dive bombers diving on their fleet at the battle of Midway during the Second World War...

"We got a few," said Bill.

"Mind if I check your licenses, duck stamps, shotguns, and birds?" I asked.

"Like we got a choice," said Bill in a grouchy, biting tone of voice.

"No, not really," I responded, matching his tone of voice. I more or less expected that kind of greeting from Bill since I had pinched him twice before for game violations in years past.

With that greeting and salutation out of the way, I checked their licenses and hunting gear. They checked out all legal-like so I began checking their birds. When finished, I found they had limits of ducks, but only seven white-fronts between the three of them!

Horsepucky! I knew my ears had not played tricks on me. Especially with all the sounds I had heard earlier of dead geese hitting the ground when flocks of white-fronts had flown over and had been shot at. But sure as Levi Garrett chewing tobacco is a good chew, they only had a total of seven geese, or two shy of having their daily bag limits among the three of them. "Where are the rest of your geese?" I casually asked.

"What you see is all we have," grumbled Bill.

"Lads, I know you have more geese than this. As near as I can figure, the three of you have to have at least twenty white-fronts down."

"The hell you say," said Bill. "If you think that, then you had best dig them up or take them out from your hind-end along with your head. That because them is all the geese we have and we are now ready to leave, so make it quick."

Up to that point in time, I had been in the wildlife law enforcement business for almost ten years. My mother hadn't found me under a turnip leaf and I sure as hell didn't like being treated like one who had. Especially from a smart mouth, known to me as a "game hog," duck-dragging outlaw, like Bill.

One thing all you readers need to understand.

Throw down a glove and a challenge to a conservation officer type, and he or she will pick it up. Especially when he or she is an experienced officer to such a degree they can tell many species of birds by just their calls, among many other things. And on that particular morning, I had heard more than enough to hold someone's feet to the fire until I smelled the bottom of their soles scorching, if you get my general drift. Plus, you readers need to remember that wildlife dies without making a sound. The only voice it has many times is that of the badge carrier in the field. And if that badge-carrying chap isn't squallin' like a smashed cat, then they are part of the problem and no better than the poacher themselves... Meow.

Figuring the men had hidden the extra geese along their rice check somewhere, I sent Shadow out to find them. Soon she came back with the look, "Where else do you want me to look now, Boss? Because mud bath or not, the rice check they are standing by is clean."

I knew my ears were better than that and they had told me there were extra geese somewhere. Especially with my definite counts of whumps of geese hitting the ground after the numerous barrages of shooting by my three outlaws. Knowing what I heard to be true, I double-checked the decoy area to see if there were any more geese scattered therein or under the goose shells themselves. Nothing surfaced. Then I walked back to the rice check on which my lads now sat calmly smoking cigarettes with smug looks smeared across their faces because I had so far found nothing illegal. Those smart-assed looks did nothing but increase my desire to discover what I knew to be true, so now, the hunt was really on...

"Let me see the soles of your boots," I abruptly asked.

"What the hell for?" asked Bill, with a sharpness to his voice announcing he didn't care for me or my kind one wit.

"Just do it, please," I requested.

Then the three men, with a lot of grumbling lifted up their hip boots so I could see the soles of their boots. All three were wearing a Red Ball brand of hip boot. Probably purchased at Chick Montgomery's Sporting Goods store in Colusa, I thought.

Then I began looking all around the area checking for the men's boot prints in the soft rice field mud. I could see where they had walked into the area to shoot. I could also see where they had rummaged through the decoys throughout the morning's shoot retrieving their dead birds. But there were also two suspicious sets leading off to the north out of sight into the fog. Advising the men to sit tight, I began cold-tracking the two men's footprints leading to the north.

Realizing I was backtracking the footprints, Bill said, "You just go ahead and follow those footprints, Terry. You will find nothing more than two fresh "game warden dumps" Carl and I took earlier this morning. So go ahead and follow those footprints to our dump sites if you feel so inclined. Take a good smell and help yourself to anything warm and gooey you find while you are there as well. Maybe we ate those over limits of geese you keep dreaming about," he chided. Remember that throwing down the glove issue I talked about earlier?

Ignoring his cutting remarks, I walked into the fog tracking the two sets of suspicious footprints. Sure as the Mississippi River has been more or less ruined as a natural river by the Army Corps of Engineers, my tracks led to two fresh "dump" sites among some parked farm equipment. However, before taking their dumps, the tracks led in among two Hardy Harvesters and a set of bank out wagons, equipment that had been used in the recent harvesting of the rice fields in and around in which the three men now hunted. Following the footprints with the Red Ball brand, I discovered they led to the same bank out wagon. There they stopped, turned around, and walked back towards their shooting positions alongside the rice check where I had discovered them hiding once my presence became known.

That is pretty strange, I thought. Why walk over to a bank out wagon and then return? It was then that I noticed a muddy boot print on the top of one of the bank out wagon's tires... Crawling up onto that bank out wagon and looking into its bed, I observed what my ears had told me all along. Therein lay a pile of freshly killed white-fronted geese! Clamoring over the side and down into the bed, I tossed out the geese. Then exiting the bank out wagon, I gathered up as many of the 23 white-fronts as I could carry and headed back to the men. I was now carrying that glove that had been thrown to the ground in front of me earlier as well...

Arriving back at the three seated men with a full duck strap over my shoulder and two hefty handfuls of geese, I dropped them at their feet. Then I returned to the farm equipment for the remainder of the geese without saying one word to the now, from the looks on their faces, worried men. That was, if the looks on their collective faces "said anything" as to the pregnant moment they found themselves in close at hand.

Arriving back at the men who were now quietly looking at me as I emerged from the fog carrying the rest of the geese, Bill said, "Them ain't our geese and you can't prove it."

"That is not what your fresh footprints are telling me," I said firmly.

"Them ain't our geese and you can't frame us with them," said Bill.

"Well, let's look at the facts. Your footprints are the only ones in this area. I have been here since before sunup and you three were the only shooters in this area. I checked all three sets of your boots and they are the Red Ball brand. Those same brands and foot sizes of the tracks at the bank out wagons match those boots on your feet. The geese I discovered in the bank out wagon are freshly killed and are of the same species found in your decoys and along the rice check you were using as a blind."

"Before this is all said and done, I will 'stick' these geese, including the seven you folks claimed, with my thermometer. I will bet a month's pay, they all more or less have the same body temperatures. Lastly as I approached you men, I counted at least twenty white-fronts, identified by their calls, hitting the ground just after you shot. What other conclusion can the Federal Magistrate in Sacramento or I draw, gentlemen? A conclusion that can only deduce that those birds found in the nearby bank out wagon are your birds as well?" I said. Gee, did that "glove" fit or not? Unlike the one at O.J. Simpson's trial, the glove I had picked up fit...

"They ain't our geese and we will fight you in court," snarled Bill.

"That is your right, but the three of you will be cited into Federal Court in Sacramento for this violation. And since you are denying that the geese are yours, let me see all of your boots, please," I said.

"What do you need our boots for?" asked a member of the trio of shooters, a man named David.

"I intend to match those boots up with the footprints by the bank out wagon with plaster casts and use them as evidence. So please remove your boots, gentlemen, because they are now government evidence in this particular matter," I said.

"You can't just up and take our boots," said Bill.

"If you think I can't, just you watch me," I said, with a tone of finality in my voice that was not to be misunderstood, even by a hardhead, killing son-of-a-gun like Bill.

"Can we talk among ourselves?" asked David.

"Sure can," I said as I moved out into the decoys so the men could have some privacy, suspecting just why they now wanted to discuss the matter among themselves. But before they conferred back at the rice check out of my earshot, I made all three of them remove one boot which I held as evidence. Without doing that, I figured if they ran off into the fog with all their boots on and got to a place where they could change, poof would go my boot print evidence. Like I said, my mom didn't raise a turnip... David and a man named Carl Johns argued briefly with Bill. Then David walked out to me where I stood quietly in the decoys looking at my three shooters.

"Them is our geese," he said.

"I didn't think any of you wanted to go to Federal Court in Sacramento over this. Especially with your previous waterfowl violation records. However, I do appreciate your honesty in coming forth over this violation," I said.

"There is one condition to our owning up to the goose-killing, though. If you can't keep that condition, then we want to go to trial," said David.

"What is that?" I asked, curious as to where this line of thinking was going.

"You promise not to tell anyone you caught us breaking the law and catching us with this over limit of geese," said David.

"That is no problem. I don't share information with anyone as to whom I catch breaking the law. However, you must realize that once I file the citations, they become a matter of public record. As such, anyone snooping through the records may find out about the three of you being tagged for killing an over limit of dark geese," I said.

"I know that and we will take our chances. However, you must promise not to tell anyone, especially anyone who lives locally, about what happened here today," he continued.

"Done," I said with a grin, whereupon the three local outlaws trooped forward and were cited for joint possession of an over limit of dark geese, to wit, 21 dark geese jointly over the limit (jointly because I did not see who shot what geese and in what numbers individually). Then I let my lads have back their remaining boots, but not before I had taken a point-and-shoot camera and had taken pictures of the soles of their boots and their suspicious footprints in the rice field mud with their boots laid alongside the tracks for comparisons...

After my chaps left, I cleaned the geese so they wouldn't spoil. By cleaning the birds there in the field, it lightened the load of evidence birds I had to carry. As for my dog, she got to eat warm goose guts until she looked like an oversize cracker barrel. That was her "expected" reward for having to get up so early, take a "mud bath," and work the waterfowl hunter circuit at such odd and unusually long hours. However, the next day the back of my truck sure paid the price for the gusto over her warm goose guts appetite. That was one time I wished I had a fire hose instead of just a garden hose in which to wash out the back of my truck! Hell, even Shadow looked embarrassed over me having to wash out the bed of "her" patrol truck! But that dog had saved my life years earlier on the Hoopa Indian Reservation when I was a rookie California Fish and Game Warden one night while on deer spotlighting patrol. So as far as I was concerned, she got her way in the "chow" department. That was the very least I could do for that great old dog and constant field companion for eleven years.

If you readers want to read that story, you will have to find it in my sixth book titled, The Thin Green Line (Chapter 8, "Dim Eyes, an Old Dog Named Shadow, and Bright Memories"). To my game warden "types" reading these lines who have been in similar situations with "their" dogs, be prepared. That chapter will bring tears to your eyes along with your own dog-related "Bright Memories..." Even as I write these words, I am finding it hard not to find tears in my eyes as well. It must be the dust in the air that is making my eyes water, eh?

As for my three goose-shooting chaps, they each forfeited $450.00 in Federal Court and the geese went to three needy families in the nearby small Sacramento Valley Towns of Colusa and Williams.

True to my promise, the names used in this story were created and not the real shooters' names. Two still remain alive to this day and I never again caught those chaps breaking the law. However, "Bill" was a consummate "duck dragger," and that type of dedicated and almost instinctive killing was in his blood. I doubt he ever stopped doing what he did on the dark side of the law. That was until he died from a massive heart attack! I wonder if he ever realized that God created all the critters and someday he would have to confront that "Person" for all the wildlife blood he illegally spilled... Especially after his many years operating as an illegal commercial market hunter of waterfowl in the Northern Sacramento Valley in the late '50s and early '60s.

It is to that point of commercial market hunting I must digress for all my unwashed readers. Commercial market hunting, especially for waterfowl, began after the end of the Civil War. It progressed across this United States as did the expansion of our peoples on the land. That destructive practice was correlated with the building of the railroads and the growth of our cities. This illegal practice of commercial market hunting of wildlife species, especially for waterfowl, peaked in the late Nineteenth and early Twentieth Centuries with the advent of multi-shot pump and auto loading shotguns. Until public opinion turned against this trade in animal parts in the late Nineteenth Century, market hunters were considered respected members of their communities.

In fact when I worked in the Northern Sacramento Valley in the late '60s, old time market hunters still found sympathy from many of the local citizens for their earlier destructive killing and marketing practices. Waterfowl taken during those heady days were sold to local bars, hotels or more commonly to middle men who then plied their sales trade in the larger cities where the demand for duck dinners was high. Duck dinners commonly consisted of one- half the duck carved off the carcass with the wing and leg attached in the late 1800s. Typically, those dinners sold for $3.00 per meal or about $60.00 dollars in today's money. Waterfowl commonly sold for $3.00 per canvasback, $2.50 per redhead, $1.50 for mallards and Northern pintail, $2.00 for geese and less for lesser species of ducks. Arkansas, alarmed over the reduced populations of ducks, geese and swans in that state because of market hunting, passed the first game law prohibiting the market hunting of waterfowl in 1875!

That was followed with the passage of the first federal law, the Lacey Act, initially prohibiting the marketing of wild animal species in interstate commerce in violation of state laws. That federal law was later expanded to include prohibitions by other federal, state and tribal laws trafficking in animal species as well.

The federal Migratory Bird Treaty Act passed in 1918 put the final nail into the coffin of the remaining market hunters. Although such destructive commercial killing practices continued on a more limited basis into the 1960s due to lenient courts, non-existent state and federal law enforcement budgets, state and federal prosecutors who found wildlife crimes to be victimless crimes hardly meriting their time as prosecutors, and the existence of a market for animal species, better conservation day were ahead.

Times have changed considerably and now any market hunting activity is met with heavy state and federal enforcement efforts and tough prosecutions. Market hunting as we once knew it is now locked in the silence of the past...

I know the "Good Book" says the critters were made and set on this earth for our use. However, I don't think the "Good Book" used the word "Abuse" when it came to our dominion over God's critters. Gee, Bill. What did God say to you about all the critters you took illegally when you arrived after your heart attack? That is, if you ever got that far skyward...

AN ADVENTURE WITH A TUNDRA SWAN

Exiting my home in Colusa one winter morning before daylight, I was greeted once again by a thick, wet blanket of tule fog. Dropping the tailgate, I let my Labrador retriever, Shadow, into the bed of my patrol truck. Fastening the tailgate, I hauled my miserable carcass into the cab of the truck for another day's adventures during waterfowl season in the Northern Sacramento Valley, but not before draping my right arm around my dog's big neck and giving her some loving attention. Turning the ignition key, I heard the powerful 383-cubic inch engine with a four-barrel carburetor roar to life. Watching my gauges, I let the oil pressure rise into the "normal" operating range.

Throwing the four-speed into second gear, truck, Dog, and I left the driveway for whatever adventure awaited us that fine foggy day. And what a unique day that would soon turn out to be! In fact, that turned out to be the only day in my professional life where I actually got my tail-end physically kicked, big time, and in short order... And, I got my tail-end kicking that day for being just a nice guy and trying to do the right thing...

Turning north onto the Princeton Highway, I headed for the Sacramento National Wildlife Refuge to the northwest. As I carefully picked my way down the highway through the heavy fog towards the refuge, I hoped I would not meet a rice harvester coming my way. Since they always took up a lane-and-a-half on any highway and usually were not well-lighted, things could get exciting fast when one was met head on and that went double on foggy days. However, I made my way safely to the refuge's southern boundary and shortly thereafter found myself sitting at the intersection of Road D and Hunter's Creek in Glenn County. Getting out from my truck, I let the dog out to take "care of business." While she sniffed out every mysterious smell, I quietly listened for Mother Nature's telltale signs of the waterfowl world in close proximity as they characteristically steamed back and forth overhead in the dense fog, lost as usual.

For the last ten days, the Sacramento National Wildlife Refuge had been a migration rest stop for several hundred Arctic or tundra swans (named whistling swans in those days), not to mention hundreds of thousands of ducks and geese. The tundra swan was a species of North American waterfowl which was totally protected in that day and age. And it seemed every time they left the protection of the refuge, numbers of that species had been falling illegally to knothead waterfowl shooters' guns, many times because they were mistaken for lesser snow geese, especially in the dense winter tule fogs. How that happened I never could fathom. The snow goose is considerably smaller, has a different, very noisy call, and black wing tips. The swans were much larger, usually flew quietly or only whistled as they flew, and lacked the black wing tips commonly found on snow geese. And for the other non-mistake swans being killed, as is many times the case, they were illegally taken because they were a large, tasty-eating, protected game bird, especially those birds of the year. That was the reason for my presence that fine foggy day in Glenn County during waterfowl season next to the swan concentrations on the refuge.

Days previously, I had discovered many swans heading west from the refuge's protective boundaries onto several flooded and harvested rice fields onto which to feed. I also had numerous outlaws from the Town of Willows hunting that area and figured it was just a matter of time before they "crossed swords" with Mother Nature. Therefore that area was being graced with my magnificent pitcher's mound-sized carcass that fine foggy morning so long ago.

I had discovered earlier in my law enforcement career that one could have lots of wildlife and man separated and running around without many problems. However, once that combination of man and wildlife mixed, that was when much of the illegal killing occurred. And when that mixing occurred, that was when Mother Nature needed members of the "Thin Green Line" or conservation officers like myself to step in and lend a hand. In short, folks, you can have all the laws and regulations you want on the books. However, if there aren't badge carriers incountry to enforce those laws, and in adequate numbers, you have nothing but a mess of "toilet-paper- with-printing-on-it." I am always amazed at the lack of wisdom or common sense shown by many politicians who think they can save money by reducing those numbers of officers in the conservation law enforcement community because they have so many laws on the books. Politicians do this with the misguided notion that all they need are some laws on the books and that will take care of itself. Hogwash and what is left on the street on the fourth of July after the parade and the horses have gone by! What is needed is someone carrying a badge and gun and who is tougher than woodpecker lips to enforce the regulatory word. Then drag those violating chaps before the judicial system, which hopefully is lacking any activist liberal judges, in which to carry out the true tone and tenor of the law of the land. That would make for a damn fine start to some of our world of wildlife problems...

Without that kind of badge carrier, one will end up with reduced numbers of bison, Pacific salmon, Atlantic salmon, whales, grizzly bears, passenger pigeons, and the like. Do any of those species, their current day numbers and life histories, bring back any memories over what I just said? Those species were reduced in numbers over the years due to man's inhumanity to wildlife because of the lack of controls or just plain common sense. That alone should lend credence to the need for that fraternity representing the wildlife's "long arm of the law." Someone needs to tell the "idiot stick" California Governor from Austria (who was present when these words were being penned) that he needs to brush up on his American natural history (a subject now poorly taught, if at all, in our public schools of today) before it is all gone. If he had any sense at all, he would see to it that his conservation officers need one heck of a lot more support in their numbers if the natural resources from that great state are to have any kind of a chance at survival for those yet to come to enjoy. 'Nuff said! 'Nuff said, but little listened to or understood in this day and age by many of our liberal, Democrat, jug-headed, tax and spend politicians... But, I digress...

Standing there quietly that morning in the dense tule fog, I soon became aware that once again the air was filled with thousands of confused migratory waterfowl. It was evident by their calls and wing-slapping collisions that they were pouring off the Sacramento National Wildlife Refuge by the hundreds of thousands as they headed southwest. And I would bet a wooden nickel that every one of them possessed an empty gut and a desire to fill it. They knew where the best rice fields were located and fog or no fog, everyone was in a hurry for breakfast. It was to mornings like that where I was glad to be alive and able to bear witness to Mother Nature's bounty. Today, for the most part and as these words are written, those days and numbers of many of those migratory birds are now long gone. Maybe another tribute to man's inhumanity to the world of wildlife, eh?

Far to my south, I heard the soft thumping of shotguns in the dense tule fog. Standing there, I waited for about another two or three minutes to see if they continued. That was standard law enforcement practice for me which was to head for the "sound of the guns" because that was what the action usually was. Then there it was once again. No two ways about it, I thought, that shooting was from at least three hunters and from the sounds of it, they were having the shoot of their lives. Loading Dog back into the bed of the truck, I started working my way south in mile increments. At the end of each mile, I would stop and listen once again for the sounds of my suspect shotgunners. Once relocated, I would again move south and repeat the echo-locating process every time my suspect shooting occurred. By now, the air was a mass of thousands of confused waterfowl calling and looking for a place to light down and "gather up some morning's grits." Even my dog was now looking skyward at the sounds of semi-lost birds in awe. No two ways about it, I thought, I lived for days like that. Even today, I still carry the wonderment of those amazing times now, for the most part, lost to the ages' moments in my soul. They were wondrous times. I have often questioned if they will ever return? Then my mind runs to the time when the thunderous flocks (at one time the largest flock of birds in the world, estimated to be between three billion and five billion in number) of passenger pigeons once graced this country's skies. This species was destroyed by man in the age of black powder guns and are now gone forever. The last one, Martha, died in the Cincinnati Zoological Gardens in 1914 and is now stuffed and in the Smithsonian Museum of Natural History...

Soon I found myself back in Colusa County in the McDermott Road area. Pausing once again, I soon located my three busy shooters having the time of their lives in the Delevan Road area. Standing there in the heavily misting fog, I soon honed in on the approximate location of my shooters who were creating one hell of a business for the Winchester or Remington shot shell industry, if you get my drift.

Looking for a place to hide my truck, I found an out of the way place next to three parked rice harvesters. Grabbing my field gear and Dog, we began walking past the harvesters into a recently harvested rice field from whence the heavy shooting came. Passing my last harvester on foot, I was surprised to see a black Ford three-quarter-ton truck tucked away out of sight behind that piece of farm equipment. Recognizing the truck as one belonging to one of my Italian outlaws from the Delevan area, I began grinning. The truck's owner always had a hard time counting when it came to killing a limit of ducks or geese. Well, if I had my way, today was going to be his "lucky" day. I was an excellent counter of dead ducks and geese and would be there to more than help my Italian buddy, if he needed help with his numbers... With the fog as my friend, a feeling from my guardian angels that something was amiss, and three sets of fresh tracks heading out into the muddy rice field from that hidden truck to follow, so went yours truly and his trusty dog, Shadow. You know—the warm duck and goose gut-eating-make-a-big-pile- the-next-day-in-the-back-of-my-truck, dog. You know, folks, even as much as that dog loved eating duck and goose guts, she never once hard-mouthed a retrieved bird. Not even a dove or a snipe. And for you unwashed, one can go on a snipe hunt. There really is such a critter living in the wild and they are damn good eating, providing one can hit the little, fast flying devils...

Walking out across that rice field, I was truly amazed at the numbers of ducks, geese, and swans in the air. Several times I had to duck as small flocks of American wigeon (medium-sized ducks) came blazing by in the fog like Federal cannon shot at Gettysburg (really, folks, if you ever get the chance, go to the Gettysburg Battlefield. And if you are a student of history, get out from your vehicle and just stand still and listen once you are on that battlefield's hallowed ground. If you are "historical," you can actually feel the energy resonating from that area as you stand there! You can really tell something ethereal happened in that area and can still feel its physical presence. It is called the heartbeat and soul of America. Trust me. Go there and see for yourselves. You won't be disappointed. But once again, I digress...) Proceeding onward, I headed for the sounds of the rapidly firing shotguns. My shooters had not let up and, from the sounds of their heavy shooting, were still a good one hundred yards distant. Picking up my pace but still being careful not to lose my cover in the fog, I hot-footed it south. To my way of reckoning, if my three gunners were any kinds of shooters, they should have limited out already. Not wanting to let them kill the entire world of waterfowl, I continued my fast pace following their footprints as I now began breaking into a sweat. You readers laugh. It is not easy pushing a monster-sized carcass across a sticky, muddy rice field. But, the hunt was on and I was still in the game as were my possible bad guys.

Crossing over another heavily grassed over rice check, I could see where my lads had knelt in the mud at the edge of the check and from all the fresh, empty shot shells lying around, had quite a shoot there earlier that morning. That was not all I found. Lying in the grasses at the edge of the rice check were 17 freshly killed mallards and Northern pintail (yes, there is a sub-species of Southern pintail)! Stopping for a quick examination and count, I could see my shooters' tracks still leading further south into the foggy rice fields. Taking out my Buck knife, I slit a web from each left foot of the birds in such a way the cut would hardly be noticed. That way if my shooters backtracked on me and got to those birds before I got to my suspects, I could still identify them as from my earlier cache of hidden birds once I ran across them later on. Taking out my notebook, I quickly recorded the birds' numbers and species. Then off Dog and I hustled once again before my shooters had killed everything in the air with feathers.

Slowing my pace and opening up the front of my hunting jacket so I could cool off, I again began cold tracking my three shooters' footprints in the soft mud. Coming to another rice check, I saw once again where they had knelt earlier and shot ducks. Again, I discovered a mess of freshly killed mallards, Northern pintail, and this time a few American wigeon (yes, there is a European wigeon). There were 15 freshly killed ducks in that pile. There were also five Pacific white-fronted geese, one tule white-fronted goose (a very rare, larger and darker sub-species than a Pacific white-fronted goose) in the pile, and a totally protected, freshly killed arctic or tundra swan! Again, I slit the webs on the birds' left feet for later identification and duly recorded the same in my notebook.

Now seeing that second pile of dead ducks, geese, and the swan set my heart racing. The limit in those days was eight ducks and six geese per person per day. My lads now had 32 ducks, six geese, and a swan down. Clearly an over limit of ducks if there were only three shooters and they were still shooting like they owned the Winchester or Remington shot shell factory... Suffice to say the hunt was now on, really big time, especially with the totally protected, dead swan in the bunch! Not seeing any advantage in letting my three game hogs kill the rest of the ducks, geese, or any more swans in the valley, I stood up and approached my shooters last know location straight away and at a trot.

It was then I heard the unmistakable whistling sounds and heavy swishing wing beats of a flock of swans coming my way from behind. Standing there in an open field shrouded by fog, I hoped I could flare them away from my three shooters' nearby killing field with my obvious presence. No such luck. That flock of about twenty swans came right over the top of me like "ships of the line" from the days of old and not twenty yards high. I could hear them whistling softly among themselves and the heavy swishing of their great wings as they labored in flight now directly overhead. Then not forty yards below me, it sounded like the whole Union Army line had opened up on George Pickett's Rebs at the Battle of Gettysburg. It was clear my lads were using unplugged shotguns and the swans were now paying for being incountry and flying so darn low.

Running towards my three shooters location to preclude any more illegal shooting, I broke through the fog just in time to see three swans fall like rocks from the sky and a fourth fluttering down obviously wing tipped! "Hey," I bellowed, "Federal agent!" Man, you never saw such action on the parts of my three shooters. Every one of them started uncapping their Browning semi-automatic shotgun magazines and trying to replace their plugs (a device required by law limiting a shotgun to only three shells). "No such luck, boys," I yelled. "Leave those shotguns alone and put them down!"

For a moment none of the men moved and then seeing me quickly rambling into focus through the fog, they knew in a moment who the heck I personally was. Down went the shotguns in various stages of disassembly and then the three lads just stood there in resignation. Meanwhile, my crippled swan dug himself out from the soft rice field mud where he had fallen and then tried to take off once again. With a wounded wing there was no way he could fly, and soon my dog had him by the back of the neck and was holding the madly flopping bird down.

"You boys leave the shotguns where they are and give me a hand with that swan," I barked. Soon, the four of us had the huge cob (male swan) in hand so he would not damage himself or his primary wing or major flight feathers any further. Walking back to their shotguns with the swan tucked in under my right arm, I made sure all the guns were assembled and remained empty. Then I had the three of them pick up another 22 dead ducks, four geese and three more swans they had previously shot in the rice field. Walking back the way we came with me carrying the crippled swan under my right arm, we picked up all the remaining dead birds and headed for our parked trucks. As for the wounded swan, he tried to grab me a few times with his bill and then settled down and went along for the ride safely tucked under my arm.

Back at our vehicles, I issued citations into Federal Court in Sacramento to my lads for using unplugged shotguns, taking and possessing over limits of ducks, and taking protected migratory nongame birds, to wit, five Arctic or Tundra swans. There was a lot of grumbling by my lads, especially when I made them gut out all the birds so they wouldn't spoil. But I figured that was the least I could do for all the havoc they had wreaked on the world of waterfowl that fine morning so long ago.

As for the huge crippled swan, I just let him loose into the cab of my truck for safekeeping for the time being. I did so because I figured I would take the crippled bird to the nearest national wildlife refuge and release him there with the hope his wing tip would heal up since it was only slightly damaged. Plus, if I had put him in a burlap bag I always carried for evidence birds, he might further damage his primary wing or flight feathers while trying to escape. And he would need those if he was to have any chance at recovery and continued his migration, I reasoned.

Then I returned my lads' shotguns (weapons were hardly ever confiscated in federal court in those days so I did not seize them unless the shooter lacked sufficient identification. In those cases of lack of identification, the weapons were seized to guarantee the miscreant's appearance in court and then returned). Finally, I issued them their respective citations, and with a wave of my hand, the pile of seized ducks, geese (the under limit of geese were seized because my lads were using unplugged, shotguns which meant all the birds were taken illegally and therefore seized as evidence), and swans, Dog and I headed for the Sacramento National Wildlife Refuge. There I would put the seized ducks, geese, and swans in my evidence freezers kept at one of the refuge outbuildings for trial if needed. As for my live swan, I had plans on releasing him on the closed portion of the refuge in good habitat so he could heal up in peace.

Getting back out onto the Maxwell-to-Willows Highway, I headed for the refuge. What a grand sight that made. Picture this if you were a passing motorist. A rather large but beautiful-looking man (me, of course) driving the truck with a huge swan standing in the front seat on the passenger side with his long neck and head sticking a foot or so out the partially rolled-down passenger side window. The swan was as quiet and peaceable as you pleased. In fact, he appeared to be enjoying the ride and so was I. I had caught three Delevan lads who needed catching, made a hell of a mess of good cases, and had rescued a fine specimen of a male (or cob) Arctic (or tundra) swan. Damn, my day couldn't have been any better!

Then my day turned to that evil-smelling stuff you find on your shoes when walking in the public park. You know, that stuff that people don't clean up, left behind by their "wannabe" dog, let- yap-every-time-they-take-a-step, pets... I had a small, soft rubber gorilla hanging from my cigarette lighter knob on the dash of my truck. It had been given to me by my brother-in-law, Dee Barbea, a California Highway Patrol Officer. There always existed a friendly competition between the "Chippies" (highway patrol) and the "Tule Creepers" (game wardens) in the State of California for years. Dee had discovered the gorilla in a store and had cleverly painted it up to look like a game warden. Then he shipped it to me indicating I looked like the rubber gorilla. Liking the damn thing, I hung it on the cigarette lighter knob in my truck, figuring what the heck...

Tooling down the foggy highway all fat (well, let's just say thick), dumb, and happy that morning, I noticed the swan had now spotted my jiggling gorilla hanging from the cigarette lighter knob. For the longest time, all he did was just look at it with his head all cocked off to one side. Then all hell broke loose! For some reason, that damn swan, took offense to my gorilla. Without any kind of warning, he attacked! You know, folks, there isn't a lot of room in the cab of a three-quarter-ton truck when it is filled with a 320-pound federal agent and a twenty-pound swan in full flight. And I do mean in full flight! Here I was, going down the highway at fifty miles per hour with a swan in full attack mode on my poor, stupid, minding his own business, rubber gorilla! And I do mean attacking! That swan was trying to fly in the cab of my truck as he whipped the hell out of my rubber gorilla with his bill and wings! Can any of you imagine what it is like being in a cab with a monster-sized federal agent trying to slow down his truck while a massive swan with his flailing six-foot wing span violently fills the cab? Well, it ain't purdy.

That darned bird put knots all over my head from his hard wing bones and gave me a bloody nose before I could even pull over and get off the highway! In the meantime, the swan tore my soft rubber gorilla all to hell and managed to crap "green" all over the inside of the cab at the same time. Soon I had blood running down the front of my shirt and swan poop plastered to the side of my head and stuck in my right ear! Dang, I even had swan poop on the inside of my windshield! I don't know what that swan had been eating, but he sure had a bad case of the "Hershey squirts" that smelled every bit like rotten anchovies left out in the summer heat! By the time I got stopped and had my "passenger" under control, I had two cars parked along the side of the highway watching a twenty-pound swan whipping the hell out of a 320-pound federal agent! And to make matters worse, Shadow, my dog in the back of truck, rolled around "laughing" at me and my clumsy attempts at trying to "retrieve" a swan. Hell, when she had caught the swan in the field, she didn't have any trouble... I am sure to this day, that dog was laughing at me in a disrespectful manner... I know for a fact that afterward she sure disapproved of how I smelled and looked...

I finally got the obviously unhappy and ungrateful swan under control, putting him into a burlap bag for safekeeping (at that point, to hell with the primary wing feathers!). That ended the flying in my cab thing... As for my gorilla, he was a real mess. I only found part of his body and one leg! Arriving at the refuge with a bloody front to my hunting coat from the nose bleed, I dumped the swan off into a nice pond where he could live in peace. Then I stashed my evidence birds in the freezer and cleaned up. The rest of the day I continued working the tule fog making four more large over-limit duck cases. But boy, the knots on the side of my head sure let me know I had been in a fight and had come off second best... In fact, they were so large in size that I couldn't even wear my hunting cap. That was one of the very few times in my career I got worse than I dished out.

My three chaps posted bail in Federal Court to the tune of $850.00 each. Additionally, all had their hunting rights revoked in the United States for the rest of the year.

Afterwards, Chief Federal Judge McBride for Northern California, who was located in Sacramento, called me just before Christmas. In that call he requested I deliver all the closed case ducks and geese I previously had commercially picked, cleaned, and wrapped, as well as my unpicked ones. Delivering over six hundred ducks and geese to him, he got to act like Santa Claus and deliver the fruits of my labors to needy families in the City of Sacramento area for their Christmas dinners. Now folks, that was one of the very best federal judges I ever had! On top of that, he was one good Christian man. May the good Lord take a liking to him...

As for that swan, while picking up Judge McBride's Christmas birds, I discovered he had been caught, killed, and eaten by the coyotes on the Sacramento National Wildlife Refuge. Now that ungrateful thing knew how my gorilla felt. Merry Christmas, you damned swan...

THE "PIED PIPER"

Rising early as I usually did during waterfowl season, I looked out the kitchen window to see what was in store for me weather-wise. It was another winter day in the Northern Sacramento Valley blanketed with tule fog. Since I had been working 16-hour days for the last 15 days, I decided to take a day off. Take a day off and go duck hunting, that is. But I would still carry my badge, gun, and cite book just in case I ran into an unfortunate or two with their hands in Mother Nature's cookie jar. Rattling around in my kitchen, I threw together a "lumberjack's breakfast" as I gathered together my hunting gear. A hunting jacket full of 10-gauge, 3 1/2-inch shot shells, several duck and goose calls, my 10-gauge double barrel shotgun, a "PB&J" sandwich each for Dog and me, and six cardboard foldout Johnson goose decoys completed my kit. Then chow was ready and I fell to knowing that might be my only hot meal for the day. That repast was finished off with a rather generous slice of my bride's homemade rhubarb-and-strawberry pie. No better way to start a day than with a piece of her world's best homemade pie, I thought with a sticky-faced grin. Then since she wasn't there in the kitchen to keep me corralled, I had a second generous slice. Well, to you readers trying to keep me corralled, that first piece of pie was so good and went down so fast, I had to have a second piece. You know, so I could taste it...

Breakfast done and Dog fed, out the door we went into the tule fog for a relaxing day hunting waterfowl together doing what I loved, namely the sport of kings or hunting North American waterfowl. Some "relaxing" day that one soon turned out not to be... Letting Dog into the cab of my truck for a warmer ride to our shooting grounds on the north end of Line Dennis's rice farm, off we went. Arriving 15 minutes later, we disembarked into an area on the north end of his farm lying just to the west of the Delevan National Wildlife Refuge. Walking out about one hundred yards into a recently harvested rice field, Dog and I could hear the excited noises the ducks and geese made on the nearby refuge as they prepared for another day in the Sacramento Valley. All that did was put a bit of haste into my step and sped up my heart rate in anticipation of the exciting tule fog duck hunt to follow. Finally arriving where I wanted to set up, I laid my shotgun safely down on a rice check and walked thirty yards out into the field. There I set up my six Johnson goose decoys and Dog made her usual mess right where I wanted the birds to fall. Oh well, "sometimes one eats the bear and other times the bear eats you."

Returning to my shotgun and the cover the rice

check offered, Dog and I hunkered down and waited for legal shooting time to arrive. In the meantime, we were entertained with the sounds of thousands of confused birds leaving the comfort of the refuge during the morning lift-off as they looked for a place to load up on waste rice grains left in the fields by the combines. Come one-half-hour after the arrival of legal shooting time (I always made it a point never to shoot during the legal one-half-hour prior to shooting time because of those problems associated with bird identification), I made ready. Reaching into my hunting coat, I brought out two 2 3/4-inch, Alcan paper reloaded shot shells containing No. 4 shot and slid them into the tubes of my double barrel. Then I readied my mallard call and pintail whistle for the next flock of low-flying, confused birds due to the dense tule fog.

Soon I heard the sounds of a large flock of ducks passing high overhead. Warming up my duck call, I charmed the socks off the "tail-end Charlies" of that flock. Sure as all get-out, I heard the familiar slapping of wings as the flock of ducks shifted and reversed course upon hearing my call from the rice field below. Soon they returned overhead in the thick fog only this time much lower as they looked for the feeding ducks on the rice ground below. Waiting until that flock had just passed, I gave a "highball" call and readied my shotgun. Seconds later, I was smack dab in the middle of about one hundred mallards rocketing about looking for their "buddy" calling to them from the ground. In fact, they were so close that I had to wait until they passed by me and got out about 35 yards distant before I cleanly shot and killed a nice fat drake mallard. I only shot once at passing ducks for two reasons. I was shooting a double barrel shotgun or one holding only two shots. If I wounded the bird at which I was shooting, I wanted another barrel to kill him and not let him stagger off and suffer a lingering death. Second, I was out for a memorable morning with my dog and the ducks. I didn't want the shoot to end too quickly. With that shot, the ducks headed for a safer place and Shadow made a picture-perfect retrieve. Man, let me tell you, the morning was off to a beautiful start. First with a great breakfast topped off with two slices of my bride's out-of-this-world homemade pie. Then good duck calling, a perfect shot and a picture perfect retrieve by my dog. Life was good and about to get better! Moments later, I repeated the above action two more times as more confused birds soared overhead and now three beautiful drake mallards in full winter plumage, highlighted by their bright red-orange feet, graced the ground by my spot on the rice check. It was great to be alive!

Then my day turned into what my dog had left earlier in the decoys... Out from the heavy fog came the shapes of four other duck hunter wannabe's. Seeing my six folding goose decoys in the middle of the small field I had chosen, like any good sportsmen, they stopped. Stopped, I assumed, because they didn't want to infringe or intrude on my shooting area. They held a short parley and then the four of them, unlike good sportsmen, lined up against an adjacent rice check just off my goose decoys and settled in for a morning's shoot as well! Damn, I was flabbergasted. It was not sportsman-like to shoot off someone else's decoys unless invited. I couldn't believe what I was seeing and, to say the least, was a bit perturbed. Realizing they also wanted to work off my duck calling as well as my decoys, I made a decision. Walking out into the field, I picked up my decoys. Then Dog and I headed out deeper into the farm tract and thick fog so we could duck hunt by ourselves and not be disturbed.

Finding another likely looking area sixty or so yards distant from my first spot, I set up my decoys once again. Then Dog and I headed for the nearest rice check and waited for another flock of fog-confused birds to drift by. The next group of birds turned out to be a flock of the great-eating Pacific white-fronted geese. Grabbing my goose call, I charmed the socks off the whole flock and was soon swarmed by about thirty geese looking for a safe spot to set down. Picking out a mature goose (they have a lot of dark black feathers on their bellies, hence their other name being "Speckle-Bellies"), I made a one-shot clean kill. In the meantime, as Dog went to retrieve my goose, I could hear my four "sportsmen" banging away like Cox's Army off in the distance. Hearing more white-fronts coming, I reloaded the shotgun and waited. Once again, I did my magic with the goose call and soon had a confused-by-the-dense-fog flock of geese almost in my lap. Another single shot and a fat mature white-fronted goose lay among the decoys. So far, five shots had been fired by me that morning and five birds were now in the bag. Not bad for an old and tired, beat-up wildlife officer, I thought, with a foggy wet-faced grin of pure enjoyment and utter relaxation.

Then once again, my day turned to crawdad poop! Out from the gloom of the fog came my four "sports." Apparently liking my goose calling and earlier decoy set, here they came once again. Once again they plopped their tail-ends down on a nearby rice check! In fact, they were so close, they could now shoot directly off my decoys... Now I was starting to get a little steamed. Especially since this was a classic example of poor sportsmanship, not to mention, dangerous as well. I was shooting a 10-gauge 3 1/2-inch magnum shotgun, and its killing range with my two full choke barrels was a good seventy yards. If I wasn't careful, I might "harvest" a knothead instead of a goose... And if I did, I wasn't sure how to "clean" him. Then, I would suppose, I would have to use a lot of butter and garlic to make him taste good. And even with enough garlic and butter, I doubted I could make him taste good! I grimly thought as an ugly afterthought...

Then a huge flock of ducks swarmed into my field and before I knew it, my sports had killed a mess of them before I could even shoot. That was followed with much whooping, hell-raising and hollering over their kills as they ran around in the rice field picking up their dead and dying ducks among my "borrowed" goose decoys.

Disgusted, I once again walked out into the field, picked up my six folding goose decoys without saying what I thought of my sports so they could hear it and headed even further back into the depths of the Dennis farm to be rid of these idiots once and for all. Walking a good one hundred yards, I once again set up shop in the swirling mists. Soon I could hear the roar of thousands of ducks and geese coming off the refuge in their late morning "lift-off or rise." Within moments, the air filled with dozens of flocks calling for someone on the ground to give them a heads-up as to where the best morning grits could be found. Hearing a flock of Northern pintail sail closely by (identified by their unique fluting calls), I got busy on my mallard duck call and pintail whistle. After a few passes, the flock was soon within gun range. That time, I picked out a mature drake pintail and dropped him cleanly with one shot. With that fine shot and watching my dog make another picture perfect retrieve, my hackles over the previous poor sports behavior were slowly laying back down. Once again I was enjoying myself in the sport of kings and no longer looked like a car-hit-chicken over my four "sports" and their behavior. Then a flock of lesser snow and white-fronted geese came scooting by and a couple of quick goose calls later, I had an interested flock. Did I say flock? How about one thousand or so birds milling all around me, flying, landing, or zooming by! That kind of experience in the wild, with just man and his dog, is a glorious memory for the ages! One that is uniquely lodged in a man's soul, to be retrieved years later when "age and times on a man's carcass are tough" and his "summer" is just about gone, if you get my drift...

That time I killed another mature white-front along with a lesser snow goose. However, the birds were so thick in numbers and making so

Wildlife's Quiet War | 79

much noise, they didn't really much pay attention to my shooting. Soon I had about five hundred geese on the ground in my decoys and more on the way! What a spectacle! Keeping Dog at my side and not letting her retrieve my two dead geese just killed, we just drank in the spectacle of Mother Nature's greatness up close and personal-like. Like I said earlier, moments in time to be used as food for one's soul when one is long in the tooth, short on time and close to that boundary of eternity... That spectacular event went on for the next ten minutes or so as more and more birds responded to the din being created by the masses of noisily feeding birds on the ground.

Then I got a faint whiff of that damn crawdad poop once again! For you unwashed, crawdads move into flooded rice fields to feed in the summer months. Then when the rice fields are drained prior to harvest, many crawdads are stranded and without life giving water, die. Hence the smell of crawdad poop in the harvested rice fields in the fall of which I write. With a roar, my now several thousand ducks and geese rose into the air in a huge alarmed mass. That was followed by a thunderous barrage of shots fired at them from the far side of the field as my four sports made their presence known once again! With both Dog and me stung by stray shot from that close- at-hand shoot, I bellowed out my displeasure as would a bull moose in rut when disturbed!

"Sorry," came a lame apology in the dense fog at the far end of the field. "We didn't see you there," came the voice once again.

Now my nose was really out of joint. It was almost like I was a "Pied-Piper." Everywhere I went my four rubes trailed along. Every time I used my duck or goose calls it seemed they were drawn to their sounds. Well, I was not going to let these chaps spoil my day any more than they already had. While Dog picked up my two downed geese, I once again picked up my decoys. Then without a backward glance, Dog and I walked out into a field and fog another two hundred yards further away that time! Finding another good-looking rice field, I set up my goose decoys one more time. I also took my dead ducks and geese and placed them in my decoys as well. As I did, I would take a stout piece of rice straw and stick one end in the mud. Then I took a dead bird's head from my previous kill and stuck it on top of the rice straw. Then the carcass was laid out all natural-like. That way, I made an even better-looking decoy set. With that, Dog and I headed for the cover of the nearest rice check some 25 or so yards distant.

There we sat down on a rice check and it was then I remembered our PB&J sandwiches.

Digging them out, I gave Shadow hers and I commenced eating mine. Shadow, like any other Labrador, tried wolfing down her sandwich. Of course, the extra thick peanut butter (is there any other way to make a PB&J?) stuck to the roof of her mouth. Then, some of the craziest damn shenanigans occurred. First, she tried to lick her stuck PB&J down off the roof of her mouth. No such luck. Then she tried sliding her face in the rice field, first on one side then on the other, trying to dislodge her sticky repast from the roof of her mouth. Finally giving up in frustration, she returned to me with a "help wanted" sign written all over her face. Damn, I loved that dog! She was a "people" and as human as one could get. My Labrador dog-loving readers know of what I speak... Digging the sandwich off the roof of her mouth, she quickly made sure the damned thing never "attacked" her ever again...

By now several hundred thousand ducks and geese had lifted up off Delevan National Wildlife Refuge and were milling around in the fog at every point on the compass. Talk about the "call of the wild." It was so noisy one could hardly hear himself think! Since I still had four ducks to go to fill my limit, I got to work on my mallard call. Once again, I had the air full of mallards in short order and within close gun range. Four more shots later and I had a beautiful limit of drake mallards along with a single drake pintail to grace my duck strap whenever I decided to leave for home. Grabbing my goose call, I went to work on the geese since I was still shy of my snow goose limit for that day. Moments later, I was once again in a literal "snowstorm" swirl of white snow geese. In fact there were so many swirling around at such close ranges, I couldn't shoot and only be guaranteed of killing just my limit. Then the flock grew even denser causing Dog and me to lie down on the rice check for protection from all the confused, low-flying bodies zipping by close-at-hand as they looked for places to land and feed. For the next twenty minutes, Dog and I were literally in a veritable blizzard of hungry ducks and white, lesser snow geese. And the more they came, the more noise they made. And with that, the more others came to the sounds of those on the ground!

Soon Dog and I were surrounded by thousands of geese and ducks on both sides of our rice check. Just to give you readers an idea of the numbers of birds in the air still coming in, 1 got hit at least a dozen times by falling duck and goose poop! It didn't pay for one to look up, if you get my drift. And to you less fortunate waterfowl hunting readers out there, you can just lick your lips and imagine... It really was just like that in the 1960s and '70s in the Northern Sacramento Valley.

Now my readers can see why I worked sixteen-hour days and seven days a week just to "hold the line" against those so inclined to break the law because of such bountiful wildlife resources! And now you can also see why I still had commercial market hunters and "duck draggers" by the score to worry about whenever I was out and about... And that didn't take into account the action by the regular field hunters, those sports hunting on my three-hundred-plus commercial and private duck clubs, and those wealthy shooters in the adjacent Butte Sink Duck Clubs. Like I have said many times in my books, when it came to getting the job done, Custer had better odds... But, I digress.

It was then that Dog and I were bombarded once again with the proverbial "crawdad poop" as all hell broke loose! My four rubes had heard all the noise from the excited ducks and geese landing and flying into my latest area of enjoyment. And as if my rubes were "piped" in once again by a "piper," they had sneaked up on the nearby feeding hordes of birds. Then unexpectedly their first shots were laid out across the heads and necks of the masses of feeding birds. When the many thousands rose into the air in alarm to be rid of the flying lead dangers, their masses were dumped into by more close-at-hand aerial shooting.

That did it! You can only poke a bear just so many times before you get the bite taken out of your last part over the fence... Holding my position behind the rice check, I waited for the low-flying shot to dissipate and my rubes to show themselves. That took some time because, once they realized just how many birds they had killed in the ground sluice and in the air, they took guilty pause, hidden behind a rice check.

That was alright with me though, I thought. They had poked the "large one" (that's me) one time too many and now it was time for my lads (the four idiot sportsmen) to "pay the piper!"

Finally I saw four heads poke up over the rice check as they looked at the "snow white" blanket of dead and dying snow geese in the rice field to their front. Additionally, the ground looked like it was covered with white maggots. There were so many crippled ducks and geese trying to waddle off and hide in the grasses along the rice checks that it looked like the ground was alive and moving in its agony. Then with a whoop of joy, over the top of the rice check came my lads like troops in the trenches during the First World War. But I moved nary an inch. There were so many cripples all over the place, I figured I would let the four of them run them down for me. That way, they would recover more birds and be all pooped out when the "magnificent one" (that's me) made his grand, Robert Redford the younger appearance (that would be me once again).

For the next twenty minutes, my four lads scampered around gathering up their ill-gotten booty. In the meantime, Dog and I had crawled along the rice check behind them almost to their original firing position. There we waited to see what our lads were going to do with their gross over limits. I didn't have long to wait. Each man selected a limit of ducks and geese from the pile and laid them off to one side in the field like those were to be taken home. Then they gathered up the rest of the over limits of birds and hid them under some rice straw by their rice check. Back they came to their limits and loaded those birds into their game bags and onto their duck straps. Then grabbing the extra geese by their necks that wouldn't fit in their game bags or on the duck straps, they headed back to the rice check from whence they had just shot.

However, now there was a small rock in the road. Well, many would say a pitcher's mound, if they took my ample size into consideration... Just as they got to the rice check, I stood up in all my Teutonic magnificence, minus the spiked helmet of course. Boy, with my sudden appearance, you talk about four lads looking like a bunch of African meerkats. I had dead ringers, with dead being the operative word...

"Morning, lads. How was the shooting?" asked the "Pied Piper," as he held up his federal credentials and gold badge for all the world to see.

For the longest moment, no one said anything. Then the one with a potbelly larger than mine said, "We did good, officer. We all got our limits."

"Well, lads, I would like to see some hunting licenses, duck stamps, birds, and shotguns, if I might," I said, like nothing was out of the ordinary.

For the next several minutes, my lads complied. In fact, they hardly said anything as if wanting to be rid of me just as soon as possible. Gee, I wonder why? Then it came time to check their shotguns. Every one of them were unplugged or capable of holding more than three shells, as was forbidden by state and federal laws.

"Well, boys, we have a problem. It seems all of you used unplugged shotguns to take your birds. Since that is a violation of state and federal laws, you will be issued a citation and will lose all your birds as well," I quietly advised.

"What do you mean we will lose all our birds?" asked "Potbelly."

"Well, lad, the birds were taken illegally with unplugged shotguns. Since that type of taking occurred, all the birds are illegal as well, and are to be forfeited to the government," I quietly said knowing the best was yet to come (Remember the hidden birds under the rice straw back in field at the edge of the rice check?).

"Can't we keep just a few? We came all the way from San Francisco and slept in our car all night so we could hunt today. And now you tell us we can't even keep our birds?" Potbelly continued in a whine.

"That is the way it is, lads, sorry," I continued, as I walked up to the rice check and sat down. "Now, do you lads want to tell me anything about the over limits you took?" I asked.

For an instant there was abject silence. Then all hell broke loose as everyone was talking all at once denying my accusation.

I quieted all the lads down with a wave of the hand, and I am sure, followed by a look on my face that would have stopped a tarantula dead in its tracks from jumping on a small nearby critter. "Men, let's not embarrass yourselves any further. Why don't the four of you walk over to that pile of rice straw and gather up all your extra birds you hid under there just moments ago." That said, the look on my face and then theirs, said it all.

After a moment's hesitation, the four culprits glumly walked over to the rice straw pile and began bringing me back arm loads of freshly killed ducks and geese. In the meantime, I told

Shadow to "get the duck." With that, off she went gathering up the other crippled birds my lads had earlier overlooked. When I had all the birds gathered up by the lads, I made them walk the rice checks looking for more wounded ducks and geese. One hour later, I had 113 ducks and 55 dead geese in a pile. The maximum lawful limit in that day and age for my four lads, was 32 ducks and 24 geese. As one could see, they were a tad over...

"Now, lads, let us set to gutting all these birds out. That way they won't spoil and that also makes them lighter to carry," I quietly said as I looked over the piles of broken bodies.

For the next hour, my lads from San Francisco and yours truly gutted and hauled ducks and geese back to my vehicle. Once finished, I commenced writing up my chaps for taking migratory game birds with an unplugged shotgun, taking over limits of ducks and geese, and for joint possession of over limits of ducks and geese. While in that process back at my vehicle, Line Dennis, the landowner, drove by and, seeing all the activity on his farm ground and recognizing me, stopped.

"Need any help, Terry?" he asked, as he looked over my four glum-looking chaps.

"No sir, got her under control," I said. Then I thought of something. "Line," I asked, "do these lads have permission to hunt on your land?"

"Hell no! Is that where you caught them, Terry?" he asked, with rising anger in his voice.

"Yes, sir," I replied.

"Can you call the sheriff? I want those men arrested for trespassing," he continued now getting a bit worked up.

"Line, I can do better than that. Even though I am a U.S. Game Management Agent, I am still cross-credentialed as a deputy state fish and game warden. As such, I can write them a state citation under the Fish and Game Code for trespassing if that is what you want," I responded.

"Write them up, Terry. No one hunts on my land without permission," he said. "And if they ever do, they sure as hell aren't allowed to kill everything in sight," he grumbled as he looked over the pile of broken duck and goose bodies lying in the back of my truck.

Finishing up with my federal citations, I dug out my state citation book from the truck. The four lads were soon issued state citations under the Fish and Game Code for trespassing on private property. With that and evidence tags all around for the seized birds and shotguns, we parted company. I later took the evidence birds to Angelo Jaconetti in Colusa, a commercial bird processor, for picking and wrapping. Then I headed over to the Williams Justice Court and filed my state trespassing citations.

Two weeks later, each of my lads forfeited $750.00 in Federal Court for the migratory bird violations, and $150.00 in the Williams Justice Court for the trespassing charges. A rather expensive outing, I must say, especially in light of the fact I only made $1,000 per month as a U.S. Game Management Agent in those days. By the way, those birds seized that day were also some of the "Christmas" birds Chief Federal Judge McBride gave away to the needy for their Christmas dinners in the City of Sacramento area. Since none of the men had any previous wildlife violations, their shotguns were all returned.

When I came home that evening after my storied day off hunting ducks, I cleaned up in the garage and fed Shadow a giant can of dog food. As she retired to her doghouse for a well-earned snooze, I went inside my home. I was met at the open door by my long- suffering bride and the great smell of one of her famous home- cooked meals.

"Have any luck today?" she asked, as she gave me a kiss.

"Sure did. Got a limit of ducks and a few geese and gave them to the Yamamoto's. Had a great and beautiful hunt. Never missed a shot. Other than that, it was as quiet as this tule fog is when it comes rolling in..." With that I sat down at the dinner table ready to eat. Putting the napkin on my lap, I noticed my bride staring at me with one of her beautiful, "I know better," blue-eyed stares. A stare that fairly shouted, "Don't feed me that "quiet as a mouse pissing on a ball of cotton" out there crap."

Quickly looking away from her knowing look before she caught me fibbing, I had to laugh inside. I could only lie to her twice a year and get away with it. Once on her birthday and once on Christmas so she couldn't figure out what I had gotten her for a present. All the other times, I tried not to worry her about the profession and the day's events. So sometimes, "white lies" were called for about the many crazy things that happened to me while on the job. Especially the numbers of outlaws I sometimes faced down while alone (which was almost all the time—welcome to the real world of the wildlife conservation officer). However, that evening she caught me sure as one does a carp when waving a gob of worms placed in front of its nose when it is spawning time in the warm water shallows.

Grinning, I said, "Well, I did have a little action this morning with some Bay Area chaps. It was just one of those days, Honey, when everything I did seemed to attract attention. Kinda like being a Pied Piper, only this time with rather large 'rats.'" Ignoring her quizzical look, I settled down to a great dinner after a wonderful day in the rice fields of Colusa County. Come to think of it, that was the only time in my career in which I called in a batch of outlaws with a set of duck and goose calls along with six old beaten up Johnson goose decoys...

THE BURLY BUNCH FROM BURLINGAME

Returning to Colusa County from a weeklong stint in the San Joaquin Valley Delta working the ultra-rich island duck clubs with California Fish and Game Warden Dennis "Buck" Del Nero, I could see the makings of another thick tule fog in the offing. Forgetting the blanket of fog in the Northern Sacramento Valley for a moment, I let my mind drift back to my week of duck club work with my old and dear friend from the fish and game academy, Warden Buck Del Nero.

Once again it seemed everything we "touched" as conservation officers had turned to gold. Illegal swan shooters, folks shooting waterfowl illegally over baited areas, duck clubs shooting gross over limits, untagged birds in duck club hanging facilities, the taking of protected migratory non-game shorebirds, you name it, and we ran across it. In fact as a culmination to our week's work of sowing hate and discontentment among the outlaw ultra-rich who paid little or no attention to the conservation laws of the land, we had hit the jackpot. On one duck club we had seized an

18-cubic foot freezer chock full of illegally shot, picked, and cleaned wild ducks. On another San Joaquin Delta island holding two wealthy duck clubs, we had seized 665 illegally taken ducks and geese from their hanging facilities! Man, those were the days when the "catching" was out of this world... Then, we had tangled with a wealthy duck club that was owned by the Mafia which, as we were soon to discover, was loaded with huge over limits of ducks and geese. That discovery was followed with the offer of a bribe to look the other way by the club president or our pick of the "Ladies of the Night" frequenting the club. But I will save that story for another telling. Just so there are no wild rumors floating around as a result of those words, no, Buck and I did not partake of the bribe money or any of the favors from the Ladies of the Night...

Sure as God made little green apples, my boss, Jack Downs, and Buck's boss, Captain Jim Wictum, as a result of the that week's law enforcement efforts, would be called in on the carpet once again for all the hate and discontentment Buck and I had sowed across the wealthy duck clubs in the San Joaquin Valley Delta. Called in on the carpet by G. Ray Arnett, the very political to my way of thinking, California Fish and Game Director who, it was alleged, liked to be invited to hunt on such wealthy duck clubs. "Hunting invites" on such wealthy duck clubs that soon dried up when Buck and I rode roughshod over the game hog outlaws clipping their wings and curtailing their excessive trigger finger actions... It didn't matter that Buck and I had a one-hundred-percent record of convictions in Federal Court from all our waterfowl enforcement "ramblings." What was causing the politicians of every color "internal gas" was the fact that our enforcement efforts had a certain cramping of style on the ultra-rich who felt they were above the wildlife laws of the land. Oh well, I thought, if the "fat cats" aren't squalling like smashed cats, then Buck and yours truly weren't really doing their jobs as well as we should have been doing...

Letting my mind get back to the present matter at hand, I listened to the powerful throbbing "Swiss watch-like" rumblings of my 383-cubic inch Dodge engine as I thundered along the Interstate 5 freeway. It would be good to be home and back in the Northern Sacramento Valley, I tiredly thought after our 18-hour days in the Delta. Back again from the "wildlife wars" to see my family and fix up around the house that which would need fixing after my absence. Then my thoughts went to my long-suffering bride, Donna, a fulltime school teacher (and a damn good one, I might add), a mother of two "tom-cat-wild boys "Mr. Dad" in my absence, and homemaker all wrapped up in one super "Best Friend" and mate. No matter how one looked at it, she was the one family member who always pulled "more than her share of the wagon." What a God-given "catch" and blessing she was, I happily thought. Finally turning into my driveway and being met by my faithful Labrador dog carrying one of my old socks around in her mouth and "all happy to see your body wiggling," I was home...

Before dawn the next morning found me thundering north on Princeton Highway in a "London-like" thick pea soup tule fog. Another good day for the duck hunters and game wardens, but a bad day for the winged critters, I thought. Looking in my side view mirror, I could see my dog Shadow's large ears flapping in the cool moist air as I lumbered down the road. What a dog, I thought. If I didn't know better, I would say she was smiling and happy to be once again in the back of "her" patrol truck (I had left her home from my previous week's work because those types of covert duties Buck and I had planned were no place for her).

Later, eventually turning and tooling westward on the Delevan Road, I noticed an unusual and extremely fancy motorhome setting off in a harvested rice field by some other parked farm machinery. Flopping that bit of information into the back of my mind, I continued down Delevan Road as I headed for my day's planned patrol area west of Interstate 5 because when that time of the year rolled around in the winter, my ducks used to move west across the Interstate and hit the rice fields in that western part of the Northern Sacramento Valley. The local wildlife outlaws, understanding that ancient waterfowl phenomena, usually did the same. Hence, my presence in that area that fine morning so long ago.

Returning home later that evening on Delevan Road, I once again noticed my large and expensive motorhome still parked out in the rice field. Only this time its interior lights were on, and I noticed several large bunches of ducks and geese hanging in duck straps along the outside of the motorhome. Well, they are getting some shooting, I thought as I stored that information into the annals of my mind. Arriving home, I was met at the backdoor by the voices of my growing sons who were squabbling over a remaining chicken leg on a plate at the dinner table. I had to smile. Sons are good, I thought as I entered the warmth and took in the great smells coming from the kitchen in my home. There I was met by my beautiful, blue-eyed bride with a smile that said, "I am glad you are safely home." I was glad to be home and out from the foggy damp air as well. That was followed with a hug and a smooch, with my boys calling for their dad to "kiss her again, Dad," which I happily obliged.

The next morning before daylight found me backtracking my route from the day before. I had been pretty successful the day before on the west side netting five lads with over limits of ducks who were killing in such a manner that they really needed catching and I happily obliged. I was now hoping for another repeat performance with anyone else who had their hands illegally in Mother Nature's cookie jar. Passing my motorhome from the night before, I noticed my lads were up and getting ready for another hunt in a damn thick tule fog day. Only this time, I noticed all the ducks and geese that had been hanging outside their motorhome the evening before cooling out had now disappeared.

Once again that information went into my memory banks as I continued towards the western side of the Interstate. This time I was heading north and west. I had heard a world of shooting coming from the west side of the Town of Willows and figured I had better take a look, to ascertain if my lads were staying within the duck and goose limits of common sense and legality since many from that town had a historical penchant to do otherwise when it came to the world of wildlife.

Hours later, passing my motorhome at the end

of a long day working the lads west of Willows, I noticed four rather large-sized lads cleaning a pile of ducks and geese in the headlights of their RV. They had several plastic five-gallon buckets between them and into those went the guts from that day's kill. Taking a closer gander as I slowed my truck, I could see that again my lads had done quite well. Just like before, that information went into my memory banks for later retrieval especially if I found the lads from the motorhome hunting the next day.

Once again, I had done quite well on the west side, I thought as I slowly continued down Delevan Road in the evening fog. That is, if one can count eight chaps apprehended with over limits of geese and ducks along with three others possessing no federal duck stamps.

Tule fogs were good for three things to occur. In those days if a wildlife officer got off his tail-end and worked, he would be rewarded with numerous good waterfowl-related violations. Second, it was hell on the ducks and geese for all the facefuls of lead shot they received when low flying in the confusing fog. Third, all the duck and goose seizures I was now making were filling up my evidence freezers at the Sacramento National Wildlife Refuge like there was no tomorrow. If nothing else, it gave more "duck and goose fodder" for Chief Federal Judge McBride to distribute during the Christmas holidays to needy families in the Sacramento area when he "played" Santa Claus, I thought with a smile.

Then I noticed my duck gutters rising up from their work area as I passed their motorhome and hanging their day's bag limits once again on the side of their vehicle to drain and cool out. If they had several good days' shooting in the tule fog, they could now be over the legal limit. Now really interested, I threw on my cut-off switches which dumped off all my lights and stopped and watched my lads with my binoculars. Moments later, they all piled into a sedan parked at the motorhome and headed for what I suspected was the Town of Maxwell for some drinking, a warm dinner, or both.

Waiting until I made sure they were gone, I hatched a little plan. Slipping out from my vehicle and its place of hiding off the main road, I walked into their RV's parking area. There, I checked their birds hanging on the side of the motorhome. They had limits alright. Hell, who wouldn't have in this fine tule fog hunting weather, especially if they could hit the side of a barn. Then for some reason, the inner devil took over in me. As I was later to discover, it was a damn good thing he did... Taking out my Buck knife, I slit all the left-footed webs on their ducks in such a manner it wouldn't be readily noticed.

Then since their birds were properly tagged for temporary storage in accordance with federal regulations, I left the scene. But in the back of my mind was a nagging question. What had happened to all the other birds they had hung on the side of their RV days earlier? Because if they had kept them, they would now be over the possession limit, quickly rattled through my mind (a possession limit in those days was one daily bag limit).

The next morning as I headed west of the Interstate for the third straight day of sowing hate and discontent among my valley's local outlaws, I passed my motorhome. The lights were on inside, and after stopping, I could see through my binoculars several individuals in camouflage dress fixing breakfast. Damn, Terry, I thought. If those lads are going out again today, they bear better watching because they already have a horde of birds killed from the two previous days! Crossing the Interstate, I pulled over and waited for a spell. Finally figuring I had sat long enough for my "motorhome" lads to get into the field for the day's hunt, I returned to the scene of my parked RV and surrounding idle farm equipment. No one appeared to be at the motorhome so I boldly drove in among the idled farm equipment, parked, and dismounted.

Looking around, I saw a Burlingame,

California, fireman's patch on the window of the motorhome. There was another like advisory on the license plate carrier. Well, one thing is for sure, I thought, it appears we have a rig belonging to a fireman from the Burlingame area. At least, I would think the FBI would call that a clue... Looking around for any evidence of ice chests full of ducks sitting outside, I found none. All I discovered were a mess of feathers in front of the motorhome where the lads had gutted their birds from the evening before. Additionally, there were numerous splotches of dried blood on the side of the RV where duck straps of birds had hung earlier as they cooled and drained out. Other than that, the area was cleaner than a redbone hound's chow bowl. Oh well, I thought, my four lads are just storing their birds inside their motorhome for safekeeping.

Then I heard a number of shots ringing out several hundred yards to the south of the motorhome. That area was nothing but harvested rice fields, and if a crab has a shell, I bet that shooting is coming from my Burlingame crew, I thought. Forgetting my earlier planned trip west of the Interstate, my instincts were now with this motorhome crew. They had killed plenty birds previously and were now in the fields shooting once again. Suffice to say, my lads may be working on huge over limits, I thought. That suspicion, the increased sounds of shooting, and the "holy hell" my guardian angels were raising from within told me to get my miserable carcass moving in that direction, otherwise there wouldn't be a single duck left for posterity...

Swinging my truck further around behind the two rice harvesters and a bank out wagon so it would be better hidden, I got the surprise of the morning! Hanging in and among the idle rice harvesters, almost out of sight, were nine bunches of ducks and geese! Getting out from my truck, I walked over and commenced a bird count. Each bunch was tied in groups of 15 birds by a heavy wire. All had been gutted and hung out of sight to cool in the damp foggy air! In total, as I was soon to discover, were 30 assorted geese and 105 ducks! Talk about surprised! All I could do for a few moments was just stand there looking at "my bird nest on the ground" because a legal limit of ducks and geese for my four shooters, at a maximum, was 24 geese and 32 ducks! These lads were just a tad over the limit... Closer examination revealed that many of the ducks had their webs on their left feet with little splits! Gee, I wonder who had done that earlier with his Buck knife? Once all the over limits of birds were cut down, they were quickly photographed, seized and stashed in the back utility box of my patrol truck out of sight as evidence of my four lads' wrongdoing.

Locking the doors on my now-hidden among the farm machinery patrol truck, Dog and I took off on shank's mare towards the sounds of the shotguns "rattling" away to the south. Shotguns that more than likely "spoke" to the possible location of my four possible firemen from the motorhome.

After one hundred yards of harvested rice field hustle, I slowed and then began sneaking closer to my suspect four waterfowl gunners in the dense fog. As I walked, from the sounds of the huge numbers of confused birds in the air and the gunnery display I was hearing to my south, the day's "show" was in full swing. Stopping to catch my breath and cool out from my walking labors in the heavily rutted and still muddy rice field, I listened once again. I was able to echolocate onto the exact area from which my gunners were having such a great duck and goose-killing field day.

After catching my breath and cooling out, Dog and I began our final "run for the roses" before my chaps killed every living thing flying around them. Especially now, in the light of their over limits seized earlier from the parked farm machinery by their RV. Striding directly for the heavy and continuous sounds of gunfire, I was soon upon my waterfowl killing field and those pulling the triggers.

As I broke out from the dense fog, I first noticed a large bunch of goose and duck decoys cluttered about the freshly harvested rice field. Scattered in and among the decoys were dozens of dead ducks and geese with their heads and necks propped up with rice straw to increase the numbers of decoys in their set. The mixture of dead birds and decoys made for a real draw to the confused birds still flying overhead. Now out from the fog's covering embrace, I spotted four rather large, huskily built shooters strung out along a rice check. About the time I spotted them, they spotted me in all my beauty and grace emerging from the fog...

"Hey, you dumb son-of-a-bitch! Those are our decoys. Go find another place to hunt. This spot is already taken," thundered a husky voice from my group of four shooters.

Ignoring my "greeting and salutation," I continued picking up their dead ducks and geese in such a manner that was sure to "draw a crowd from my shooters." A crowd I would not have to run to ground once they discovered who I was if my little "pick up all their dead birds" plan worked. I was right. Instantly, here came four burly guys right at me with the "bits in their teeth," if the serious looks on all of their faces meant anything to the casual observer.

"What the hell are you doing, asshole? Those

are our birds and if you know what is good for you, you will leave them be," said the biggest of my four burly shooters. And I do mean burly, stout-looking lads. All sported mustaches right out of the 1800s and were built like brick outhouses! Now in those days, I was not like the old and broken down wimp I am today. I stood a stout six feet four inches in height in stocking feet, weighed in at a lovely and of course beautiful 320 pounds (beautiful to a cannibal, that is), and could heft over 450 pounds in a dead lift if necessary. However, approaching me had to be at least a collective nine hundred pounds of burly, testosterone aroused "beefsteak" right off the range, if you get my drift!

Turning, I parted my hunting coat so the lads could see my "hog leg" and held up my federal gold for all to see. Then I quietly announced, "Federal agent, gentlemen. I would say from the looks of what I am seeing lying here on the ground in front of your shooting positions, you lads have a small problem. For sure, there is an over limit of ducks and damn close to that in geese, if you are not over that as well," I said, in a matter-of-fact tone of voice meant to defuse the situation and add a little perfume to the air to diffuse all the strong testosterone smell being emitted from my four shooters...

"Who the hell did you say you were?" said the largest "fire horse" of the group.

"Federal Agent Terry Grosz," I said in such a manner that all could clearly understand.

With those words, my four burly lads stood down from their aggressive behavior and now began looking and acting a little concerned. I would have looked concerned as well if I had been them. From all the ducks and geese lying in and among the decoys, the area looked like a waterfowl battleground. And from the looks of it, the ducks and geese had not won that battle...

"Lads, I would like it if you would safely unload your shotguns so I might check to see if they are legally plugged. Please make sure their barrels are pointed safely away from the group to preclude any accidents. Then I would like to check your hunting licenses and duck stamps. Lastly, I will need a bird count to ascertain if you lads have gone over your daily bag limits," I said, so as not to be misunderstood in my mission or requests.

"Yes sir," said one that I was soon to discover was the group's unofficial leader named Dale Henshaw. "We are all firemen from Burlingame," offered Dale, "and we don't want any trouble. Especially from the 'feds,'" he continued.

"You lads won't have any problem with me unless you have a few too many birds over the limit. And in case that becomes an issue, it can be settled with a simple citation," I continued as I closely watched my lads especially over my latest words. They were a hefty bunch and I sure as hell didn't want to "dance" with any of them unless I had to. Especially if there was a "hanging in the wind" coming their way for having such large over limits of ducks and geese in their possession.

With that, as they trooped by, I checked their shotguns as numbers of birds continued making low passes over their field of decoys looking for a safe place to land and feed. Their shotguns checked out legal-like as did their licenses and duck stamps. Then began the real test of their intentions as I gathered in all their ducks and geese. They were 14 over the daily bag limit in the duck-killing department and four over in the goose arena once I had finished! As I counted out the birds in their presence, I don't think any of them could have passed any gas, especially as I got closer to their prescribed daily bag limits. When I counted the "overs," I knew there would be no gas passing in that bunch that fine foggy morning.

"Well, boys, we have a slight problem. The lot of you are 14 ducks and four geese over the daily bag limit. Since I don't know who took what, all of you will get a citation for joint possession of over limits of ducks and geese," I said. Then I just looked at the lads to see if they were to remain gentle as a hummingbird or were going to collectively plant my last part over the fence deeply into the rice field mud along with all the crawdad poop and duck droppings...

"Does this mean our fire captain will find out about this?" asked one Richard Bowen.

"Not on my account," I said. "Possession of over limits of waterfowl is a misdemeanor. But all of you need to be aware, once I file these citations in Federal Court in Sacramento, they will become a matter of public record."

"We can handle that," said Dale, with a look of relief flooding across his face. "Hell, this is one time we can piss in the wind and not even get wet," he continued, with an even-bigger, "I-know-something-that-you-don't-know-officer grin."

In that grin, however, I could plainly discern something even more sinister. That look said, "He may have caught us here with a small over limit, but he hasn't got us with what we have hidden back at the motorhome."

By then the tule fog was beginning to lift and I could just make out their motorhome some two hundred yards distant. Then I got an idea to preclude any future unpleasantries in the field, especially if they were aware of what I knew about what was so incriminating back at their motorhome now lying in the back locked box of my truck. The fact was they would have to stand before the "mast" for those over limit violations as well before the day was done.

"Lads, I will need some help with all these birds. Since they were illegally taken, they can't be possessed. So, my plans are to gut them here to lighten up the load as you folks pick up your decoys. Since you all have over limits, your hunting is done for the day. However, if you don't mind, I could use some help carrying out all these birds."

With those words, the mood of my burly brigade of four firemen from Burlingame turned a bit sour. "Well, officer, since we can't have any of the birds, you are on your own," said Dale with a sly smile. To my way of thinking once again, that "smile" spoke to his knowledge of the mess of incriminating birds still hidden back at the motorhome. The more quickly they could leave me behind staggering along with my load of evidence birds, the more quickly they could load up those hidden birds before I arrived at their motorhome (or so they thought) in their rig and escape. And upon escaping with their huge stash of birds still back at their motorhome, or so they thought, that would just put the icing on the top of their cake as they disappeared off into the sunset.

Nodding at the response I got with my request

for assistance, I said, "That being the case, I will keep your hunting and driver's licenses until I get back to your motorhome. Once there, I can issue all the citations and answer any questions at the same time."

Dale nodded that would be fine with him and the boys. Then out of the corner of my eyes, after a hurried conversation among themselves, I watched the four men hurriedly packing up all their decoys. As suspected, I figured they were in a hurry because they wanted to get back to their motorhome before I did. Then they could gather up all their hidden birds among the farm machinery left to cool out and hide them in the motorhome. Following that, after receiving their citations, they would split with a load of illegal birds having pulled the wool over the "goofy and dumb as a stick" federal agent's eyes. Well, my mom, God rest her soul, didn't raise a turnip. Matching my pace with the four men, I was ready to go just as they were ready to leave. Then across the wet and muddy rice field the five of us more or less "quick-timed." They wanted to get to their vehicle first, and me, I needed to keep pace to preclude any funny business, like them discovering all their previously killed birds were gone.

Now in those days, I was in great shape even for a fat man. I had a set of legs that would match a

Clydesdale's along with lungs like a blacksmith's bellows. Soon, even with the load of gutted birds I was carrying, I began to outdistance my four burly lads from Burlingame as they struggled with their awkward loads of decoys through the sticky adobe-like rice mud. Then I really poured on the coal as the thick fog began manifesting itself once again. With my legs churning and birds swinging from my duck straps, I quickly disappeared into the mists ahead of my now-wheezing, somewhat burly lads who were not in as good of shape physically as was the "dumb as a stick" federal agent.

Arriving at my truck before my four men in the field, I hurriedly drove it around to the back side of their motorhome like that was where I had it parked all along before they could see what I had done. That way, the lads would not figure out I had discovered their previous stash of ducks and geese in the harvesters. Then taking off my now thoroughly soaked and sweaty hunting coat, I placed it over the newest seized pile of birds in the bed of my truck. Lastly, I got on the radio and made a quick call. Then I moved around to the back of my truck and began slowly tagging all my recently seized ducks and geese with evidence tags as my four lads finally emerged wheezing from the mists as they fought the gooey rice field mud. (The rice field mud had been churned to all get-out each evening as the harvesters returned to this same spot in the field for daily maintenance and parking for the night.)

As my men caught their collective breaths, I said, "When you lads are ready for me to issue your citations and return your licenses, let me know." Then I continued filling out my evidence tags on the recently killed birds like all was quiet on the Western Front.

"You can start right now with me," said Dale, as he tried to smugly hide his little secret of the over limits previously hidden out of sight on the back sides of the harvesters.

Soon the others appeared after they had put away their hunting gear in the motorhome and gathered around my patrol truck for the paperwork to follow. As they did, I noticed out of the corner of my eye a white Sheriff's Office patrol car slowly emerging from the fog and coming down the road. Then it turned into the area in which sat the motorhome. Driving up to the motorhome, one Del Garrison, Deputy Sheriff and good friend, stepped out and just stood quietly there by the side of his patrol car as I attended to business.

Good old Del, I thought with a grin. Del was a big man. Quiet as all get-out, but as mean as a "she-grizzly" when aroused. Now let my four burly firemen raise any hell, I thought with a grin. If they do, at least my fanny won't be the only one mashed flat in the rice field mud along with all the crawdad poop... Hell, for that matter, now that Del was on the scene, I could still hear the dying sounds of the cavalry bugle as he stood quietly by his patrol car...

"Now, gentlemen, are there any questions? As all of you can see, I am issuing you state citations into the Williams Justice Court because of your cooperation instead of taking the lot of you into Federal Court in Sacramento. That way there will be less chance your fire captain will discover the lot of you killed over limits of ducks and geese. Are there any questions?" I asked once again, knowing the best was yet to come. Little did the men know, I had a rather "soft headed" female, lower court Federal Magistrate sitting on the bench in Sacramento. She didn't have the foggiest idea as to scope and degree of violations in the world of wildlife. So, in this rather serious instance, I took matters into my hands. The Justice Court Judge in Williams was one hell of a fine man and a great judge. He was a landowner and also a dyed-in-the-wool duck hunter. Judge Gibson clearly understood the variances within the magnitude of taking and possession violations. That was why my burly lads were not going to the Federal Court in Sacramento. As I have said many times, wildlife dies without making a sound. The only voice it had many times was that of a conservation officer. Therefore, my lads were going to the Williams Justice Court. At least there, the illegally taken ducks and geese would have a fair and final just word in the justice system relating to their untimely demise. All the men just shook their heads as to not having any questions as they continued eyeing Deputy Garrison trying to figure out how the hell he had figured out what was happening and had gotten there just as the action was being concluded.

"Well, if you lads have no questions, I have one," I said. "In the utility box in the back of my truck sits another 105 ducks and 30 geese. Birds that I strongly suspect were taken by all of you earlier. Especially since I have been watching the four of you each evening cleaning such large bunches of ducks and geese. After the four of you left for the field this morning, I drove into this area and discovered those birds hanging out of sight on the harvesters to keep cool. And since all are tagged with your names, as prescribed under state and federal law, it would be hard to disown those birds along with those ducks and geese the four of you took this morning. Any of you know which of you shot the over limits in that bunch of birds in the back of my truck seized from their places of storage on the rice harvesters?" I asked.

For just a second, there wasn't a sound from

my firemen other than the lot of them collectively sucking wind. Then all hell broke loose as every man jack of them all at the same time denied knowing anything about the birds, even in light of all their identifying tags. I let the men vent for a minute or so and then dropped my bomb square in the middle of their "noisy firehouse defense."

"Gentlemen, as I said earlier, for the last several days I have been passing by this area. Every day I noticed you folks had fresh birds hanging from the side of the motorhome. In fact, last night I observed all of you cleaning that day's birds in front of the motorhome's headlights. When finished, the just cleaned birds were hung in their duck straps on the side of your motorhome to cool out. They were hung out in such a manner and in plain view that a search warrant was not necessary or required if and when inspected by an officer of the law. Then all of you went into town, I presumed, for dinner or a couple of drinks. When you did that, I came back to your motorhome and marked the left foot on each of the most recently killed ducks and geese. I did so by splitting one of each bird's webs on its left foot. Also, remember you lads had properly tagged those birds as required by federal law (printed name, date, where taken, signature of the taker). Surprisingly, those are the same birds being held in my patrol truck. Now, you lads can deny all of that, or you can come clean and admit to those gross over limits of birds taken earlier and possessed by the four of you as well."

By now my lads were in complete shock. It was obvious the men were rubes when it came to violating the fish and game laws and lacked the ability to hold a stiff upper lip when presented with the ugly facts of pending apprehension. As I later discovered through their subsequent admissions, they had planned on taking an even larger number of birds back to Burlingame all along. There they had a local Chinese chef lined up who was going to prepare all the birds for a firehouse family annual wild rice fed duck and goose feed.

"Can we talk among ourselves, officer?" asked a now more-contrite Dale.

"Be my guest," I said.

After huddling for a few moments, Dale turned saying, "What do you want to know?"

"I want to know who took the birds, when and why," I said.

"All of us took the birds over the last several days for a family feed back at the firehouse," said Dale quietly. "As to who shot what, we don't know. We just party-hunted (a not-so-uncommon event by some shooters in today's world of wildlife. In short, everyone shot until they had all the birds they wanted without any consideration as to who shot what or the daily bag limits).

"Is that true, lads?" I asked. All the men shook

their heads affirmatively. Then I said, "All of you will be receiving a formal complaint in the mail, since I didn't see all of you taking those birds seized here this morning from the farm machinery after I talk to the Colusa County Attorney and Judge Gibson at the Williams Justice Court. I would suggest, when notified as to the court's action, that all of you take care of the matter posthaste."

"How much do you think it will be?" asked Richard Bowen. "Don't know, gentlemen. That will be up to the judge. But if I were a betting man, the fines will be stout enough that it will cause each one of you to take pause and remember this hunt the rest of your lives in case you have any future inclinations to do the same," I advised. "Especially since we have two different illegal shooting situations requiring several sets of charges in which all of you will be held accountable," I said.

With that and no further questions, the four beaten men boarded their motorhome and left the area. As they drove out of sight, I walked over to my friend Del Garrison who was still standing quietly by his patrol car as if nothing out of the ordinary had happened.

"How did I do, Little Buddy? Did I do good standing there looking all important-like?" he asked.

I just patted the shoulder of my bigger-than-life friend. How I do miss him to this day! He was always there for me so many times over the years when I was a state game warden and later as a federal officer. And many times the odds were not in our favor but he was always there. He later died from the complications of diabetes. When he died because of that disease and his many amputations, he was only physically half a man. However in my heart and soul, he will always be bigger than life to me. Being a diabetic myself, I am sure I will see him some day later on hopefully in a better world... Then maybe we can talk over old times over a piece of my bride's terrific homemade blueberry pie and the diabetes be damned!

My four burly firemen from Burlingame later forfeited $1,000.00 each in the Williams Justice Court for taking and possessing a gross over limit of ducks and geese. Additionally, Judge Gibson revoked all their hunting rights for a year in the United States.

I guess one could say that for the planned Burlingame firemen's family dinner, they had better have had a great Chinese cook. I don't know how "crow" tastes, but it has to be worse than rice-fed ducks and geese from the Northern Sacramento Valley. But as many of you know, those Chinese are some of the world's best cooks.

After all, over a billion people can't be wrong... Who knows, maybe their Chinese cook had a great recipe for crow...

Chapter Two

THE FIRST ANIMALS OFF NOAH'S ARK

THE MOURNING DOVE, to many American sportsmen, is one of America's most prized of the game birds. This small, fast-moving "winged rocket" of the uplands, grain fields, and weed fields hunting venues has become the harbinger of the rest of the fall and winter hunting seasons to follow. Usually hunted during the late summer because of its early southward migration patterns, it has become a cherished "first out of the bag" for the season's hunting sportsmen. However, hunting this winged rocket is not an easy task. When flying, it cruises along in an erratic flight pattern about 45 miles per hour, and the national average is about seven shots taken for every bird added to the sportsman's game bag!

However, in some parts of the country, like

the southeastern United States, a sub-cultural dove hunting tradition of primary importance has historically manifested itself. One in which great plans are laid for the sporting event soon to follow on the dove season-opening weekend. Guest lists are drawn up to return favors rendered previously, historical shooting fields are readied (read illegally baited in many instances), individual shooting positions are laid out, cold refreshments planned for by the proverbial barrel, a gathering of the clan, and at the end of the day, an epicurean event is laid out many times in the grandest of fashions. Epicurean events such as BBQ's, rivers of cold refreshment, every culinary accompaniment laid out in the finest Southern tradition, all liberally spiced with grandiose stories of shooting hits and misses during the morning's hunt, floods the senses. A great time had by all, except the great-eating, fast-flying, luckless dove which had the misfortune to fly lethally into a stream of No. 7-sized lead shot at the wrong moment!

In the western United States, the opening weekend of the dove season is somewhat less worshiped and more subdued. However, in some wealthy corners, a tradition similar to that followed in the southeast is still mirrored. But for the most part, the day's event is heralded with armies of less fortunate and sub-culturally disinclined sportsmen flooding into any available piece of dove-holding real estate for whatever "winged" fortune smiles on the shooter. In the end, several million of the feathered, excellent-eating rockets of the air fall to the sportsmen's guns before they can migrate to their southern climes.

In my day, however, not all dove were taken equally in all of the United States. That is, sadly to say, not legally. Many thousands fell over killing fields illegally littered with "bait" in the form of grains of food favored by the dove in such a manner as to attract the little game bird into the area so baited, many times in unholy numbers. This allowed the dove to be taken illegally, in many instances, in just as unholy numbers by the gunners gathered within the "shooting arena" (note for the record, I don't call them hunters because of the lack of fair chase).

Because of this lack of fair chase with the use and aid of bait placement, the federal government outlawed its use in the taking of migratory game birds in the 1930s. Thereafter for many years, the use and aid of bait to take migratory game birds was declared illegal. Those caught using and gunning with the unfair advantage of bait were usually dealt with harshly in the federal court systems. However, in some state court systems, that was not sometimes the law of the land. Since the illegal killing of migratory game birds was considered a victimless crime and many times laced with political overtones of favoritism at the local levels, sentences were less than severe for those breaking such laws. In those instances the illegal efforts by those seldom touched by the local, and sometimes lax, heavily politicized state court systems just multiplied.

Still, many members of the Thin Green Line persisted in pursuing and apprehending those societal elements illegally killing those of the voiceless in the winged world. Many times they did so at great peril to their careers due to the liberal thinking of the times by the local populace and from the actions of many "touched," crooked, powerful politicians as well. Peril came in the form of reduced promotions for doing one's job and arresting those of the wealthy or politically powerful breaking the baiting laws. Peril also came in the forms of being moved after such enforcement actions so one could no longer enforce said laws or just plain fired by the powers to be in some southern conservation agencies where politics ruled...

I walked into that picture in the spring of 1970 as a U.S. Game Management Agent working for the U.S. Fish and Wildlife Service after having worked as a California Fish and Game Warden for an exciting and adventurous four-and-a-half years previously. It was a new career position for me, prior to the meddling adventures of President Nixon initiating the destruction of the then U.S. Game Management Agent's historical immunity from such political forces hell-bent on having their ways when it came to breaking the wildlife laws of the land. But that story of cutthroat crooked federal politics and the proposed moving of U.S. Game Management Agents for enforcing the baiting laws on the wealthy or politically affluent, especially in the States of Illinois, California, Louisiana, and Maryland, is for another time and book. Thanks to Michigan's conservation minded Congressmen John Dingle, such vindictive actions, once he became aware of such activities, were nipped in the bud and not carried forth... But like I said, a story almost now forgotten, for another time...

Picking up my madly ringing office phone several months after becoming a new U.S. Game Management Agent, I said, "Good morning. This is Terry."

"Tiny (my nickname due to my size), this is Jack (my new boss and the Agent-in-Charge for Northern California who was based in Sacramento). What do you have planned for the next couple of weeks?"

"Nothing other than to continue picking up thousands of dead ducks killed by botulism (a bacterial poisoning), with the airboat (part of my game management agent duties) on Delevan and Sacramento National Wildlife Refuges," I responded. To you unwashed, botulism was a deadly killer of ducks, geese and other shorebirds in the Northern Sacramento Valley in the 1960s. Warm, shallow water, alkali conditions, rotting organic matter, reduced oxygen levels and the like created a bacterial "soup" on many of the valley's national wildlife refuges (before the refuge managers figured out how to manage the water depths on their refuges thereby alleviating most of the problem ... deeper, colder water meant less "toxic soup" opportunities). A metabolic by-product from the bacteria created a deadly poisonous environment for the ducks, geese and other water loving shorebirds inhabiting the area. Ingestion of the toxic soup by the critters led to paralysis and eventually death. Then in death, the bodies attracted flies. The flies laid their eggs on the carcasses and that soon lead to millions of maggots. Then surviving critters ate the wiggling maggots who were not bothered by the toxin but were super charged with the botulism toxin. The deadly result was even more winged critters died. Hence our "game management" job in picking up the dead and burying them so the deadly toxin could not be spread further.

"Good. I have another detail for you. The new

agent for Stockton, California, Case Vendel, won't be on line for another several weeks. Since the opening weekend of dove season is fast approaching, I need you to shift your duties to that area to work dove hunters until he gets moved and comes on-line. Plus that entire area, due to all the Italian influence, has a history heavy in the illegal use of bait in which to gun doves. Why don't you get your tail-end down there and see what you can stir up and give the state officers a hand if they need it," he continued.

"Any area in particular you want me to work, Chief?" I asked.

"No, hell no! When you get there, you will find the whole area loaded with every kind of bait covering every piece of available ground used to hunt dove. Those damn Italians have a motto that "if it flies, it dies." That goes double for those hunting dove in that area as well," he replied with a tone of deadly seriousness in his voice. "Plus, the Italians are damn good cooks and they really love eating their dove," he added as an afterthought.

"Ok, Chief. Give me a day to clean up and put my airboat away so I can get squared away for this detail. Then I will be "in the saddle" and on my way," I replied with a tinge of anticipation in my voice over a new type of adventure. Little did I realize, Jack had just handed me a law enforcement whirlwind of unreal proportions.

You see, there were only 178 U.S. Game Management Agents in the entire nation at that time. We were terribly short-handed (the same goes for the now special agent force today), fiscally challenged (the same goes for the agent force today), and faced with many law enforcement responsibilities in the world of wildlife (the same goes for the agent force today-get the point?). Because of those hard facts and the associative reality, we all quietly sang Custer's song dedicated to the U. S. 7th Cavalry, titled "Garry Owen," as our main musical theme while at the workplace. I think my readers, especially you history buffs, will get my drift... So into that whirlwind I went to see what illegal "sheaves" I could "reap," being that the dove was somewhat biblical in scope, if one believes in the story of Noah and the great flood.

THE SAN JOAQUIN VALLEY'S BAITED KILLING FIELDS

Two days later I kissed my long-suffering bride good-bye and gave each of my two sons a hug as I told them sternly to mind and watch over their mom. Then I left Colusa for the Stockton area some several hours distant. Checking into a Motel 6 ($6.00/ night in those days—read "cheap") because our law enforcement division at that time was low on funding (still a common problem as these words are written because of poor leadership in the Fish and Wildlife Service), I began doing what I did best as an experienced conservation officer.

First, I spent a day surveying the area using my knowledge about what constituted the most likely looking dove habitat. As I was soon to discover, that action on my part didn't carry much water. Hell, there were dove in every nook and cranny in that part of the country wherever I looked. Changing tactics, I began laying out on a map the best areas I found for dove concentrations over the next three days. Damn, I never saw so many dove as I did those following days. They were everywhere and by the tens of thousands! They abounded in the walnut groves, vineyards, wheat fields, safflower and sunflower fields, asparagus fields, wood lots, weed fields, and everywhere else in between! And I do mean by the literal thousands! Next, I tried a proven method I called "casting." Bailing out from bed before daylight to catch the dove's morning "lift-offs," I began moving around the area looking for early morning dove flight concentrations and activity.

Soon things began clicking and looking up. Without making it too obvious, I began mapping out the heaviest dove morning concentration locales on my field map (read, feeding areas). However, that activity proved to be problematic as well. There were dozens of such concentrations of dove sailing into all kinds of likely looking habitat like there was no tomorrow. Then I began mapping just those areas that looked like they were inhabited by swarms of bees from an overturned hive. You know, where dove were noticeably densely flying into and out of an area. Even the FBI would have called that kind of unusual activity a clue. In a word, that law enforcement method clicked.

"O-Dark Hundred" the next day found me moving in and around those fields where I had observed swarms of dove moving into the area as well as dozens of the birds sitting in long strings on transmission and telephone lines as if waiting for their chance to feed. Eureka! Using that "tricks of the trade" method, I began finding all kinds of swatches of recently placed bait! And I do mean bait, like by the ton in some instances! And I mean finding bait by the "long ton!" I discovered several large fields holding at least ten tons of plainly dumped-from-a-truck, rows of safflower seeds (a seed used for cooking oil production). It was very easy to see because the dump sites were plainly laid out between rows and rows of truck tire tracks and swarming with dove and pigeons (rock dove). And that was when safflower seeds sold for $270.00 a ton! Before it was said and done, I had discovered 39 major baited areas! And that didn't count the 27 other minor baited areas I had collaterally discovered as well in my stumbling around from place to place...

Following my discoveries found me on the phone to my boss in Sacramento. "Jack," I said. "I need some help. I have more damn baited areas than I can shake a stick at. I have found over 60 baited areas, 39 of which are monster major sites. I realize I am a rather large-sized chap but with so many baited areas, that spreads this miserable carcass of mine a little thin, if you get my drift."

He just laughed. "Tiny, I told you to expect a hatful of hornets. And it appears you have discovered what I suspected. Oh well, remember what the Texas Rangers used to say: 'One Riot, One Ranger.' There is no extra help available. Every game agent in the country has his hands full of the same problems throughout the rest of the western and southeastern United States. You are on your own unless I can get some help from the agents in Idaho since they don't have a dove season (some states did not have a dove season because many, it is rumored, still remembered the dove was the first bird off Noah's Ark. As such, it was not to be taken in the sport of hunting...). But don't count on that help forthcoming. Those guys have their hands full as well, especially in the southern part of that state with all their illegal eagle killing by the sheepherders. Keep me posted if something gets ugly, political or out of hand. Other than that, do what you do best and that is to catch as many of those cheating sons-of-bitches that you can. However, remember once those lads shooting over the baited fields discover who you are, they will scoot off like a mess of "mercury quail" through the fingers of even your big old hands." I was later to discover, no truer words were ever spoken.

Suffice to say, I got as much help as Custer did on the Montana prairies in 1876, when it came to working the San Joaquin Valley's baited dove fields. Oh well, as they used to say in Texas, "One Riot, One Ranger."

THE WEED FIELD

The baiting laws regarding dove during my time as an agent basically stated that it was illegal to take any migratory game bird over a baited area. In those days, the baiting laws were considered "strict liability" laws. If you were there doing something illegal, you were a "had dad." There were no legal requirements requiring that one had to know he was breaking the law. Just simply breaking the law did one in. Case in point, they were conservation laws meant to conserve the natural resources... And "take" was defined as any migratory birds being taken (hunted, captured, killed or pursued, or attempting to do so) going to or from that baited area. Today, because of howling and gutless politicians protecting their at-one-time illegally gunning constituents in states such as those "sports" in California, Maryland, Texas, Florida, and Illinois, those laws have now been weakened and watered down federally. Basically as I now understand it, unless the fields hold foreign seeds (seeds not of the current crop) or added bait where the shooters show culpability as to placement or knowledge of the illegality, you don't have much of a case to work with. No longer are the laws strict liability.

Once again, man's greed has overcome common sense and fair play. The history books are already replete with man's foolish decisions and greed relating to the natural resources of this great land of ours. This one on baiting will just be another deadly "rock in the box" pointing to the "greatness" of mankind and his natural ability to soil his own nest... But once again, I digress.

Dove season for 1970 was soon upon me as I readied my gear for a long day in the field. I figured I would first work a ninety-acre weed field loaded with safflower and wheat grains. Because of the foreign seeds in the weed field, it would be an easy case to prove no matter how one cut it. That would be my opening day mourning dove shoot's activity. Then for the afternoon shoot, I had selected a burned and freshly harvested fifty-acre wheat field loaded with safflower seeds. If I was able to catch all the violating chaps in those two fields, I figured I would be one spent lad come the end of the day. Man, was I ever so right in that angle of thinking.

Parking my patrol vehicle a short distance from what I called the "weed field," I raised the hood like I was broken down and placed a note under my windshield wiper advising I would be back soon with a wrecker. That way, I hoped my ruse would throw off any nosy or suspicious landowner. Off into the adjoining walnut grove I scuttled like a large land crab. Since the walnut grove bordered the weed field, I figured that is where my shooters would park their vehicles. They would have shade and a place to return for drinks and lunch when the morning's shoot waned and be out of the field of fire during the shooting activities. I had earlier discovered a pump house at the edge of the walnut orchard that looked out over the weedy field and the area where my dove gunners-to-be would be located. There was also a large, loose sheet of corrugated roofing alongside the pump house. I planned on lying under that so I could watch the day's events in the weed field and not be seen. It was for that cover I headed in the early morning's cool of the San Joaquin Valley and the action my first baited dove field would bring on the opening day of the hunting season.

Wildlife's Quiet War | 135

Banging around in my carry bag were the tools of my trade. Items such as binoculars, spotting scope, cite books, water, evidence tags, camera, bug spray in case I needed it, and chow in the form of an Italian salami. Therein also lay my "Plan B." To all my readers, everyone needs a Plan B just for everyday living. And if one is a conservation officer, he or she needs a good Plan B always close-at-hand.

In a small packet in the carry bag resided a number of printed five-inch-by-seven-inch Plan B cards. Each read: "NOTICE: A federal officer is watching those shooting over the adjacent baited weed field! He has recorded all the license plate numbers of said vehicles parked in this area. He is also filming all the shooters by their deeds, including facial shots of all the illegal shooters." (A small white lie — I didn't have such a camera). "If you leave this area without first being contacted by this federal officer; your vehicle will be impounded at a later date and sold by the government for being an instrument of a crime, to wit, taking migratory game birds over a baited area, a violation of federal law under the Migratory Bird Treaty Act. " (Another small white lie — the car taking and sale portion that is.)

I figured when the shooting got hot and heavy and the gunners were looking skyward at the incoming birds in the pre-dawn, I would sneak among the parked vehicles and affix the cards under their respective windshield wipers. That way when my magnificent presence made itself known on the "battlefield," that little warning just might take the "fleet" out from the flying feet of many of my runners. As it turned out, my little ruse pretty much worked as I had planned. Only five of my vehicles sped off not heeding the warning when I dropped the hammer later on. I figured the next few days of them having "curdled milk" over the worry of losing their vehicles was plenty of punishment for their heavy trigger fingers shooting migratory game birds over a baited area and for not being apprehended. Truth be known, I really couldn't remember all the faces and who was shooting or not in the baited area. So, the license plate numbers ruse was as worthless in a court of law as a mess of teats on a boar hog... By the way for the record, that old saying, "useless as teats on a boar hog" doesn't hold water. Scientist have discovered that the number of teats on a boar hog is really important. The more teats the boar hog has, the more teats his female offspring will have. The more teats a female hog has, the more piglets she can raise. The more piglets raised, the more money the farmer can pocket. So, that old saying really doesn't hold much water but it sure sounds good when used... Oh well, I thought that point would be important to all my non-farm-type readers who are reading these lines...

Lying down under my sheet of corrugated tin with little of me sticking out to be seen, I made myself comfortable. Setting my binoculars and notebook off to one side, I grabbed my salami and began my breakfast as I lay comfortably in the soft, recently plowed ground under my cool sheet of tin. Then a big bug-like object dropped onto the exposed back of my neck and began crawling towards my head. Thinking it was a stink bug which can bite, I made my move. Without a thought, I reached up and smashed the critter. Then shaking it off my neck and onto the ground in front of me, I illuminated it with my flashlight to see what it was. Like I have said many times in my previous books, God loves fools, little children, and game wardens. Lying there in the soft, diffused, slivers-of-light- through-my-fingers from my flashlight was a rather large, smashed flatter-than-a-flounder, female black widow spider! Bailing out from under my tin roof and turning it over, I discovered two more of the deadly spiders by their egg clusters. They, too, suffered the fate of their first ill-fated kin. Just another day in the normal life of a "tule creeper." Thank God for my guardian angels looking out for my miserable carcass... If that damn thing had bitten me on the back of my exposed neck, well...

Shortly thereafter, vehicles began noisily arriving in the walnut orchard behind me. Most parked not fifty feet from where I lay with my mashed-as-flat-as-a-car-hit-chicken, dead black widow spiders. Then as nearly as I could tell in the early morning's darkness, 43 chaps hurriedly exited the walnut orchard, walked out into the adjacent weed field and took up their more than likely pre-arranged gunning positions. It was then, as vehicular traffic abated and the darkness of the morning was still my friend, I rose and hurriedly sped among their vehicles, affixing my little five-inch-by-seven-inch "greetings" under their windshield wipers. Finishing, I scuttled back to my hiding spot like a rather large land crab, crawled under my tin roof out of sight and waited. I didn't have long to wait for the anticipated action to start.

Soon I could hear the soft sounds flying male and female dove make as they flew overhead and settled into the baited area for their morning's free breakfast of safflower seed and...lead shot! Now, some of my sharper readers caught what I just said. How the hell did he know the difference in sexes of the dove in the early dawn's poor light while lying under a sheet of tin roofing? Easy. A male dove makes a whistling sound from an alula or special set of feathers on the leading edge of its wings. A female dove is basically lacking such a sound or it is much reduced when flying. Just like hummingbirds. Bet you folks didn't know that either, did you? For all my readers who missed that clue, be aware. If you are not alert, I might just try and pull the "world of wildlife" wool over your eyes later on when you least expect it or are not really watching the swirling of events going on around your feet...

Suddenly it was as if the whole world erupted! Dozens of shotguns roared forth their "morning's greetings" into the surprised dove looking for a free meal. Several times shot "rattled" off my corrugated tin, black widowless cover...

That was my signal and I got down to the business at hand. Hurriedly recording brief descriptions of my shooters and dove killed, my eyes "scampered" from shooter to shooter within the binoculars. As I said earlier, it was illegal to take migratory game birds over a baited area. For me to prove my cases in a court of law, I had to show that my shooters were taking or shooting at dove over a baited area. That I quickly accomplished with my binoculars, notebook recordings, and my lads helping by pulling their triggers. Soon the shooting got so fast and furious, it was all I could do to just record my shooters and their illegal acts. In fact there were so many shooters and dove falling from the shooting that it became impossible to record who was killing what and how many. But that was well and good because I was between my shooters and their methods of escape. And now I had the recorded evidence I needed for any court of law when it came to illegally shooting over a baited area. I didn't have it all, such as number of shots fired or numbers of dove killed, but I had enough to get me through any court of law with a conviction and that is what counted.

Once I had satisfactorily noted every shooter in my weed field shooting at or killing a dove, I made my move. Made my move because there was no use in letting my lads kill everything under the sun just to hang large over limit charges on their miserable carcasses as well. In that particular baited field, it was more than possible to kill four hundred to five hundred dove before the day was done because of the way the birds were pouring in regardless of the shooting noise, sight of the shooters or intensity of activity.

The dove were so used to feeding there unmolested (the bait had been placed there at least a week earlier and left alone) that even with close-at-hand shooting they continued flying into the field, landed, and fed. Even in the presence of shooters walking around retrieving their recently killed dove in plain view the birds continued like a swarm of bees flying into harm's way. In their eagerness to eat, many were shot on the ground as they fed. It was plain to see why the government had outlawed the use of bait many years earlier. No two ways about it, it allowed killing to occur far in excess of the biological production of the species. Man was just too darned greedy and stupid to realize the damage he was causing to the resource to stop what he was doing. In short, to hell with those humans yet to come who might like to experience such wonders in the world of wildlife...

Rising from my position in the walnut orchard, I walked to my closest shooters like I owned the place. Approaching my lads, I quietly identified myself and requested and received their hunting licenses. Then telling them to stop shooting and not mention who I was under threat of going to jail for shooting over a baited area, I moved on to my next bunch of hapless shooters still blazing away.

Remembering Jack's earlier words about "mercury quail" once the alarm was sounded, I headed for the biggest groups of shooters (note I don't call them hunters or sportsmen). There, I quickly repeated my earlier procedures. That way I figured I would grab the largest number of lads before someone realized there was a German Teutonic "turd in their baited field punch bowl" (but even I had to admit "he" was a beautiful-looking turd...).

After grabbing off 22 hunting licenses from my

surprised shooters, the shooting began to abate and then got as still as a field mouse looking at a rattlesnake from just inches away. With the realization there was a badge-carrying-turd-in-the-punch-bowl in their midst, my shooters began slowly drifting back towards their vehicles like nothing out of the ordinary was occurring. However, I noticed every one of them greedily keeping their illegally taken birds as well as keeping their eyes on me!

In a surprise move, I abruptly turned and headed for my cutoff position where I could intercept every shooter as they exited the field for their vehicles. That cut-off maneuver stilled my now surprised "walkers" for a moment. Then my walkers turned into "runners" just like Jack had said as they "jack-rabbited" for their vehicles. In that "herd instinct" panic, I managed to grab off another six chaps and procured their licenses before the rest melted into the walnut orchard surroundings. Cutting directly back to the vehicles at a dead run, I grabbed off five more chaps' licenses in their process of hurrying to their means of escape. Then I turned my attention to the now occupied vehicles before they could get away. That I did by placing my most beautiful carcass directly in front of the moving vehicles in the orchard. That worked pretty well up to a point.

Then here came a Ford pickup hell bent for

leather with nothing but "escape" on the panicked driver's mind.

"Get the hell out of the way," bellowed the slightly tipsy driver as he aimed his vehicle at my magnificent carcass standing on the narrow orchard roadway. He lowered his head like a bull and put the pedal to the metal! His engine fairly screamed. Seeing he wasn't in the mind to heed my held-up hand holding my badge, I reverted quickly to my best John Wayne Plan C. Pulling aside my hunting coat, I exposed my sidearm and took a firing stance in case the Ford kept on coming at me like I was a jack rabbit in the road. That subtle little maneuver worked beautifully when the lad driving the vehicle observed my pulled-back coat exposing my gun hand resting quietly on the butt of my .44 magnum. I also think the look of finality on my face had some bearing on my driver's decision to stop. Dirty Harry could not have done it any better! Skidding to a dusty stop barely twenty feet in front of me, the driver bailed out from his vehicle and puked. I guess he had too much bad tasting John Barleycorn to drink out on the dove field, eh? Soon that situation was somewhat under control, but I had a hunch I had not seen the last of the mouthy fellow from the Ford. That feeling would soon bear fruit of a different flavor come the afternoon...

As it was, several vehicles drove off in great

haste sliding around me as they left a cloud of dust hanging thickly in the orchard. With the amount of red spider (leaf parasite) in the area and the dust being raised (acting as a carrier for that parasite), that had to have made the walnut farmer real happy...

By then, most had more than realized the turd in the punch bowl was one of those damn "federal agents." After the exhibition of "sportsmanship" in the dove field that morning by the many shooters, that federal agent was in a ticket-writing mood. Three hours later, I had issued 36 citations for taking migratory game birds over a baited area, five citations for using unplugged shotguns, and four more for over limits of dove in possession. In addition, after several individual questions per hunter, I discovered every one of my lads knew the field had been baited! Real sports that bunch especially after learning the field had been baited specifically for an illegal hunt... While my lads gutted my now-evidence birds so they wouldn't spoil in the late summer heat (wildlife taken illegally cannot be possessed), I collected my five-by-seven cards off their windshields for possible later use in another like situation. Then I walked the shooting area looking for cripples and dead birds. In that endeavor, I picked up another 55 unclaimed birds scattered about in the weeds. In total, I

Wildlife's Quiet War | 145

had seized or picked up 178 dove! Finishing up with my mess of "high-quality sportsmen," of whom 33 turned out to be Italians from the area, I contacted the landowner. In that meeting, I advised that I couldn't stop him or his friends from shooting migratory game birds over the baited area. But if they continued shooting over that field and I caught them, I would pinch every man jack of them. I also advised no legal hunting could occur over the area until ten days after the last of the lure or attractant had disappeared. The farmer, who admitted to baiting the field for his friends, later chose to disc under the entire weed field that very day. Oh by the way, that farmer received a federal citation for 18 U.S.C. 2 (Aiding or Abetting) for placing the bait in the field and inviting his friends over to illegally shoot a migratory game bird (dove) over the area.

Each chap cited for shooting over bait later paid $150.00 in Federal Court in Sacramento for that violation. For using an unplugged shotgun, that cost the owner of said firearm another $50.00. Those with over limits paid $35.00 for that violation plus an extra $25.00 per bird over the limit. Not a bad morning's work I must admit for my first baiting cases as a federal officer. The dove were all iced down to preserve them and later donated to the Sutter County Sheriff's Office to feed the prisoners. To those of you who know how good-eating dove are, I would say those prisoners ate pretty darn well when it came to their safflower-fed dove dinners from the San Joaquin Valley. Especially if that had been accompanied with mashed potatoes, gravy, fresh spring peas, hot biscuits and maybe a good bread pudding with lots of raisins and heavily seasoned with cinnamon, sugar and nutmeg... Man, I am sure glad God made me a chow hound!

THE BURNED WHEAT FIELD

As planned for the afternoon shoot, I headed for a nearby burned wheat field that I had discovered earlier that was also heavily baited with safflower seed. For that operation, I had a different Plan B. My battle plan was to go into the field with all my illegal afternoon shooters just "like one of the boys." There I planned on getting in among them as another shooter. I figured that when I had enough evidence for a court of law I would drop the hammer on those shooters I could quickly capture as well. However, that operation would also call for a Plan C. In that plan, I would take afield an empty double barrel shotgun (empty, so no one could say I was shooting illegally or trespassing and hunting on private property). That would allow me to get close to my shooters with a minimum of attention and then I could put the grab on them from just "next door." Or so I thought still being a rookie at working this baited field thing...

Arriving at the wheat field just as the afternoon shoot was beginning, I drove my undercover, looking all normal-like, patrol vehicle in among the other shooters' vehicles. Since my vehicle was unmarked and carried a regular license plate, I figured I had the edge. I was also dressed head-to-toe in regular dove hunter's garb so I could really look the part. Getting out, unlimbering my shotgun and taking my time, I noted four fellows immediately to my right shooting dove over the nearby baited wheat field. Reaching back into my car like I was looking for shot shells, I duly noted my four shooters in my notebook lying on the seat. Grabbing up my shotgun, I walked onto the edge of the baited field of gunners. As I walked onto the field and headed for a place without someone else in the immediate area, I took stock. There were 51 shooters all banging away at the afternoon flight of dove as they came into the heavily baited field. Knowing there was no way to round up all those lads, I selected an area of the field holding 19 shooters in a large, close knit group. I figured I could capture this group quite easily when I decided to drop the hammer on my illegal shooters mashing all their greedy fingers as they eagerly "dug" around in Mother Nature's cookie jar...

As I worked my way towards the group of 19 shooters, I kept my eyes skyward as if looking for dove. Every time one would come close, I would pretend not to see the critter until it was too late for a shot. When I had worked that ruse to death, I began seeing the dove just a little too late as I raised up my shotgun like I was going to shoot and then changed my mind because the bird was now out of range. When that ruse went south, I pretended to be having troubles with my shotgun's firing mechanism. Finally in false disgust, I broke it down in front of God and everybody, especially my "selected" 19 shooters, as if trying to repair the errant double barrel firearm. By then, I had managed to observe every man jack of my party of 19 shooting at or killing dove over the baited area. In short, just the evidence under the Migratory Bird Treaty Act for a conviction that I would need in a court of law.

"Hey, that asshole is a federal agent," came a voice from the far side of the field.

Turning, I saw my "voice" as that of none other than the "puke" with the Ford pickup I had "touched" earlier in the morning back in the weed field shooting over bait. Within moments of the man's warning outburst, the shooting had all but stilled as most everyone looked around for the federal agent "turd in their baited field punch bowl."

"There he is," continued the voice as he now pointed me out to the crowd of illegal shooters. Now you talk about a turd in the punch bowl, it was plain for all to see it was a large and evil-smelling one if what the puke said was true...

Observing my puke from the Ford and his handful of dove quickly leaving the field, I stored that picture in the back of my mind. For you see, it is not nice to piss off Mother Nature or her minions, much less piss on one... Since I had observed my puke shooting and now walking off from the baited field with a handful of dove, I would make it a point to see to it he was once again charged with taking migratory game birds over another baited field. See, I told you it was not nice to piss off Mother Nature... If my puke thought his fine was high for the first violation, imagine what it would be like for a second such violation in the same day!

My group of 19 were now all standing within capture range after hearing the words from the puke. Taking that as my cue, I headed directly for my chaps before they could bolt like a bunch of spring colts in the pasture. Holding up my badge, I said, "Hold it right there, lads, Federal Agent. I have recorded all the license plates from your vehicles and anyone who runs will find his vehicle impounded by federal authorities for later auction." (I lied. My little statement was what one could call a "force multiplier," especially if it held them in their tracks like that of a deer in the light of a spotlight on a moonless night.)

Those in the group of 19 who had started drifting off after the earlier words of warning from the puke now froze in their tracks. Then it was too late for their escape. I was among my group of shooters and it is human nature to "hold" when "Johnnie Law" was in such close proximity. At least, that was generally the case in those days. Today it seems when the law is at hand and you are in the wrong, many people will choose to run. I kinda liked the simpler days of old... As for the others in the field, it looked like the start of a race at the Daytona Speedway. Shooters were running every which way but loose for their vehicles. Those already at their vehicles were streaming from the area like the devil was hot on their trail! There was enough dust in the air from all the fleeing vehicles that it looked like an old fashioned "redneck" stock car race on a dirt track at the fairgrounds in Georgia on a Friday night.

But I couldn't be bothered with "spilled milk." I had my hands full with 19 lads wondering if they should run or what was coming next. Gathering all my lads around me, I had them stack their dove at their feet as I once again identified myself. Then taking note of the number of dove at each man's feet, I began the paperwork. A while later when I was finished with the paperwork, I had each man clean his dove and pick the ants off them so I could save them for donation (the ants had gathered on the carcasses when I had the lads pile them on the ground by their feet for easy counting). As I confiscated each man's dove, he was issued an evidence receipt for his birds.

Ah, folks, you will have to wait for a bit... I am listening to a CD on my computer blaring out the skirl of bagpipes as these words are written. They are playing the last song my son and I "heard" together as they took him off in a hearse to be cremated. I just am plain damn having a hard time writing these words as that song brings back sad memories of my 35-year-old police officer son who died in the line of duty before his time, leaving a lovely wife, two great children and his broken hearted parents behind with only memories... Damn... I used to love bag pipe music but not any more... I apologize for the break in the story but it just happened and stalled me in my literary tracks.

Continuing on, each man later forfeited bail in Federal Magistrates Court in Sacramento. As before, each man paid $150.00 for taking migratory game birds over a baited area. Those with over limits, of which I had five, paid $35.00 for the violation and $25.00 per bird over the limit. The two men found to be using unplugged shotguns each forfeited an additional $50.00. The two chaps discovered hunting without a valid hunting license each forfeited $35.00 in addition to their other violations. As for the puke with the mouth who gave me away on that baited wheat field that fine afternoon, he was once again "dumped." I had an Information (Complaint) filed on the lad and he was made to appear in Magistrates Court in Sacramento. When I saw him that time, he once again looked like he was about to puke. A $500.00 dollar fine and warning to never again appear in Judge Ester Mix's Magistrates Court made the chap fairly turn green for his second violation of that day (he paid the standard $150.00 for the first violation). I never again ran across that tough guy who puked after my first car stop on the baited weed field or the mouth who gave me away on the burned wheat field later on that same day. Probably best I didn't for his sake. Once again, I more than paid for the gas and oil that day... But, my day wasn't finished, not by a long shot in a manner of speaking.

THE MOTEL 6 PARKING LOT SURPRISE

Stopping at a convenience store later that afternoon, I took on a load of fuel and several bags of ice for my evidence birds residing in my ice chests. After icing down my two ice chests of dove, I headed for my motel for a shower and some rest. Parking my car in the slot next to my room, I began unloading my gear. Alongside me were four lads, obviously hunters from the looks of their garb, unloading their gear as well. As hunters will do, the question came up on how each other did. My lads did so out of general interest and me asking the same question doing so with the law enforcement motive in mind.

"We did pretty good," said a tall lanky chap. "How did you do?" he asked.

Without a word, I beckoned my four lads to the backseat of my unmarked patrol car. When the men were all eyes, I opened up the ice chest in the backseat. It contained several hundred dove from my day's labors. Stepping back, I let my lads take a long look. I did that for several reasons. First, I wanted to see what four sportsmen would say about an obvious over limit by a "game hog" who was obviously all "hind-end" for doing such a thing Unfortunately over the years, I have discovered many folks will look and say nothing out of the ordinary or to the law over what they observed! Second, I had done this before at other times in other parking lots under like circumstances. Several of those times my actions had borne fruit of an "over limit kind from other shooters," if you get my drift. So, nothing ventured, nothing gained to my way of thinking. As expected, other than a bunch of *whoo-ees* over the huge numbers of birds, nothing! Those reactions were compounded when I had the men follow me to the trunk of my car and showed them another ice chest full of a huge number of iced down dove as well.

For a long moment none of my four "all-eyes" chaps said anything. Then the lanky one said in what I considered a heavy Texas accent, "Them's nothing, boy. Follow me." With that he gestured for me to follow him into their motel room. Once inside, I saw four ice chests. "Lanky" opened up the first ice chest saying, "Them we got four days ago." Then opening up a second ice chest, he said, "Them we got three days ago." All the while proud of himself and his hunting prowess and that of his compatriots, he commenced showing me like ice chests full of dove from two days earlier, and finally those taken during the first legal day of dove season!

"Where did you guys get all those dove?" I asked like a big-eyed dumb guy.

"Oh, on a friend's ranch several miles from here," said Lanky with a proud smile.

That proud smile turned to mush when I chose that pregnant moment to "roll the gold" on them. Then all of my chaps burst out in raucous laughter. When they quit laughing, I stood there like a dumb head. What the hell is so damn funny? I thought. Their hind ends are hanging out so far, they never again will be ever able to take a respectable dump, I thought...

Finally Lanky, who I was soon to get to know as Dave Robinson from Oakland, said, "That is a great joke. Acting like a cop and all."

Pocketing my badge, I said, "Gentlemen, my name is Terry Grosz. I am a United States Game Management Agent whose primary duties are to enforce the regulations under the Migratory Bird Treaty Act. Since that includes dove, I find that you chaps are a tad over on the lawful possession limits of dove allowed. That being said, all of you will be cited for possessing over limits of dove and the birds will be seized." Man, with that revelation, it had gotten so quiet in that motel room you could have heard a stink bug passing gas the next county over.

Suffice to say, that day did not end so well for my four chaps. Later each man was assessed $500.00 each for possessing over limits of dove, to wit, sixty over per man in Magistrates Court in Sacramento (the maximum fine allowed under the old Migratory Bird Treaty Act for fines; seldom was jail time levied in those days.). I did find one thing strange, though. Even though the men had shot dove early before the season had legally opened, they had stayed within the daily bag limit for each day they had illegally shot. Go figure... Also to my game warden-type readers, you probably noted that I did not take my four shooters for "taking dove during the closed season," but had written them for possession over limits. That was because I could not prove "take" other than what they had said. Proving "possession," however, was a piece of cake since the ice chests holding the over limits were in their motel room.

The next day I hooked up with Buck Del Nero, California State Fish and Game Warden from Stockton, and many more lads fell to our "scavenging" the dove fields in the San Joaquin Valley. That relationship did not end there. Buck and I had gone to the fish and game academy together years earlier. While there, our friendship grew and years later we stormed across the duck marshes in his Stockton district as well. Many battles, political and otherwise, were fought, but you readers will have to read those stories in one of my earlier books titled, For Love Of Wildness. Those stories will be more than worth your time when read... However, be prepared for what you read. It won't be pretty, especially when the killing got ahead of me and before I could get it shut down and those pulling the triggers corralled and "stump broke."

TRAPPING DOVE AND OUTLAWS IN BEAR VALLEY, COLUSA COUNTY

One of my wildlife management duties as a U.S. Game Management Agent was the annual trapping and banding of mourning doves. Information gleaned from those activities would then be passed on to the U.S. Fish and Wildlife Service's Migratory Bird Management Office for dove population evaluations. Ultimately, that and other biological data would be used to set subsequent dove hunting season dates and bag limits. Having recently been assigned a dove-trapping assignment as a new officer and given a banding quota of five hundred dove, I began looking for a safe and secluded area in which to trap because I didn't want anyone to discover and rob the newly captured dove in my traps in the process. I finally settled on a piece of real estate in western Colusa County in Bear Valley owned by my rancher/farmer friend, Terrill Sartain. The Bear Valley Ranch was a 66,000-acre piece of fairly deserted and arid real estate that held a sizable population of mourning dove. Hooking up with my old friend Cliff Fulton, a Colusa County Reserve Deputy Sheriff and Reserve California Fish and Game Warden who was patrolling Sartain's ranch as a second job, off we went. Locating several likely trapping areas along creek beds, scrub oak, and cheat grass fields, we set to work setting out my live traps. Soon I had 18 large, fine mesh wire figure-eight traps baited with safflower seed set out ready for business. Now all I had to do was wait a day for the birds to find the bait, have them greedily walk into my traps, and I would be off and running to meet my banding quota for the Service.

Mid-morning the following day after the dove had fed, Cliff and I headed out to check my traps. My first trap was a total surprise. At one end inside the trap huddled twenty or so unable to escape, horribly frightened dove. At the other end laid a fully fed, four-foot- long rattlesnake with two very suspicious bulges inside his ample carcass. Two of my trapped dove I suspected were represented by those damn bumps. It was plain that the snake had come upon my dove trap and spied several hapless feathered dinners contained therein. Finding the small entrances on the side of the trap, entrances that allowed easy entry but foiled any exit, the snake had made himself quite at home. While there, it managed to polish off two of my hopelessly trapped, scared-out-of-their-wits mourning dove.

That dove-eating snake, later sautéed in olive oil, onions, fresh mushrooms and fresh garlic, along with a side of some of my world famous mashed potatoes (loaded with sour cream, cream cheese, butter, and spices), and a fresh, as only

Wildlife's Quiet War | 159

California vegetables are, green salad, made a hell of a nice meal that evening for Cliff and yours truly... In fact, from then on, Cliff and yours truly never passed up a rattlesnake lawfully captured in the serpent-infested Bear Valley. And later, each of those subsequently discovered snakes came to know olive oil and fresh garlic up close and personal like, after they had been promptly dispatched of course... Eat my poor little old doves will they!

For the next week during daylight hours, Cliff and I trapped, sexed and banded over five hundred dove. Then at night, the two of us worked the many ever-present deer spotlighters using the Bear Valley deer herds as their own personal shooting gallery and meat market. However, I was always on the lookout for better banding spots as the two of us roamed around, especially when I began re-trapping some of my previously trapped and banded dove returning to their original earlier trap sites.

It was during one of those times of exploration that I stumbled onto an unexpected bonanza. Driving further along Bear Creek in the dry Bear Valley geography, Cliff and I spotted an unreal number of doves roosting in the nearby oak trees. As we drove up, they exploded from the trees like a covey of bobwhite quail. Since dove never congregated in such numbers without a damn good reason, my old game warden senses went into high alert. Further examination of the area in the location of the flocks of tree-dwelling dove revealed an unexpected bonus and welcome surprise. The area in which we had discovered so many dove had been previously baited with wheat! Now, there is no law that says one cannot place out food for migratory birds. One just can't shoot the migratory critters over it.

Well, hellfire and damnation soon followed! The ground around the baited area was littered with freshly spent 12-gauge shot shells from an earlier shoot (I could tell from the smell of freshly burned powder when smelling the spent shells)! Seeing "a bird nest on the ground" or a close-at-hand law enforcement opportunity, Cliff and I quickly hustled our "last parts over the fence" out of the area in case our illegal shooters came back into the area unexpectedly and discovered us.

Wednesday and Thursday of that week, Cliff and I banded birds in the morning and then staked out our newly discovered baited area until dusk. No one showed. However, come that next Friday afternoon, that "waiting" for our illegal dove shooters became a cat of another color.

To our joy, a large motorhome appeared in the area and soon located itself under the shade of a stand of trees in an oak grove adjacent to our baited area. Emerging from the motorhome came four lads with drinks in hand and expensive Cuban cigars stuck in their faces. I remember looking over at Cliff with a grin which was matched by one of his own. "Hot dog," I thought. Meat on the "hoof" and they didn't have a clue there were a couple of real good "grillers" incountry. But to our surprise, our lads never fired a shot that afternoon. They set up their camp and in the evening just sat around a campfire drinking and having a good time. That was the way we left them later that evening.

Cliff and I still had work to do that evening. We had to pull each of our dove traps in case we got tied up with our chaps shooting over bait the following day. I especially didn't want another rattlesnake-dove-eating episode to occur on my account. Nor did I favor my dove being trapped and then unable to get out of the Bear Valley hot sun to drink after feasting on the dry safflower scattered in and around the trap site. If that happened, the safflower previously ingested would expand and burst in their crops causing a sure-fire slow death. Then the two of us headed back to the ranch for dinner and some sleep before the much anticipated morrow's dove shooting events.

Come daylight the next morning, Cliff and yours truly were in position to observe our chaps and yet not be seen. Man, did the two of us get another bonus surprise! Two of the lads emerged from the motorhome right at daylight with rifles! Then back into the forest of oaks and cheat grass fields they went. Within an hour, Cliff and I heard one shot! An hour later, our two rifle-carrying chaps returned with obvious dried blood on their hands and forearms (as seen through our 60x-power spotting scopes)! It was plain to us these two had just taken a closed season deer (the only big game in the area and before the later arrival of feral hogs)! Since they had not returned with the critter, I suspected it was now cooling out in the shade of the oaks where no one would look. Well, they had that little ditty wrong! I knew two chaps that would look until they found that deer and then the "poo" would hit the fan big time!

After a while, out from the motorhome bailed our four chaps with their shotguns in hand, more cigars stuck in their faces, and sporting big grins. Walking over to the wheat-baited area some forty yards distant, they spread out along a line of trees. Soon their shotguns began popping and the dove boiled out from their roost sites in the oaks like someone had once again overturned a hive of bees.

Using our binoculars, Cliff and I had a clear view of the activity and began recording the actions of the shooters and the numbers of dove killed. When we had all the evidence we figured we needed for a criminal case, we abandoned our positions and hotfooted it back to my new patrol truck hidden in the oak forest a quarter of a mile away.

A beast, if you will, was my new truck. A new three-quarter-ton, stick-shift, Dodge pickup (that "tanker" cost the government $2,000 in those days!). Across the rear of the bed near the tail gate laid a 750-pound steel plate and in the front of the bed, just behind the cab, was a large tool and accessory box along with a specially built 75-gallon gas tank. For rubber on the ground, the truck sported ten-ply tires. For a mill, well, a 383-cubic inch engine with a four barrel carburetor provided the "frosting" on that "cake." That truck could safely run on gravel roads up to 93 miles per hour before it began to "float." I never lost a chase in that truck, including one in which I ran down a Porsche 911! That chase took me twenty plus miles on a gravel road through Bear Valley but in the end I had my illegal, closed season dove-killing Porsche driver. The way I figured it, unless the lads in the motorhome had a thousand-horsepower mill under their hood, there was no way they could get away from me that fine day if a chase was in the offing. Plus, it is a little tough to outrun Motorola, if you get my drift...

Swinging out from our hiding place, Cliff and I began our "run for the roses." As we drove down the Bear Valley road in plain view a short distance from where they had parked, I saw our four lads quickly laying down their shotguns and begin walking back to their motorhome like nothing out of the ordinary had occurred.

"Mark their shotgun locations," I said to Cliff, who, being an experienced officer for many years, really needed no such instruction. He was one hell of a good officer and a World War II veteran. He had seen so much in Europe that little now fazed him, especially when it came to four guys trying to act innocent and all pretty-like. May God rest Cliff's soul these many years later. He was a good man and a "blood brother" to my now-older Special Agent supervisor son, Richard, who is currently stationed in North Dakota.

Turning off the main dirt road onto the two-track trail leading to our four culprits still making "we are innocent" haste for their motorhome, I just smiled. It was always amazing to me just how guilty one looked when trying to act all innocent and beautiful-like.

Pulling up alongside their motorhome, Cliff stepped out. Since he was in charge of security on the Sartain ranch, he began asking the men if they had their identification allowing them to hunt on the property supplied by the main ranch office. Each of the four men were all happy-like and quickly produced the required paperwork. Since dove season was on, Cliff also checked the men's hunting licenses. They were in order as well. Then Cliff asked them why they had laid down their shotguns when we came into view since dove season was open.

One of the men, a chap named Donald Jackson, replied, "We had just decided to come in and get some lunch and a few drinks. No one else is in the area, so we figured our shotguns were safe and left them at our hunting spots for retrieval when we returned. That way we didn't have to carry them to and from our hunting locations."

Since I was the senior wildlife officer in charge, Cliff looked over at me to now proceed as I saw fit. Walking around the front of my truck, I identified myself to the men. Then I just looked at them for a long moment for the effect it would have on their guilty souls. You know, like a rattlesnake would look at a mess of trapped dove before he went into the hot garlic and olive oil in a cast iron frying pan...

"Gentlemen," I said. "We have a slight problem. The area over which the four of you have chosen to shoot dove is baited." When those words were uttered not a man moved. In fact, they reminded me once again of my terrified dove huddled at the end of my first trap looking at the snake that had just eaten two of their brethren...

Then the explosion came! There was instant denial from all four quarters as the men let me know in no uncertain terms I was dead wrong. I just let the lads get it out of their systems, then shut off the grumbling denials with a wave of my hand.

"Gentlemen, let me continue," I said. "Several days ago, Officer Fulton and I discovered the baited area over which the four of you just shot this morning. We collected the needed evidence and staked out the area in case those putting out the bait returned. We observed the four of you arrive yesterday afternoon and then shoot the area in question this morning." Man, it was then that I saw a flash of sick looks zip across the faces of the two lads we suspected had shot what probably was a deer earlier in the day just after daylight. You know, that kind of a look when you are a small critter who has fallen into a southern marsh and has managed to quickly crawl out of the water onto a log only to realize the log is moving and it ain't no log but a hungry gator with bad thoughts on his mind and possessing an empty gut...

Continuing, I said, "Well, there is a way to settle this 'hoorah.' What say the six of us return to your shooting area. There Officer Fulton and

I will show you the bait used which was wheat. Since wheat is foreign to this area of cheat grasses and oaks, all of you will have to admit it looks suspiciously like a baited area. Once that walk-about is concluded, we will pick up your dove, shotguns, a fresh sample of bait, and then return to your motorhome. There Officer Fulton and I will issue all of you citations for taking migratory game birds over a baited area. At that time if any of you feel we are wrong in our assessment, you can later challenge these charges in a court of law which will be the Williams Justice Court located in Williams."

For the next thirty minutes or so, Cliff and I took the lads to look over the baited area. There we showed the now very quiet men the wheat strewn all over the ground. During that process, the men finally admitted they had spread out the wheat in the hopes of having a great dove shoot, along with their deer hunting (deer hunting was allowed on the ranch during the open season and for bucks or male deer only. However, at that time, deer season was closed until the following week). Being a gentleman, I thanked the men for their honesty in owning up to the error of their ways. Cliff and I then took new wheat samples to close the evidence ring on our case, picked up the dove killed by the men and a mess of freshly spent shotgun shells, and their shotguns.

Walking back to their motorhome, the men had little to say. Then getting out our state citation books, the two of us issued the men state violation notices for their little error in judgment. When finished, I asked the men if they had any questions regarding the matter. One man, a Darrel Jenkins, asked what the fine would be and I advised they would have to call the judge in the Williams Justice Court for that information. Silence followed that question and I sensed our dove baiting issue was settled.

Then I dropped the bomb. "Gentlemen, all we have to do now is finish the matter on the illegal deer." Those words hit the men like a thunderclap! The four men just looked at us like they had just seen the Grim Reaper pass by, and he had been looking right at them! Not receiving any follow-up arguments from the men, I pointed to the two men Cliff and I had seen with the deer rifles earlier in the morning. You know, the two who returned to the motorhome shortly after we heard one shot with what appeared to be dried blood on their arms and hands. Once again, none of the four captured chaps dared to even breathe. Then one of the suspected riflemen attempted to deny any wrongdoing. His denial was less than convincing and it was clearly evident by the look on his face that he knew it. Wanting to get back to my dove trapping, I cut short any further "cat playing with a mouse" discussions with a wave of my hand.

"Gentlemen, Officer Fulton and I saw the two of you (pointing out the men) depart the motorhome this morning carrying rifles. Shortly afterwards, the two of us heard one shot. Then a short time later, the two of you returned and from our vantage point using 60x- power spotting scopes, it was evident the two of you were sporting what appeared to be dried blood on your hands and forearms. Now, we can continue this little charade, or you can go and show us where the deer is and we will settle this issue with just a citation. However, make the two of us go and find that suspected deer, and we will, and then the two of you will find yourself in a Sheriff's Office patrol car en route to the Colusa County jail for taking a closed season deer. The choice is yours to make, lads," I stated.

Twenty minutes later, the freshly killed, illegal deer was in our hands, and once again Cliff and I issued state citations to the two lads for possessing a protected game animal, to wit, one doe deer. Later in the day, Cliff and I delivered the deer to Deputy Sheriff Carter Bowman located in the small western Town of Stonyford so he could give it to a needy family before it spoiled in the early fall heat. Cliff then telephoned Terrill Sartain with the word on the men's violations.

Terrill quickly revoked the four lads' rights to all hunting on his land and advised he would do so formally that day with a registered letter of their dismissal from his hunting club.

Cliff and I, on second thought, returned later to the deer's now fly-covered gut pile after our four sports had left the area. There we ran off a bobcat and retrieved the deer's heart and liver. That evening, we feasted on fresh deer liver, heart, fried spuds mixed with onions and hot peppers, corn on the cob, and cold beer. There really is something to be said for living in and off the great outdoors... And to be getting paid for our endeavors, that was our "dessert."

Oh, by the way. I did make my banding quota of 500 mourning dove that year: 650 to be exact before I quit banding. And, I made a damn nice dove baiting case with an illegal doe deer thrown in as a bona fide twist. I guess one could say I had a great time trapping dove and outlaws in the Bear Valley of Colusa County.

DOVE, SAFFLOWER AND WINE GRAPES

Early in the summer of 1971 found me once again working pre-season dove hunters in the Stockton area of California. My usual partner and local California State Fish and Game Warden, Buck Del Nero, was away at a squad meeting for a couple of days so I was on my own. That was alright though because it gave me a chance to explore and see what I could dig up on my own in an unfamiliar area, and the Stockton country always seemed to be an area full of wildlife and outlaws at every turn in the road. To my way of thinking, a wildlife officer's paradise. As I was soon to discover, that first day on my own that year would turn out to be no different than if I had Buck along. There would be plenty to do and as usual in the world of wildlife law enforcement and low budgets, it would be "One Riot, One Ranger" for all the illegal happenings...

Rising early that first morning incountry before sunrise, I headed out south and east from the City of Stockton. As usual, I was heading nowhere in particular because it seemed no matter where I went in that region of the San Joaquin Valley there was always a world of winged wildlife and outlaws to match. So, pick your poison. Thundering along in my unmarked Dodge patrol truck with the windows down for the cooling breezes it always brought, I had a song in my heart and a nose (and what a beautiful nose it was) looking for trouble. To my way of thinking, I had been blessed. In my profession as a wildlife officer, I got to see many beautiful sunrises, see lots of wildlife, meet many great sportsmen and an almost equal number of dyed-in-the-wool outlaws (some of whom later became good friends), plus got paid a princely sum for doing what I truly loved and enjoyed.

Looking back on those days as these words are written some 42 years later, I had it made in the shade! By that time in my career, I had developed into a hunter of humans and had the world's finest profession in which to practice that "hunting" trade. I was healthy, had the build and stamina of a horse, and two guardian angels looking over me and my actions to match. The "outlaw hunting" was good and the "catching" was out of this world. And on top of all those blessings, I, without a doubt, had the world's best wife who fully supported me in my peregrinations. A man can't ask for much more than that, except perhaps maybe a homemade blueberry pie or two along the way. And since I had also married one of the world's finest cooks and being a "pie face" myself, I had it doubly made. My bride saw to it that whenever I came home from the wildlife battle fields, I always had a freshly made homemade pie waiting. What a blessing my bride was and continues to this very day. With that alone, it is pretty obvious that God truly loves little children, fools, and game wardens. I will love her forever and one day...

Zipping along all full of myself and with a mouthful of good Levi Garrett chewing tobacco, I spotted a man carrying a shotgun quickly disappearing behind a tree way out in the middle of a walnut orchard! To my way of thinking that did not compute. Dove and cottontail rabbit hunting seasons were still a week away. Since I couldn't pull over at that spot in the highway without giving away my presence, I continued on down the road for a short distance. Then I turned back around and drove off the highway onto a farm road near the walnut orchard where I had seen my rapidly disappearing chap with the shotgun. Driving a short distance down that farm road to get away from the noise made on the main highway by passing motorists, I finally stopped and got out. Walking back to the bed of my truck, I opened up my ever-present ice chest and extracted a bottle of Coke and a small, hard Italian salami. Then walking a short distance away from my noisy truck (vehicles make a lot of noise as they cool down), I commenced quietly eating my typical "game warden's breakfast." But not before carefully laying my almost brand new wad of chewing tobacco on a nearby walnut tree limb for later retrieval.

No, you readers (damn, you folks are quick), I hadn't forgotten my lad in the orchard with the shotgun. I had learned early on to let the bad guys have enough rope, if they were so inclined to break the law, to hang themselves. That meant they had to break the law first and then the Great

Grotz (that's me) would charge forth in all his Teutonic magnificence and finery to put the irons on my bad guy. That particular day my enforcement plans were no different. I needed for my lad to break the law before I could do anything. That meant when that moment arose, I would move to the sound of his gun, if he was so inclined to illegally dip into Mother Nature's cookie jar. Therein would lie what I was seeking and hopefully, if I was skillful enough, I would have my illegal shooter and make his day. Enjoying my salami and putting my ears to work listening for any kind of shooting in the immediate area under surveillance, I heard nothing out of the ordinary. It was still just sunrise so I was in no hurry to make a premature move. That thought in mind, I took another bite of my breakfast and let the fatty, well spiced salami meat swirl around my tongue.

Boom went one shot back in the direction I had just driven past where I had spied my subject in the walnut orchard carrying a shotgun! As near as I could echolocate, that shot had come from my mystery chap in the walnut orchard some eighty yards or so yards distant. Taking another bite of the hard greasy salami and a deep drink from my Coke, I patiently waited knowing more was yet to come. Nothing happened for the longest time. Then I heard another boom from roughly the same location.

With that shot, I got my magnificent carcass in gear. Crawling back into my truck and carefully laying my uneaten salami remains on the dash for later retrieval, I turned over the powerful engine (damn, you readers are quick. Yeah, I forgot my chaw of chewing tobacco laying back on the walnut tree limb). Letting my oil gauge climb until it read normal, I slipped the four speed into gear and headed back onto the main highway. Once there, I turned back towards Stockton and my suspect shooter in the walnut orchard. Keeping my speed slow, I passed the suspect orchard and saw nothing out of the ordinary or anyone standing around with a shotgun. I was also looking for a way in which I could approach the orchard and yet not be seen by my shooter. Passing the orchard, I discovered a small farm road leading back into another orchard near a set of irrigation pumps. Perfect, I thought. If I have an illegal dove shooter in the adjacent walnut orchard and he sees me, he will think I am just an irrigation pump tender tending the pumps. Taking my time moving down the farm road to the irrigation pumps, I closely examined my suspect walnut orchard row by row of trees. Once again I spied nothing out of the ordinary. Parking by the pumps, I pretended to be working around them as I kept my eyes peeled on the walnut orchard to my south.

Boom came another shot from deep within the orchard! Moments later, numerous dove came winging by overhead as if spooked by the shooting. However, I still saw nothing out of the ordinary or anyone out in that walnut orchard! Sure as God made feral house cats great for the sport of shooting, there wasn't a soul out there in that orchard to be seen!

Boom went another shot out in the middle of my walnut orchard and within moments numerous dove once again flew overhead as if fleeing the shooting. That did it! I thought. Sure as God made a guy my size an eager eater, there was someone out there shooting dove during the closed season. But damned if I could see hide nor hair of that person. That's what happens when one is so busy with the "chase," that he doesn't know whether he found a rope or lost his horse...

Grabbing my binoculars, I carefully began my stalk out into that orchard. I had roughly located where the shots were coming from and made an effort to keep as many walnut trees between me and that spot as possible as I approached. Sneaking along like a shorttailed weasel after a deer mouse (yes, my readers, a six foot four inch, 320-pound chap can sneak along as quietly as a nest of mice pissin' on a bed of cotton), I picked up my pace. And I also saw that I was kicking out a whole host of dove that had been roosting throughout that walnut orchard. No wonder my shooter had holed up in that place for one hell of a dove shoot with bird numbers like that, I grimly thought.

Sneaking along towards the last heard shot, I soon spied fresh human footprints in the soft, freshly plowed dirt. My walnut orchard had recently been plowed and then disced to reduce the weeds. As such, the ground was like powder and that sure made tracking anyone a damn-sight easier. Kneeling down, I took a hard look at my human footprints. They were fresh alright! The marks they had made in the freshly disced earth were clean cut into the dirt, and the spiders had yet to make any webs in as was many times the case in old tracks. Plus, dirt from the sides of the footprints had not as yet caved into the prints as old ones will do. (Thank you, Dad, for teaching me to track like an Indian when I was younger. My dad, Otis Barnes, had been raised in and among Maidu Indians in Northern California as a boy. From them he had learned "The Way." He in turn taught me many of their ways as well which continued serving me many years later as a "hunter of men.")

Boom went another shot not more than forty yards distant in front of me and that time I had the exact location of the shot down pat. However, that last shot came from up in the treetops!

What the hell? I thought. How the dickens can that be? But sure as hell is hot and full of liberal Democrat defense lawyers hell-bent on destroying this great land of ours, that last shot came from high up in a nearby walnut tree! Bracing myself alongside another walnut tree, I glassed and glassed the area from whence that last shot had been fired. Then I saw it! My early season dove shooter was high up in a large walnut tree like a Japanese sniper from World War II on the island of Saipan. Only this time, the "hunter" on the ground had his number and big time!

Boom went my shooter once again from up in the crotch of the tree some thirty yards away. I observed a dove come fluttering down through the heavily leaf-covered tree limbs to the ground. That son-of-a-gun, I thought. He is shooting the dove out of the adjacent walnut trees after they come in to land and roost. What a great and clever idea. Too bad it is illegal to do so before the dove season has opened and the law is close at hand, I thought with a grin.

Well, I know how to drain the water from that swamp, I thought still grinning. Grabbing up my binoculars, I continued following the set of footprints across the freshly disced walnut orchard. Along the way, I spotted two places where a dove had died after being shot earlier. That evidence was illustrated by a small puff of feathers lying all around a slight depression in the soft powdered earth along with fresh footprints and several dark spots of blood. Well, here is one clever chap who is going to be run to ground... eh, tree, this fine day, I thought with a grin of anticipation as I continued my sneak.

Walking up to the "sniper's tree," I slid my hand down to the comforting cold metal of the .45 on my hip as I looked up into the tree. My shooter finally realized he had company and was now trying to make himself as invisible as possible by hugging the far side of the tree and not moving anything but his anal sphincter muscles...

"Hey! Federal agent. Dove season is closed. Come on down from there and be quick about it," I bellowed.

For the longest time my chap didn't move. I guess he figured he was still hidden. That would be hard to do, I thought, wearing that red-and-white checked flannel shirt and all. "Hey, don't make me climb up this tree and throw you out. 'Cause if I do, I will toss you as far as I can throw you from this tree. And if I do, that part of being thrown won't hurt until you hit the ground some twenty yards away."

Finally, an old man peered down at me saying, "Don't shoot! I am coming down." With those words, the man began climbing down the walnut tree. When he landed on the ground, I showed him my badge as I reached with my other hand for his shotgun. Upon checking it, I found it to be an unplugged Winchester pump shotgun, Model 97. (Winchester Model 97 shotguns are always a good bet for being unplugged. Keep that in mind, you game warden-type readers. They are also dangerous during cold weather because their small hammers can easily slip out from one's thumb when that hammer is being released for reasons of safety with a resulting discharge of the firearm.)

"I need to see a driver's license," I said, as I unloaded five shot shells from his shotgun. The driver's license was quietly proffered. "Augusto Toliferro," read the man's driver's license. "How many dove do you have down, Mr. Toliferro?" I asked. Without a word, the old man walked out into the orchard and retrieved four freshly killed dove he had hidden in the crouch of a nearby tree. Those, plus the two found at the base of his tree, came to six closed season dove. "Well, Mr. Toliferro, you are going to be cited into Federal Court in Sacramento for taking dove during the closed season and using a shotgun capable of holding more than three shells," I said.

The old man just nodded and with an infectious grin said, "Officer, I usually do this every year. In fact, I have done so since '19 and 37.' This is the very first time I have been caught, but I guess there is a first time for everything, eh?"

I just grinned at the old man's humor as I continued filling out the citation. I wondered to myself just how many birds he had illegally taken since "19 and 37."

"I own this orchard and the grapes and other orchards around this one. Can you believe when I came here in '19 and ought 5,' I only had a nickel in my pocket when I stepped off the train. Today I am worth a lot more than that, so I guess I can afford this ticket after all these years. Say, how much will this cost me?" he asked.

"I don't know, Mr. Toliferro. That is up to the judge," I replied, knowing full well he was looking at a $300.00 fine for the error of his ways. That was, if he had no previous wildlife violations on his record. So, it was best I said nothing of the fine until a records check was run by the Clerk of the Court in Sacramento.

Bidding Mr. Toliferro "good day" after finishing up with the paperwork, I advised he should wait until dove season legally started before going out once again. He just smiled once again, saying, "But, Officer, it is always more fun if one hunts dove during the "long season" (closed season), plus it seems the birds taste better." Once again, I had to grin at the old man's humor. However, the dove he had killed illegally that morning weren't grinning...

Shaking the old man's hand as I did with everyone who would shake my hand after receiving a citation, I put his evidence birds in a small plastic bag removed from my hunting coat, waved goodbye and headed for my truck. Tooling down the road a fair piece later, I had to grin. That old man had come from the Old Country and had arrived here basically broke. Just like my Grandfather Grosz did in North Dakota in '05, as well. Both men had worked hard in this great country of ours, raised their families, and died much better off than when they had arrived. A country where life is not fair but your chances are damn good for making it big in whatever you decide to do if you apply yourself And to be brutally frank, the only country in the world in which that kind of success can be achieved... Enjoy what you have, Americans, for many others in the rest of the world are doing with a whole lot less... Man, this really is the greatest country in the world, and thank you, Lord, for letting me live here and being part of it. Then I remembered my hardscrabble upbringing, many hungry days, hard work in a man's profession as a boy, and paying my own way through college. Yes, this is the finest country in the world, I thought, with a thankful grin. Freedom is the most powerful blessing in the world and don't any of you readers ever forget it!

Later in the day, I discovered what appeared

to be a freshly baited field not far from Augusto's walnut orchard. Driving into the area, I noticed dozens of dove sitting on every transmission line in the area. Then I also noticed numerous dove sitting on every barbed wire fence surrounding the immediate area. Damn, Terry, I thought. We have a baited area in this location close-at-hand (even the FBI would call all those birds hanging around in such numbers a clue. Well, maybe not...). Driving all around the rural area, I finally located what I suspected was the baited field. The whole area was surrounded by vineyards. But off in one corner of the area was about a five-acre weed field. Into that area the dove were flowing like water passing over a waterfall. Parking my unmarked patrol truck near an abandoned shed, I hotfooted it over to the weed field using an adjacent vineyard as my cover. Sure as God makes grasshoppers good brook trout bait, the area in question was baited heavily with safflower seed! Quickly grabbing up a sample for my ever present plastic evidence bag, I once again hotfooted it out of the area before I got caught by the landowner or ones who had placed the bait in the area in the first place (many times one and the same).

That next weekend was the opening day of dove season and guess where I was? That's right! Up to my eyes in some of the best-eating tokay grapes still on the vine as I watched 28 gunners dropping dove right and left over the baited field from my vineyard place of concealment. In fact, it was such a hot spot that I saw the shooters many times race out to pick up a dead dove only to have a live one land right next to them to feed! Needless to say, it was hell on wheels for the dove with many of them coming into that baited field for their "last" meal.

But this time I had assistance in working that baited area. At the "suggestion" of his captain, Buck, the local game warden, along with several younger, less experienced officers in his squad, had opted to help for the dove season opener and could not be with me. So I had instituted Plan B. With me in that vineyard that fine morning eating fresh off-the-vine, tokay grapes as well, was a fireplug of a man I had known since 1966. The man was Deputy Sheriff Glenn Ragon from Humboldt County which is located in the far northwestern part of the state. During his vacation he had come down to the Northern Sacramento Valley to hunt dove on the Richmond Hunting Club where he was a member. However, upon learning of his whereabouts, I shanghaied him for my Stockton detail and he readily agreed.

As most of my readers have learned from reading about working some of my previous baited dove areas, there are several rules to follow. Map out and know your baited area well. Get samples of the bait, identify it, and find a place in which to hide and watch the illegal shooting action without being seen. Lastly, take more officers for the detail than you think you will need. That is usually where the rub comes into play. For you see, there are only about ten thousand conservation officers in all of North America. That counts county, military, tribal, state, federal, and provincial, as well. Then on any given day, when you drop out the sick, lame, lazy, and many of the supervisors, you might only have three thousand working-grade wildlife officers on duty for that day. That is for all of North America, its hunting public, and its other 360 million folks inhabiting that same piece of real estate! Hell, Custer had better odds!

That is where Glenn came into play. As I suspected might be the case, Warden Del Nero had been assigned elsewhere by his captain. And there was no other help available for the opening weekend of dove season (it always helps to have extra witnesses to any criminal event taking place when in a court of law). Every officer across the state had his hands full and needed help. So I took poor old Glenn away from his dove hunting during his vacation and put him to work with me (being a deputy sheriff, he was an officer for the State of California; therefore, his law enforcement authority in essence was statewide). But he relished that kind of work and it only took him a second to tell me yes when asked. So there the two of us sat watching our baited dove field, all the while eating stolen tokay grapes from the vineyard (well, we had to taste them to make sure they weren't poisoned before they were made into some very good Italian wine).

When the two of us had a gut full of all the illegal killing (and tokay grapes), we sprang into action. Having worked out a plan of attack earlier, Glenn took one side of the baited area and its gunners and I the other. Before it was all said and done, we had captured 23 of the 28 shooters before the rest skedaddled like the Yankees did at the first battle of Bull Run. In short, the balance of my illegal shooters just "ghosted" off through the surrounding lands and got away.

For the next two hours, Glenn picked up all the dead and wounded birds he could find and gutted them before they spoiled. Me, I wrote citations until my hands almost fell off for shooting over a baited area, using unplugged shotguns, taking over limits, and taking protected migratory birds (kestrels, meadowlarks, robins). Many of the Italian gunners we caught that day had committed a not-uncommon hunting practice among their countrymen when it came to a shoot in a dove field. That was, "if it flies, it dies." Hence the reason for all the other songbirds and the like we found in their game bags. At the end of the day, we had a total of 54 citations issued and 373 evidence dove in our coolers, not to mention all the "dickey" birds we had seized as well! I would say we more than "paid for the gas and oil" used by my truck that fine day when it came to figuring up all the fines subsequently paid as a result of that little dove shoot. Then I hustled Glenn back to the Richmond Hunting Club near Colusa with my thanks, where he could spend the rest of the week of his vacation hunting dove and relaxing.

The following or second weekend of dove season in the Stockton area was not as grand a shooting event as had been the opening weekend. Most of the dumber birds and young of the year had been killed off in the initial fusillade and those that remained were one hell of a lot wiser. However, there was still money to be made in the Stockton area where the motto among many Italian gunners was still, "if it flies it dies." In fact, of the 23 dove shooters Glenn and I had caught the weekend before, 20 of them were Italians. But being the good cooks they are, I can see why they were such avid bird hunters, especially when it came to seed eating game birds.

Knowing that the dove field the two of us had worked the weekend before was still legally considered baited, I slipped into the area for a look to see if anyone was still gunning over the area the Friday afternoon before the second weekend of dove season. No one was there as I crept through a different vineyard knowing if anyone was there, they would be looking for me erupting from that first vineyard I had used as a hiding place. Working my way through that second vineyard eating my share of once-again stolen tokay grapes as I went, I got a surprise. No, you readers, I didn't get caught by the owner of the vineyard stealing and eating his grapes or, in the worst case scenario, getting a raging case of the trots from eating so many grapes.

In the process of sneaking through that new vineyard and trying not to be seen, I made a discovery clear out from left field. The vineyard which I currently occupied was heavily baited with safflower; and the dove were everywhere as I crept through it!

Surprised over what I was seeing, I was now in a quandary. How to get a bait sample, survey the lay-out of the area, map out the extent of the bait, and not get caught in the process. Somehow I got it done and come the weekend, I lurked in the bushes for my new baited vineyard shooters. No one showed either that Saturday or Sunday. Damn, I thought, maybe I had been seen tromping through the vineyard after all.

The following Friday, I once again slipped into

the area. That time I hit pay dirt. All around the vineyard were little shooting stools posted at safe shooting intervals. Looking inside the stools, I discovered each shooting stool held two boxes of shotgun shells for the shooter using that seat! Hot dog, I thought, come this Saturday I am going to have some dove shooters shooting illegally over the baited vineyard.

That Saturday before daylight found yours truly hidden at the far end of the vineyard away from all the shooters' stools. And sure as the goofies in Colorado will be the first to legalize the use of "Mary-Jane" as "medical marijuana" contrary to, as these words are written, barely enforced federal law prohibiting such endeavors, here came several vehicles full of dove shooters. Parking at my end of the vineyard, a dozen of the lads gathered up their hunting gear from their vehicles and walked down the rows of grapevines heavy with tokay grapes.

Come legal shooting hours and with the arrival of flights of hungry dove, the "popping" of a dozen shotguns told the hungry birds, "eat here at your own peril." From where I now hid, the air was full of puffs of feathers that were once living winged rockets of the air. Poor old Noah. If he saw such a thing happening to the first critters off his ark, he probably would have waded through all the shotgunners using the end of his staff to teach them a lesson. However, there was one "staff" in the vineyard for Mother Nature, and he now made his move after a number of dove had feasted their last on a face full of No. 7 1/2-size shot instead of safflower seed.

Approaching each surprised gunner, I identified myself, seized their driver's licenses, turned them over and wrote down the number of dove they had taken (the backs of the paper California driver's licenses in those days were blank), and then rapidly moved on to the next shooter before word got out that the law was in the field "muckin'" around. If that were to happen, there would have been lots of "jack rabbits" in the area instead of dove shooters, if you get my drift.

Soon, I had all dozen of my shooters rounded up except for one. He was off by himself at the far end of the vineyard so I took off trotting after him. Rounding the end of a long row of tall, leafy grapevines, I headed his way still sight unseen. However, I got dusted with No. 7 1/2 shot in the process as I moved into on my shooter's location. Squeezing the one that had struck my cheek and buried itself, I popped it out like a pimple as I trotted up and confronted my surprised shooter.

"Well, well, well. Augusto Toliferro, we meet again. Been killing any dove lately?" I asked with a grin over seeing my old "closed dove season shooting" friend again. You know, the one who had not been checked since "19 and 37." Well, suffice to say, he was as nice and surprised then as he had been when sitting up in the crotch of a walnut tree shooting dove during the closed season when they came into his orchard to roost.

"Terry, I was hoping we would meet once again. Say, when all my friends finish our dove shoot, we were going back to the ranch house and have a big feed. Would you care to join us and partake of a little good wine, some good steaks, sourdough French bread, and lots of fresh garlic fried in extra virgin olive oil?" Man, don't think for a moment I wasn't tempted! But I figured once I had cited everyone, including Augusto, and taken away their birds (remember, Italians love eating their dove), I didn't think I would be so welcome.

An hour-and-a-half later, I finished with all my paperwork. For the most part, all the lads were very polite and "old country," except for one who was a "big wheel" in a rather large bank of national proportions. He was a bit of a hind-end who wanted to know where I wanted to be transferred since he had a lot of connections and influence in the federal government (his bank was one of the banks bailed out in 2010 by the taxpayers and with some of my taxpayer dollars I might add).

About two weeks later, my baited vineyard

dove shooting lads, to a man, had forfeited $250.00 each for shooting over a baited area. That was, except for my friend Augusto. He forfeited $500.00 (the maximum dollar amount per offense allowed in those days under the Migratory Bird Treaty Act). His fine was a little higher because of his earlier closed season dove case to which he had pled guilty as well. Nothing like having a dry spell since "19 and 37" of not being checked by a game warden and then being checked and ticketed twice within several weeks by the same federal agent... I guess there really is a "Dove God" looking on, especially if you shoot enough of his critters and over a baited area at that.

Over the 32-year span of my wildlife law enforcement career, I made hundreds of cases involving "sports" illegally gunning over baited areas. Those cases were made in California, Nevada, North and South Dakota, Missouri, Nebraska, Maryland, Virginia, Delaware, Colorado, Illinois, Ohio, Indiana, Minnesota, Arizona and several other states I am sure I have long since forgotten. The only reason I didn't make more of the same types of cases in other states was because I never had the chance to work the wildlife outlaws in those locations since illegal baiting is so commonplace when it comes to shooting ducks and dove (note I don't say "hunting").

I am told in today's day and age, the federal

baiting regulations have since been weakened by political forces and short-sighted federal bureaucrats with greed, ego and stupidity being the driving forces in such changes. There is no way that justifies gunning migratory game birds over baited areas. Legally allowed or not, it is just plain wrong and immoral. I may be a bit harsh but, based on the gross killings I have seen over my long career working baited areas, gunners in such situations are in my opinion on the same level as child molesters. To my way of thinking, there is nothing morally redeeming about either activity.

It is now 2012. I wonder how much longer it will be before the government, under extreme political pressure, yields to "incidental take" of migratory birds such as eagles because the oil producers, wind power, solar, transmission line companies, military, and other entities so desire it within their particular fields of endeavor? I suspect that soon conservation laws won't be worth the paper they are written on. And the critters ... well, there is always more room in that dark hole, many times created by modern man, called extinction...

CHAPTER THREE

A U.S. GAME MANAGEMENT AGENT'S "STEW"

IN 1971 THE WINTER RAINS HOWLED with a vengeance into the Northern Sacramento Valley. So much so, that after ten days of incessant rains, I thought God would have to have Noah build another ark. Then it seemed the rains redoubled "their" efforts and soon the entire valley was nothing but thousands of small lakes, ponds, and wet spots with the farm roads becoming all but impassable. So impassable that if one were to take a four-wheel-drive truck out into the fields, it was curtains. In one turn of your wheels you were axle deep in sticky adobe mud. Then it was shovel time or making a call to your local wrecker to come and pull you out. And since those were the days before the advent of the flood (pardon the pun) of all-terrain vehicles (ATVs) ravaging the land, once you were off the main roads it was shank's mare, a boat, or nothing in order to get around checking the hunting public.

Then the crawdad poop left behind in the rice fields after they were drained in late summer hit the fan (yes, earlier zillions of crawdads would move into the flooded, fertile, warm rice fields to feed). The mighty Sacramento River, swollen beyond belief, flowed over her banks and out through the relief weirs (weirs or spillways adjacent to the river to relieve the floodwater's pressure on the main river system). Soon hundreds of square miles of flooded lowlands greeted the eye much to the chagrin of the landowners and wealthy duck clubs located in those now-underwater zones. But chagrin was in the eyes of the beholder. For the feathered, web-footed critters, the new expanses of watered habitat was plainly and simply a blessing because then the feathered critters could roam almost forever and for miles basically undisturbed in their new flooded lands. And with that, it brought new feeding and resting areas mostly away from the intrusion of man and his ever-present shotgun and the open waterfowl hunting season.

When those flooding events occurred, my wildlife law enforcement efforts went to seven days a week with 16-hour cold and wet days becoming the norm. This was necessary because such flood-

Wildlife's Quiet War | 197

ing spread out the Sacramento Valley's millions of wintering ducks, geese and swans throughout the newly flooded lands. When that event occurred, it brought out those walking on the dark side of Mother Nature in droves who heretofore had been unable to hunt on those flooded private lands. Under federal law, if I remember correctly, the flooded lands were now designated navigable and open to public use. If that wasn't problem enough, the floodwaters collaterally displaced thousands of resident deer, quail, pheasants, and multitudes of fur bearers all of which soon found themselves desperately trying to find any high ground upon which to seek shelter. And all that did was concentrate such now homeless species in great numbers onto any available dry real estate. In turn, that transformed such displaced critters into numerous tempting and easy targets for those walking on the dark side who took the now- flooded private lands as their own public shooting galleries. Into that mess of local outlaws from all the valley's adjacent towns strode one magnificent, very handsome, some would even say beautiful, Robert Redford-like (when he was younger and better looking), Teutonic-looking individual and his trusty dog. In case my readers do not know of whom I so gloriously speak, it was my dog Shadow and me, you meatheads... Who else would be so large, magnificent, and stupid enough to brave the flood waters in a sport canoe looking for wildlife outlaws who had the propensity to be a little quick and heavy on their trigger fingers as they more or less trespassed their ways to their heart's content?

Leaving my home one fine morning before daylight in a driving rain, Dog and I headed south for the small Sacramento Valley Town of Meridian. There I found a launch site just off the Sacramento River levee leading into the valley's raging flood waters and launched my Grumman Sport Canoe.

You know, one would think an intelligent officer would use a somewhat larger boat than a canoe when working raging, debris-infested floodwaters, but that was all I had. The Grumman was 7 1/2 feet in length and had a beam of at least 3 1/2 feet. However, that make of canoe was very stable to my way of thinking and experience. In fact, if one was careful, they could take a dump over the side and not roll the canoe! Try that on a regular canoe and one would not have to use any toilet paper, if you get my drift (no pun intended). Onto that, I attached a 9 1/2-horsepower Evinrude outboard motor to the transom as my primary source of power (other than my paddle). That was way more horsepower than the Grumman Sport Canoe manufacturer safely called for but one where I had discovered that the combination of horsepower and type of canoe were ideally suited for each other. Into the bow went my hundred-pound Labrador Shadow and a five gallon gas tank to offset my somewhat dainty 320-pounds of magnificence located in the stern. Two paddles, a life preserver, a small carry bag for my law enforcement gear, a military ammo can holding tools, a spare cotter key and shear pins, and a homemade bread venison sandwich for Dog and me completed our kit. And once again to all you unfortunates out there, the world's best homemade bread made by my bride, a slice of which when fresh out of the oven will knock your eyes out at twenty feet it is so good! Man, I can almost smell it baking in my wife's kitchen right now... Zuh!

Then Dog and I waited for daylight so we could safely navigate the deep and swiftly moving floodwaters made all the more hazardous with all the drowned wild animals and floating debris being carried therein. As we waited for daylight, I was delighted in hearing all the whistling wings and calls overhead from the hundreds of thousands of ducks, geese, and swans streaming happily to and fro over the flooded zone. This zone increased their feeding and loafing areas to the nth degree. I could also hear numerous outboard motors running around in the floodwaters in the dark. Those sounds let me know that the local outlaws, now unimpeded by fences and duck club boundaries because of the navigable flood waters, were heading out and about on their unseen missions. Missions that more than likely crept along the edge of the dark side, if the past histories of such activities went true to course.

Finally, with the arrival of daylight, it was our turn to enter the flooded area. Rolling down my hip boots in case I was spilled into the swiftly moving waters and had to swim, Dog and I moved out into this new arena of adventure. Taking my time, I moved slowly among the myriads of floating debris, rafts of rice straw, strings of dislodged duck decoys from the wealthy duck clubs upstream, two drowned deer, and every other form of flotsam and jetsam known to man in between.

As more light manifested itself, I got a real eyeful of the biomass that was moving above and around me. Deer, mice of every species, muskrats, beaver, racoons, rats of every make and model, skunks, weasels, beaver, river otter, and every other kind of quadruped known to live in the Sacramento Valley were present and swimming for their lives. In the trees sat hundreds of forlorn-looking pheasants, dozens of out-of-their-landed-element valley quail, every bird of prey known to man, feral cats, and just about anything else that could climb or fly to be rid of the dangerous floodwaters raging below. Suffice to say, every time I partook of such activities, I was always amazed at the amount of biomass dislodged by the flooding Sacramento River waters. And that didn't take into account all the finny critters swimming underneath the surface waters like the confused sturgeon, striped bass, salmon, catfish, and every other type of displaced finned critter in between.

"POW! POW!"

Moving up along a narrow line of cottonwood trees alongside the Sacramento River levee for the slower-moving water the structures provided and the cover they offered, I observed a duck boat moving slowly one hundred yards off to and above my starboard quarter. In it were two chaps wearing hunting gear. One was carefully running the outboard motor and the other was standing unsteadily in the bow with an oar. Every so often, the bow man would push driftwood or debris away from the front of the boat as he intently examined the waters ahead. Then I saw him excitedly point to his right for the stern motorman's benefit. The boat quickly moved to the right as my bow man put away his oar and drew a small handgun from a holster heretofore concealed on his hip. *Pow! Pow!* went his pistol into the water just off the bow of their boat.

Replacing his pistol, the shooter quickly grabbed a boathook from the bottom of their boat and started frantically "fishing" at something in the water next to the boat's bow. Utterly fascinated with the action of the boat's occupants, I grabbed a branch of the tree I was by to stop and steadied the Grumman. Then I grabbed my binoculars with my other hand so I could better see the action of my shooter's boat. My lad in the bow of the boat was trying to fish something large out from the water and was having a damn hard time of it. Finally the stern man let go of the motor and stepped forward in the boat to assist his partner. Together they "horsed" up a huge brown "thing" into their boat. As the men did, they bunched together and their bodies concealed from my view whatever they were hefting into their boat. Then they did a "high five" of celebration with their right hands. With that, the motorman returned to the stern of the boat and the outboard's operation and the bow man fussed with their unseen "catch" lying out of sight in the bottom of their duck boat.

What the hell did the two of them just land? I asked myself in puzzlement. It looked too small for a deer but it sure as hell was something large and brown, I thought, now really getting my curious side up.

Then my lads once again began moving slowly

upstream in the floodwaters. They went perhaps another tenth of a mile with me paralleling them from behind from an unseen position when I observed my two lads repeating the same mystery procedure. Only that time, they were unsuccessful in whatever they were trying to do. However, "beautiful I was" and "patience was my name" as I continued slowly paralleling my shooters from an unseen distance below them in my row of covering trees growing along the Sacramento River levee. Thirty minutes later my shooter in the bow of the suspect boat once again swung into action. I heard *Pow! Pow!* faintly as my shooter shot into the water just off his starboard bow. That time my bow lad was successful in landing a large, barely alive and still-kicking beaver by himself!

~~

Those damn fools, I thought, they are shooting swimming beaver displaced by the floodwaters. Well, this was certainly the right time of the year to collect such furbearers for their best pelage but they had one major problem. In those days in California, beaver could not be taken by such means unless they were previously legally trapped or a nuisance beaver and one had a state fish and game permit to do so. And displaced beaver would not be considered nuisance beaver under the reading of the law, I grimly thought.

Paddling still unseen out across the floodwaters until I was directly behind and below my beaver shooters, I clung to another tree on the far bank, watched and waited. In the meantime, boat after boat of suspicious-looking lads flowed by me as they headed upstream on the floodwaters towards the better duck clubs and hunting locations in the Butte Sink. However, I had to bide my time when working other boaters in those flood waters. I only had a 9 ½ horsepower motor. And from the looks of the motor on my beaver shooters' boat, they had at least a 25-horsepower outboard. In short, if they decided to run from me, they would be gone in a flash and I would be left in their wake holding nothing for my efforts.

Finally I got my chance. Once again my shooter needed the assistance from his motorman in landing another just-killed and very large beaver. When my motor operator ran up to the bow of the boat and was occupied with the hauling task at hand, I fired up my motor. Quickly my light canoe was up on step. In short order I closed the distance between our boats like a rocket as my two outlaws were deeply preoccupied with the still-struggling beaver. By the time my lads realized I was onto them and just might be the law, it was too late. Swinging up alongside, I cut my motor, reached out, and gently grabbed the left side of their boat.

"Morning, lads. Federal agent and state fish

and game warden (I still held a deputy game warden's commission, even though I was now a federal officer). I would like to check your game if I might," I said. At the same time, my eyes scanned the two chaps for any sign of danger and for what lay in the bottom of their boat. Both men looked surprised and of little danger, other than the bow man who was armed with what turned out to be a .22-caliber, Smith and Wesson revolver.

As I showed the men my credentials, I requested the pistol, butt first, and received the same. After unloading the handgun, I took a closer look at what lay in the bottom of their boat. There lay three dead, freshly shot beaver, including one weighing at least one hundred pounds to my way of thinking (I later weighed it at the Colusa Marina and it topped their set of fish scales at 98 pounds!).

"Gentlemen, you need a furbearer's license to trap beaver. Moreover, that license does not allow one to randomly take beaver with the use and aid of a firearm unless it is already in a trap," I said. Neither man said anything upon hearing those words. It was clear to me from the looks on their faces they knew they were out in "left field" legally. "Do either of you lads possess a furbearer's license?" I asked. Once again silence reigned and several dumb looks greeted yours truly. What I had were two chaps who had come up with the idea of shooting displaced beaver for their furs from their boat. As for following the state laws, well, neither lad had the foggiest idea of ever doing so from the looks of it. Especially figuring that any game wardens seen out in that immense flooded zone and heavy rains to screw up their day's beaver shooting would be unlikely and a miracle to say the least.

"Lads, I need to see some identification like your driver's licenses since both of you are going to receive citations for illegally taking furbearers," I said. Without a word, both men dug into their pants and soon produced their driver's licenses. Two citations later, I transferred the now three evidence beaver into the bow of my Grumman. I also seized and held their pistol as evidence as well. After issuing them evidence tags for what I had seized, I asked the men if they had any questions. You sure could tell they were still in shock over the whole affair. Since my arrival, the two of them had hardly said a word. In response to my latest question, I was greeted with silence as well. Something just wasn't right with those two, but way out there on the floodwaters I just couldn't put my finger on it. Having nothing more to say or do, I bid the lads farewell. Boy, they were sure glad to leave and get away from me. Suffice to say, within moments they had hustled their behinds out of my view.

Waiting until they disappeared from whence they came, I headed for my patrol truck parked some distance downriver. There I transferred the three heavy beaver to the front floorboards of my truck for safekeeping. I did so figuring carrying the extra weight around in my canoe in those dangerous waters was a dangerous chance I didn't need to take.

Then still questioning my lads' strange and silent behavior, on a hunch I keyed my radio mike to make a transmission. Several minutes later, I was apprised of the fact that my two silent lads were both wanted on outstanding felony warrants in Sutter County for armed robbery and breaking and entering! I tipped off the Sheriff's Office as to their last known locations and probable boat landings they might use and then let it go at that. I was later advised that the Sutter County Sheriff's Office had apprehended my two beaver shooters at a well-used boat landing further downriver. I guess one could say the god of the beaver shot that day in the floodwaters had finally and in full measure gotten his due.

Following that, I once again headed out into the floodwaters. By now I could hear worlds of shooting the full length and breadth of the flooded waterways above my launch point. To my way of thinking, the local outlaws were having a field day in the flooded areas normally reserved for the landed masses and the wealthy duck clubs. And to compound my concerns, the air was filled with numerous low-flying birds in the heavy rains which told me my illegal shooters had by now penetrated the almost refuge-like confines of the previously quiet waters of the Butte Sink, an area home to a million resting waterfowl, numerous expensive duck clubs and, now from the sounds of it, a mess of people who didn't belong. To my way of thinking that meant only one thing. Over limits being shot by my free-floating outlaws and, more than likely, extremely large numbers of birds being taken over the legal limit at that.

Time to head northeast, I thought, as I pushed off once again from the levee, but not until I let Shadow out from the boat to take care of business and sniff around some. She was a great dog to say the least, but not when she stood up in the bow of my canoe and "perfumed" the air as only as she could do! That alerted me to the fact that more was coming unless she was let out of the canoe to take care of business. So I was glad for the break to let her run and take care of some very serious, shall we say, "internal business."

Saying a quick word to my two guardian angels for my safety once again, out onto the raging floodwaters I went. However, danger aside, I was pleased. I had never made a beaver case during my career up to that point, so today was a first. Especially one in which the lads were illegally shooting them from a boat. Bottom line, this case proved to be the "meaty" portion in my building of a U.S. Game Management Agent's "stew" that fine winter day so long ago. What lay next for me was to eventually become a jewel of a case.

"SPLASH-SPLASH"

Figuring my two beaver killers were now telling everyone they came upon below my location there was a law dog in the area, I scooted even further north and east to avoid detection by other outlaws. By so doing, no one straying across the line of legality knew I was there and ready to do battle once more. Again moving along the levee where the water was less swift and the debris not so dangerous to my passage, I slowly moved northward. In order to stay alive in those unusual and dangerous conditions, I stayed very alert and watchful. In so doing, I constantly marveled at all the critters swimming every which way, trying to avoid being drowned and looking for a high place out from the floodwaters they could call home until the floodwaters had receded. Soon I took to using my paddle to dip out the poor little mice and placed them in the bottom of my canoe so they wouldn't drown figuring that when I got to a patch of dry land, I would let them go. That initially worked fine as they huddled in a soft, wet pile in the bottom of the canoe to keep warm. Then, one inadvisably ran across Shadow's tail. Being a Labrador, they have a propensity to eat many large things in one quick chomp. And when it came to eating smaller morsels messin' up one's tail, imagine how quickly those fast-moving morsels disappeared! I quit helping the mouse people shortly after that figuring they had better chances at swimming versus crossing the tail of my always-hungry dog and her lethal set of "choppers."

It was then I spotted two sports in a large duck boat off my bow about one hundred yards distant. Both men were kneeling together along the starboard side of their boat holding onto something very large in the water. There was a huge amount of splashing that I could see through my binoculars and for a moment I thought they were trying to rescue someone who had fallen overboard! But during all that splashing, no effort was being made to bring anyone on board their boat... The splashing continued as my lads kept kneeling by the starboard side of their boat within the field of my binoculars. Soon the splashing subsided and then stopped altogether. For the longest time my lads remained quietly in their kneeling positions in the bow of their boat with their hands over the side as their boat slowly floated with the floodwater's current back towards my position. Finally one of the pair stood up and looked carefully all around. Fortunately, I made a small target in which to be seen, and the bank side willow patch I was now in helped with my cover. In that "searching moment," I remained unseen in the bank of willows. Satisfied, my two lads stood together on the far side of their boat and gave a big heft upward. Immediately out from the water came a large, dead buck deer! Holding the huge animal for a moment, the men adjusted their grips and then hoisted the last of the animal into the bottom of their boat. Once inside their boat, both men took to looking all around the area once again. I could see why they were so concerned over being seen. Deer season for that area was closed!

Then the boat motor operator returned to his outboard, started it up and headed for a small island off to their right near the shore. Once there, he grounded the boat. The two men hauled the deer out from the boat onto shore and began gutting it out. With their backs to me, I began paddling unnoticed across the flooded plain. Landing somewhat downstream to their position due to the strong current of the floodwater's flow, I began quietly paddling alongside the land's stiller waters back towards my two lads still gutting out the buck deer.

Quietly pulling in behind their beached boat and still unseen as my lads continued gutting their deer, I removed their gas hose connection from their boat's motor. That way, I figured if they somehow got away from me, they wouldn't run far before their boat's motor ran dry of fuel. Then they would be an easy catch as they tried figuring out what the hell had happened to their nonfunctioning motor. However, that potential "escape" was not to be. I managed to quietly beach my canoe and was halfway out from it when my lads became aware of my presence. Turning, they had the funniest look on their faces for the briefest of moments. Kind of like what I suspected would be the look on a man's face when discovered in another man's bedroom with that man's errant wife... Both men were from the small nearby Town of Olivehurst and personally knew me from a previous deer violation in which we had crossed swords, eh, antlers, in the Ladoga area of western Colusa County the previous summer during a deer spotlighting and apprehension incident...

"Morning, Bob. Nice buck you and your cousin have there," I said. And it was a nice buck! A massive four-pointer (western count of four antler points to a side) with a body weight, field-dressed, of about 185 pounds.

Bob, out of an outlaw's instinct, made a start

for his boat and then spotted Shadow standing up in the bow of my boat some six feet distant. Realizing that trying to escape would not be such a good idea, especially with such a big dog eagerly looking on for her share of the "action," he froze. However, Jake, his equally surprised cousin, didn't have such good sense or genetics. Seeing and recognizing me, he immediately bolted for their boat. Jumping "full bore" over one side of his boat, well not quite, as he caught the toe of his hip boot on the lip of the gunnel and down he went. Face first he slammed onto the far side of their boat's rail! I saw an instant splash of red as his soft nose and face smashed into the hard metal oarlock on the far side of their boat! Bouncing off the boat's side, his face then dropped hard onto their gas tank handle. Once again, a nice splash of red, matching the color of the gas tank, flew about inside their boat. Groaning, he slid into the rainy bilge water in the boat's bottom face first and was out like a light. As he lay there, frothy red bubbles began erupting from the four inches of bilge water lying in the bottom of their boat. Bilge water that had collected in the bottom of their boat from the heavy rains and runoff from the wet coat of the deer they had horsed into their boat earlier.

"Bob," I said. "Maybe you ought to help your cousin. It seems he misjudged the beam of your boat by a few inches," I said, with an "it couldn't have happened to a nicer guy" grin.

Still in shock, Bob just stood there in the wind and driving rain. Realizing that wasn't doing his bubble-blowing in the bilgewater cousin in the bottom of their boat any good, I provided the needed assistance. Reaching down, I grabbed Jake by his belt and lifted out his out-cold-as-a-cucumber head from the four inches of bilge slop in the bottom of their boat. Then I rolled him over so he wouldn't drown. Damn, was he a mess when the light of day illuminated Jake's face. His nose was broken badly and he had at least a four-inch gash across his forehead where he had hit the boat's oarlock with a fair amount of gusto. He was also missing his two front upper incisors! Hell, I thought with a grin, I didn't know Jake was a hockey player.

Looking over at Bob, I could see that he was still standing there in shock and hadn't moved a hair. Some defense attorney he was. No wonder most law enforcement officers think attorneys are the weakest links in the chain of democracy, I thought somewhat cynically.

"Yeah, I know you are an attorney," I said to Bob, before he could apprise me of the same. "However, this one may be a tough one to argue in front of a jury of your peers," I said with a knowing smile.

Finally finding his voice, he said, "Screw you. Look what you did to my cousin. I will sue the pants clear off you for what you did to him."

"I don't think so," I said smugly. "It seemed to me he is the one who tried to escape and chose to hit the side of your boat with the soft part of his face," I continued with a wet-faced grin.

"Now, I need to see your driver's license and once your cousin comes around, I will need his as well," I said, as I walked the few steps back to my canoe and retrieved my cite book.

As I wrote out their state citations for taking a deer during the closed season, I finally figured out what the heck had happened. My two lads were on their way to some illegal duck hunting on the flooded Butte Sink duck clubs. Boating upstream, they had run across the massive buck frantically swimming for all he was worth across the flooded area trying to get to higher ground. Running their boat up alongside the hapless swimming animal, they had grabbed him by his antlers and shoved his head under water until he had drowned. Then they hauled him aboard as I sat watching the whole thing unfold from a short distance away. Hence all the splashing I had seen earlier through my binoculars. Well, this was one time the "deer god" was going to have his due, I thought. Nothing like being in the right spot at the right time. Plus, this was the second time I had caught these two over deer violations. This may be one hell of an expensive duck hunting venture gone bad for the two of them, I thought as I finished up on their big game closed season-taking citations with a happy grin spreading across my soul.

Finished with the paperwork and smiling even more inside as Jake, now fully aware of his "new look," struggled with his madly bleeding face, using an oily, wet rag from the bottom of their boat. As he did, I loaded the heavy deer with difficulty into the center of my canoe. Since my repeat offenders had little to say and no questions about the legal action to follow, we parted company. Me happily heading carefully back to my truck across the floodwaters with an overloaded canoe and a smile on my handsome pus as wide as the flood waters in that part of the country. And with that, my two deer-drowning chaps went back to where they came from to find a doctor to fix up Jake's boat-altered face. Hell, to my way of thinking, his little wreck had slightly improved his looks.

Once back at my truck, I called the Colusa County Sheriff's Office for an assist. When the sheriff's deputy arrived, I loaded the fat buck into the trunk of his patrol car. The deer later went to a family of seven in Colusa who were always struggling when it came to putting a meal on the table. Me, back into the floodwaters I sailed once again like the happy warrior I was. The day was still young and the catching so far was pretty damn good.

Suffice to say, this case had to be the "garlic and spices" to the U.S. Game Management Agent's "stew" I was quickly building. However, the next case on that rainy day on the flooded farm plain so long ago was also a "doozy."

"KA-BOOM!"

Working the flooded regions created by the Sacramento River during the winter rains as a wildlife officer was always a treat. Just working in the dangerous, fast-moving debris-littered waters was "treat" enough by itself for anyone crazy enough to be out in such a maelstrom! However, I always found that those chaps availing themselves of the shooting opportunities offered in those floodwater circumstances often left their inhibitions behind. That's right. Once out on the flooded areas, it seemed the chaps did things they never would have done under normal circumstances. Hence, it was always an adventure into the unknown when working such dangerous flooded areas as a wildlife officer, especially when the human element lifted its head up from the leaf litter... And many times, those illegal activities unfolding in front of a wildlife officer's eyes were truly something to behold. Such was my next case on that fine rainy day so long ago. That one turned out to be the "onions" in my U.S. Game Management Agent's "stew."

Working my way upstream along the levee once again, Dog and I had lots of looks at individuals taking advantage of the shooting opportunities in the floodwaters. In many places I looked, I would discover small duck hunting boats tied up and its occupants hunting the many confused ducks and geese flying about. However, nothing looked good as a "catch" in those bunches of chaps, and my usually active guardian angels were pretty quiet regarding the observed activities as well. Not finding the interest in those chaps, I gave them a pass.

My guardian angels were probably sleeping on this cold and wet day, if they had their druthers, I thought as I scooted along with a respectful grin. Especially since they weren't fluttering about inside me "telling" me to be more alert when I chanced upon certain numerous lads in the flood zone shooting ducks and geese.

Then I heard the unmistakable sounds of someone powerboat shooting the many rafting ducks resting on the floodwaters to my north. The giveaway sounds of a running-hard outboard motor on a speeding boat quickly followed by the boom boom boom of a shotgun told me someone was illegally powerboat shooting ducks. To you unwashed, that was nothing more than spotting a mess of ducks on the water and then making a high speed run into them with your fast moving boat. Once within gun range and before the surprised birds could flee, the powerboat shooter, without slowing down, would shoot into the massed birds and then recover their dead or dying feathered bounty.

Continuing moving upstream in the floodwaters alongside my helpful levee, I soon spotted my culprits. I had two chaps, one in the bow and the other operating the motor. They were slowly moving from side to side in the big floodwaters looking for rafts of resting waterfowl. As soon as they spotted a group of swimming or resting ducks or geese, they would quietly motor towards them. Then, when the ducks showed signs of being alerted to the approaching boat's presence with raised heads and swimming away actions, the boat lads would "fire" up their engine. The powerboat would be opened up into full throttle as they headed their boat directly for the birds. When the birds got up in alarm, the bow gunner would fire into the massed birds. Then slowing down, the motor operator would head into the area just shot to pick up any dead or dying ducks. This action would be repeated every time they found unsuspecting ducks or geese resting on the floodwaters. They were also aggressively moving the boat under low overflying flocks of ducks and geese and shooting into those unsuspecting masses as well.

To those of you unfamiliar with the laws of the land, state and federal waterfowl regulations prohibit taking migratory waterfowl with the use and aid of a boat under power. The use of any such powered devices (boat, vehicle, aircraft) to take migratory game birds eliminates the element of fair chase and has been outlawed for many years. That is, except for some species of crippled sea ducks in environments which are very difficult to retrieve once wounded without the use and aid of a boat moving under power. There such a practice is allowed for cripples in some maritime waters, only to avoid wastage of the crippled waterfowl because they are such good swimmers. And being such good swimmers and divers (they use their wings to aid them when swimming underwater to escape), the hunting dogs are just unable to retrieve them in all circumstances. Hence the legal use of a boat under power to avoid wastage.

Moving quietly and as stealthily as I could, I moved towards my illegal shooters using the levee bank and tree rows once again as cover. However, therein lay several concerns. As I said earlier, I only had a 914-horsepower motor. My powerboat shooting lads had a much larger outboard than that. No matter how one looked at it, one had a classic tortoise and hare race in the offing... Second, my outlaws were gifted when it came to powerboat shooting waterfowl. They had taped over their boat numbers so one could not use those identifiers as a capture tool later on if they managed to escape. Then they always made sure they stayed a careful distance away from anyone near their field of illegal activities. In short, they kept a safe distance away from anyone nosy enough to observe their illegal actions. It was obvious to me that these lads had "been there and done that before."

For the next twenty or so minutes, I tailed my lads trying to sneak as closely as I could before I made my "run for the roses." However, no matter how hard I stalked my lads, they were always one step ahead of me. By now, they also had an over limit of ducks and were working to do the same on geese. Frustration was beginning to set in on my miserable carcass and only manifested itself even further when my chaps suspected my suspicious futile efforts to close the range.

Then almost as if suspecting I was "the law," they began playing with me. They would let me get close only to speed off, but not without first giving me the "high center finger greeting" before easily moving out of range. And as if unconcerned, they continued powerboat shooting the birds realizing how puny my catch dog efforts were.

Several times, I would pretend I was a duck hunter shooting at birds hoping to get closer to my lads. That ruse didn't work. Then I would shoot when they weren't looking and speed off and make like I was picking up a duck just like a regular, illegal powerboat shooter. No such luck closing the gap there using that ruse either. Then I would motor ahead of them like I was looking for a better spot to hunt and they would just quickly motor around and ahead of me, thwarting any intercept possibilities. You know, as I have told my readers many times before, it is not nice to piss off Mother Nature or her minions. And at that point in the game, I felt like I was being pissed on...

Realizing I needed to make my move before these chaps killed every duck and goose incountry, I "pulled the trigger." I waited until they had made a big kill on a flock of unsuspecting Pacific white-fronted geese. As my chaps were hurriedly running down their dead and dying birds, I went for it. Soon Dog and I were up on step and speeding towards my two powerboat shooting chaps on an intercept course. It didn't take long for them to realize what I was doing. So, they just picked up their pace in the goose-picking- up department in anticipation of my futile efforts.

Closing the gap quickly between our boats, I felt I just might finally have a chance. Seeing me more than rapidly oncoming, they picked up their last goose and took off in a flurry of outboard motor smoke. Then they pulled a cheap shot! With laughter heard from both of the young-looking lads, they closely circled my canoe at full bore making sure I could clearly see the "high one finger salute." Closely looking at my lads, I didn't recognize either of them. No matter how one cut it, I was snookered at every turn.

On top of that, they damned near swamped my canoe with their wakes as they closely passed by on several passes! One more dangerous turn like that and I would take that to be a life-threatening move in these floodwaters with me in an unstable canoe, I thought. I had decided if they tried to swamp me one more time in twenty feet of raging flood waters, I would unlimber my .44 magnum and then, "We would soon see who took a dump in the skunk cabbage if that were to happen," as Dirty Harry would say...

Fortunately for them, that didn't happen. My two knotheads, tiring of their little game, sped off to my north once again amidst great laughter. As their boat hit its step, I heard a loud thump! Looking towards my rapidly disappearing powerboat shooters, I saw they had hit something large and submerged! The chap operating the motor was thrown forward into the bench seats, and the lad standing in the bow with his shotgun at port arms was tossed forward as well. Boom went his shotgun as the bow gunner smashed into the front decking of his boat from the collision! Directly in front of their boat I saw a huge splash of water and then panic commenced onboard once my chaps picked themselves up off the bottom of their boat.

As nearly as I could tell, when my two knotheads had struck something submerged and unseen in the floodwaters, the shock of the collision had been great. Both men had been tossed around like a couple of aspen leaves in a Colorado snowstorm. As I later discovered, the man operating the outboard had hit the bench seat to his front and had smashed the hell out of both of his knees! As for my chap in the bow, he had hit the front deck of the boat with such force that when thrown forward into that decking, his shotgun had accidently discharged. The downward force of the blast had subsequently blown a hole one foot in diameter in the bottom of the bow of their boat! Now, their boat was sinking! And a sinking boat in a mess of floodwaters is not really a nice situation to be in... Especially when the lad in the stern can't hardly swim because of a damaged knee from an earlier impact with the bench seat to his front when they had initially hit the unseen submerged object going full bore.

The lad in the stern of the boat limped himself back to his idling motor, put it into gear, cranked it up, and headed for the levee. Gee, I thought smugly, guess who is sitting in his still-floating canoe near the same levee? As they came my way, I could see a huge spray of water shooting up into the inside of their boat from the hole in the floor of their bow section. In short order, they were sinking and I do mean fast! Realizing they were heading for my levee, I happily set an intercept course. Remember what I said previously about pissing off Mother Nature or her Thin Green Line minions?

Just as my lads made it to the levee's edge, their boat sank in about five feet of cold, swirling water! That made it really simple. First, I had my powerboat shooting chaps with their well-exercised middle fingers now in my grasp. Also as their boat sank, all their birds floated off in the floodwater's current. Gee, were all those evidence birds now floating towards me for easy retrieval? For the next five minutes, I loaded up my canoe with floating evidence birds as my two lads swam to shore (the lad with the bad knee just dog-paddled his way onto the levee). Then I headed for my two now-very wet, scared, shivering lads, and their sunken boat which they had hurriedly tied to a nearby tree to keep it from drifting off into the raging floodwaters.

As I pulled into their area, I had another grin cross my face. They had been running a 40-horsepower Evinrude outboard motor on their boat as it sank. If I remembered correctly, when the boat sank out of sight, that motor had been running full-out. All I could do was smile over what that meant. That is, if the wrecked motors that had been on our boats when I was in Alaska that had been running full-out when they sank in the cold waters were any kind of example as to what happens to that motor mechanically. It sure didn't do much good for a hot running engine and its cylinders for a quick infusion of cold water, if I remembered correctly.

As it turned out, my two powerboat shooting lads were from the City of Sacramento. Both lads were just 19 and were later cited for use and aid of a powerboat in the taking of migratory waterfowl and for taking over limits of ducks, to wit, 13 over the limit. As for the boat, it belonged to the boat operator's dad, one Roger Peterson. And if I might say so myself, the metal hull of that boat had one hell of a water-generated concussion shock hole in it. In fact, the concussion from the shotgun blast had not only blown one hell of a hole in the bow but had cracked the spine of the hull back about two feet as well. No two ways about it, that boat would not hold water out or in anytime soon...

As for the lad operating the boat, he had a knee the size of a basketball. A knee that had been obviously smashed on the corner of the bench seat to his front during the collision with the submerged object. It was the prettiest black-blue-yellow-purple, blood and fluid-filled knee joint you ever saw. No more football for that chap. However, my lad in the bow had suffered an even worse fate. He had two softball-sized appendages caused when his shotgun stock had slammed violently upward upon its barrel's impact with the front hull of the boat during the collision. The stock caught him directly between the legs! Then it happened again in the same area once the shotgun had immediately discharged! Suffice to say, that stock's placement was perfect, if you get my drift. Like I said, it is not nice to piss off Mother Nature... In fact after that particular accident, it would have been hard for my lad with the softball-sized appendages to piss on anybody, if you get my drift once again...

Putting my two lads carefully into my Grumman, plus their shotguns and birds, we three slowly made our way back along the levee waters to my patrol truck. There I unloaded the two lads, their birds, and their shotguns. A quick call once again to the Sheriff's Office soon produced a ride to the doctor for my two injured powerboat shooters. However, I did notice their middle fingers didn't seem to be injured in any sort of way as compared to their otherwise-injured physical and mental states. I have often wondered how the boat operator's dad took into account the little "accident" to his boat and motor as well as having to pay a $750.00 fine for his son's morning powerboat duck shooting incident?

Now to all my readers who are also great cooks, if one is careful, they can begin to smell my U.S. Game Management Agent's "stew" beginning to come together. So far on that cold and rainy day, we have added the "meaty part, garlic, spices, and now the onions." I wondered what would be added next?

A FEATHER AND A FINGERPRINT

Leaving the levee after my run-in with the powerboat shooters, I headed upstream again into the floodwaters. Only that time I took it upon myself to randomly check every chap I observed hunting waterfowl that fine rainy morning so long ago. The first seven boatloads of sportsmen all proved out legal-like. Proceeding further upstream, I noticed something large and white floating my way in the flood waters. Motoring over to the white object, I discovered the body of a freshly killed, totally protected, tundra swan! And that wasn't all. When I turned over its lifeless form in the water, I was surprised and pissed all in the same emotion. It had been breasted out! Whoever the killer was, he had taken the time after killing the critter to breast it out for the meat. The meat from adult swans is usually tougher than an old boot while that from the cygnets, young of the year, is highly prized. Then the carcass was dumped into the raging flood waters for quick disposal. Man, that sure set the hair on my last part over the fence big time!

Changing my patrol strategy, I headed up into the fast-moving floodwaters. Only this time I made it a point to stop and watch every boatload of shooters before I checked them. In each case, since the air was also full of flying swans looking for a safe place to land, I first made sure my lads weren't illegally shooting that species. After giving each and every one of them the opportunity to shoot at the numerous low-flying species, I would make my field inspection move. If no shooting at the protected species occurred, I would routinely check my lads and move on.

After checking my third boatload of shooters using that procedure, I spied a white floating object in the waters coming my way. Once again, I discovered a freshly killed and breasted-out tundra swan! Aside for the bad news about the swan being taken, the news was good. That recent discovery meant my shooter or shooters were still above me somewhere and when we met, there was sure to be "happy federal agent" greetings and such...

As my morning wore on without finding my swan shooters, Dog and I headed for the shore once again. We both needed "to see a man about a horse," and there was the matter of two venison sandwiches in my carry bag. Making sure Shadow got the bigger of the two sandwiches, I settled back down on the shore bank and watched my floodwaters racing by.

Then, there it was once again. Another dead swan slowly drifted in close to our shore and, since Dog was through with her sandwich and eyeing mine, I had her fetch the floating swan's body. Sure as all get-out, the bird had been freshly taken and breasted out like all the others. Now, I was really getting pissed. There was no way, even in the valley's dense tule fogs, that one would mistake a tundra swan for a snow goose. Whoever was doing the swan killing was doing so with intent and malice, I grimly thought.

Having wasted enough time on the shoreline even though it had been much needed, Dog and I loaded up and headed out once again into the floodwaters. We hadn't gone another one hundred yards when here came another bundle of white floating down the floodwaters! Once again, a freshly killed and breasted-out swan was discovered. Doubling my pace even though to do so increased my danger in the small boat, I headed for the area of what was called the "bean field" in the Butte Sink. The bean field was just that. A previously farmed area full of beans that was left for the ducks and geese as another "draw" for the birds to use the Butte Sink. This was just another way for the expensive duck clubs and their sports in the area to have an even better duck and goose shoot. However, the area was also a favorite haven for resting tundra swans... Once again as I picked my way through all the floating debris I came across another freshly killed swan carcass hung up in the brush. It, too, had been breasted out. However this time, the blood had not coagulated on the carcass! That meant I was getting closer to my killer or killers and it was about time. I now had five swan carcasses in my canoe and to my way of thinking, whoever was holding all the swans' breast meat had a load to carry as well!

Then off to my north I heard several shots and saw a mess of Northern pintail climbing madly skyward. My shooters on that flock of ducks had to be close-at-hand so I shut off my outboard, lifted it out from the water so its shaft wouldn't tangle up on any flotsam, and then began silently paddling in that direction. About a one hundred yards later, I spied my shooters. There were two of them in a duck boat draped with camouflage burlap and anchored to a large cottonwood tree. Finding a mess of brush myself, Dog and I anchored in out of sight and began observing my lads. For the next hour nothing out of the ordinary occurred. My two lads killed several more ducks and a pair of Canada geese but nothing else. And even more telling, they had several low-flying flocks of swans fly right over them and they scarcely even looked up.

Figuring I still had more lads to check in the area while looking for my swan shooters, I untied my canoe, and Dog and I quietly paddled over to my two chaps who were now gutting out their ducks and geese. When I broke from the cover I had been using and moved out into the clearing in front of my shooters, they hardly gave me a second look. It wasn't until I invaded their small decoy set that they quit cleaning their birds and gave me a second, casual glance.

"Afternoon, lads. How is the shooting?" I asked, as I continued paddling in closer to their duck boat.

"Fine, and I suppose you are the gamekeeper and here to tell us we can't hunt in these floodwaters. Well, save your breath. These are floodwaters of the Sacramento River and are considered navigable by the Coast Guard. As such, we can hunt here," he said as if he was loaded for "gamekeeper's bear."

"Whoa, hold it. I am a federal agent here to just check your birds, shotguns for plugs, licenses, duck stamps, and nothing else," I said with a grin.

"Well, we didn't know and didn't want to get hassled," said a bearded man of about 50 with a build like mine.

"Well, now that you lads know what I want and these are my credentials, may I check some licenses and the like?" I asked.

"Sure can, officer," said a tall, skinny man in the bow of the boat.

With that, I commenced checking their licenses, ducks, and gear. All checked out and the men were right as rain when it came to being within their limits of ducks and geese.

Getting ready to leave, I said, "You men see anyone up here shooting at swans?"

"No sir," said the skinny one. "Killing them birds is illegal," he continued.

However, when he responded, I noticed just a slight smirk on his face as if he knew something I didn't. I also observed his partner reach for a pack of cigarettes upon hearing that question. His hands were shaking badly and before you knew it, he had dropped two cigarettes into the slop in the bottom of their boat. (Relax, folks. Those were the days when a pack of cigarettes only cost 20 cents.)

Sensing something was wrong but unable to put my finger on it, I continued making small talk as I tried to sort out what I had just observed and what it meant. And now if I didn't have enough questions rattling around in me, my guardian angels inside me were beginning to move around for the first time that day. "You lads been here all morning?" I asked.

"Yes, sir," responded "Skinny" who looked at me like a snake would a field mouse. As for his older partner, he seemed to be taking a damn long time lighting that cigarette. But by damn, for the life of me I couldn't see anything out of the ordinary! Knowing I was running out of "visiting" time, my eyes frantically scanned their duck boat for anything out of place. There were two thermoses and their mess of ducks and geese laid in a pile in the bottom of the boat, shotgun shells were contained in military ammo cases to keep them dry, several cigarette butts floated in the bilge water, some netting was spread all over to cover the boat, and a pair of chest-high waders were lying in the bow. That was it! Not a damn thing for me to go on and nothing else out of place that said these chaps were my swan shooters. Then my eyes swept the area in which they were sitting for any nearby duck blinds where something could have been hidden. Nothing out of place or suspicious close-at-hand places greeted my eyes in that arena as well.

"If you have nothing else further to do with us, we would like to get back to our hunting if you don't mind, officer," said Skinny, still watching me as much as I was watching him.

I was running out of time and I knew it. To hang around any longer would just invite a complaint to my superiors over me ruining their hunt, I thought.

Finally the sun shone on the manure pile behind the barn. The unused chest-high waders. They were more or less tossed into the bow of their boat to be used as necessary. If one had a boat he wouldn't need any chest-high waders would he? ran through my mind like a short-tailed weasel chasing a deer mouse.

Then I saw it! On the lip of the top of the chest-highs was a single small white body feather no bigger than a wood tick! Right next to the feather on the inside of a folded piece of the boot so the rain wouldn't wash it away was a single bloody fingerprint! Terry, I thought, you didn't check inside the chest-highs!

"Gentlemen, before I leave, I would like to check those chest- highs. They have a white feather on them and a bloody fingerprint. As such, I would like to check inside those boots for any birds before I leave," I quietly said. To my way of thinking, that shorttailed weasel was getting closer to the deer mouse...

"No need," said the skinny one. "We haven't used them all day, so no need."

But just the way he said those words told me he had something to hide. Also, my guardian angels were now really raising hell over the possibility of a "kill."

Since the skinny one hadn't moved since I had started this line of conversation, I did. Sliding my canoe further up along the side of their duck boat, I reached out for the chest-highs.

"Them is my boots and you keep your filthy hands off them!" said the skinny one.

"Sir, as I said earlier, there appears to be a white swan breast feather on that boot along with a bloody fingerprint. Since you lads are hunting waterfowl and I have had swan shooters in the area breasting them out this morning, that would be a perfect place in which to hide swan breasts. So with that probable cause and under the Open Fields Doctrine, I will make a field inspection of that pair of boots if you don't mind."

With those words and a look not meant to be misunderstood, I reached in and grabbed the tops of the chest-highs. Dragging them towards me, I was surprised by their heavy weight. My grip on the top of the boots, because of their unusual weight, was not sufficiently strong enough and they slipped out from my hand! Realizing I had something substantial in the innocent-looking chest-high waders, I now grabbed them with authority and dragged them over to me. Opening up the top of the booted area, I discovered a large slab of dark meat identifiable size-wise to that of a slab of breast meat from a swan! Dragging the boots closer, I finally took out ten slabs of breast meat (two slabs per breast) from the boots!

In the meantime, not a word was uttered by my two chaps. The short-tailed weasel had just caught the deer mouse...

"Either of you chaps care to tell me what happened?" I asked, as I emptied out the slabs of breast meat into the bottom of my canoe.

"We was hungry," said the skinny one. "This was our first good duck and goose shoot all year, and since we were here and figured folks like you because of the rotten weather would be elsewhere, we shot a few swans as well. They is supposed to be good eating so we thought we would give them a try. I guess that wasn't such a good idea, huh?"

"Not if you get caught," I quietly said. "I will need to see some driver's licenses, gentlemen, if you don't mind."

Both men were issued citations into Federal

Court in Sacramento for possessing protected migratory nongame birds, to wit, parts from five tundra swans. Both men later pled guilty and were fined $500.00 each (the maximum allowed under the Migratory Bird Treaty Act in those days). I later distributed the swan meat to several Mexican families living on the eastern side of Colusa County who had rather large families and who were always short on grits and long on hungry stomachs. Being that they were Mexican farm laborers making very little, they sure had a need for the meat and I was happy to oblige. Especially since between the two families there were 13 kids!

Today, as of 2012, tundra swans can be lawfully taken in several states in the United States. Their overall populations are such that biologically they can safely be legally hunted under strict regulation.

By now, all my readers have to be really smelling the U.S. Game Management Agent's "stew" I was "building." Let's add the "celery" into the stew from this case and hope I make some more in which to complete this, a most interesting and unusual stew. Just imagine how good this stew would taste on such a rainy, cold day, with a mound of biscuits to accompany a freshly homemade pie made by my bride...

A BOATLOAD OF DECOYS

Wrapping up the slabs of dark-colored swan breast meat in my extra raincoat so it wouldn't get dirty, Dog and I headed for the western side of the Butte Sink. Finding a small piece of real estate that wasn't underwater, Dog and I beached the Grumman. Getting out I stretched my legs and let my backside, flattened from sitting on the hard aluminum seat, return to normal curvature. Dog, on the other hand, tended to her business and then began exploring our island.

Ping went the sound of a .22-caliber rifle bullet further to my northwest. Looking in that direction for the longest time, I saw nothing but a couple of pheasants winging their ways towards my small island. Then both noisily clattered into the limbs of nearby leafless trees without a whole lot of grace. Perching high up in the branches, both birds just nervously looked down at Dog and me but were reluctant to fly once again due to their limited long-distance flying powers.

For my readers' sake, pheasants, like chickens and turkeys, are unable to fly great distances because of limited blood vessels in their major flight or breast muscles. Hence, their white meat breast muscles and lighter, dryer taste. Whereas migratory birds like ducks, geese, swans have an abundance of blood vessels in their major flight breast muscles. Hence, their darker color, stronger taste, and ability to fly greater distances (more blood vessels means faster oxygen recharge and quicker reduction in lactic acid build up when using one's major muscle groups). Therefore, the flight distance differences between migratory birds and species of upland game birds like turkeys, pheasants, quail, and all species of grouse.

Grabbing my binoculars from the Grumman, I examined the flooded tree line from whence came my two pheasants. I observed nothing out of the ordinary but a lot fast-moving water. Ping went the .22-caliber rifle off in the distant tree line once again. Again I looked carefully but was rewarded with nothing out of the ordinary.

Urrhr! came the interrupting sound of a slow-moving outboard motor off to the east. Swinging my binoculars into that quadrant, I spotted a large, flat-bottomed boat with two occupants coming my way. One man sat in the bow with a shotgun at the ready and in the stern sat the boat's motor operator. Between the two men was a small mountain of something in the center of the boat covered with a tarp. Switching my eyes to the boat's hull, I could see "she" was riding low in the water from the heavy load she was carrying.

What the hell would those two he carrying under that tarp that made their boat ride so low in the water? I asked myself. Surely it couldn't be a monster load of dead ducks and geese, I thought offhandedly. Curiosity always being a wildlife officer's long suit, I boarded Dog and pushed my Grumman off into the swirling, muddy, fast-moving floodwaters again. Lowering my outboard motor's shaft and propeller into the water, I gave its starter rope a pull. My little outboard spun to life, and Dog and I headed over to our two lads with the heavily loaded, slow moving boat on an intercept course (my .22 shooter now forgotten for the moment).

About three minutes later, I slowly approached the side of my suspicious-looking flat bottomed boat. "Hey, you son-of- a-bitch, back off! Can't you see we are loaded heavy and don't need you or your wake to mess us up or cause problems," yelled the man in the bow.

Slowing the forward progress of my Grumman which left little wake on its best day, I said, "Federal agent. I would like to check you boys for ducks, shotguns for plugs, duck stamps, and hunting licenses."

"We aren't hunting," bellowed the voice from the large one in the stern of their boat operating the outboard motor as he tried to steer away from my approaching Grumman.

"Well, I beg to differ with the two of you," I said. "Both of you are wearing camouflage clothing, wearing duck and goose calls, and the man in the bow is in possession of a shotgun," I fired right back. Continuing I said, "Additionally, both of you are in a duck boat and in the lower end of the Butte Sink, an area known for its excellent private duck clubs and waterfowl hunting. So pull over into that grove of flooded cottonwoods and heave to because I aim to check the both of you."

With those words, both men in the boat just looked long and hard at each other for a pregnant moment. It was based then on their "looks" and their boat riding lower in the water than it would have normally that I felt something wasn't right in this henhouse. All you readers, especially you wildlife badge-carrying types, need to remember that "chance favors the prepared mind." In the present caper, something was just not right, favoring further examination by yours truly in all his Teutonic magnificence...

Swinging my canoe beside my now-anchored alongside-a-cottonwood-tree lads, I took out my credentials and identified myself again. Then ignoring the well-covered bulge in the middle of their long boat, I commenced checking their quickly proffered hunting gear and licenses. And for two chaps who had not been hunting, that also included checking their limits of ducks and geese lying in the bottom of their boat!

"Those you fellas' decoys?" I asked offhandedly after spying several decoy anchors peaking out from under the edge of the tarp in the bottom of their boat.

There was a moment's hesitation, and then the lad who had been operating their outboard motor finally said, "Yeah."

Ping went the suspicious sound of a .22-caliber rifle being fired from the large grove of trees to my northwest once again. Damn it! I can only do one thing at a time. You shooting the .22, just keep it up. When I finish here, I will be happy to pay you a visit as well, I grimly thought, figuring that shooter was up to no good.

Sliding my canoe further alongside the center of their boat, I lifted up the edge of the tarp. There in front of God and everybody lay piled high about three hundred high-class, very expensive duck and goose decoys! You know, the kind one finds on very elite and high-class duck clubs. Duck clubs like the ones found in the Butte Sink in whose waters the three of us now quietly sat like three rain-soaked muskrats. One rain-soaked muskrat with a grin and the other two wet as hell muskrats with frowns and tight hind ends...

Ping ping went two .22s from across the floodwaters to my northwest. Now I was really getting pissed. I felt I more than likely had at least two chaps shooting their .22s at something illegal, and here I sat with a potential theft case in the offing. One which I could not leave at the time because that would mean my chaps would disappear into the rain squalls, and I would still not be at the bottom of this "hoo-rah." Trying hard to ignore the clattering .22s to my northwest, I continued with the examination of my two fellows in the loaded boat.

Reaching in and pulling several of the expensive duck decoys over to me, I flipped them over. Painted on the bottom of the first decoy were the words, "Sacramento Outing D.C.," a duck club to our east! "Either of you two members of the Sacramento Outing Duck Club?" I asked. Silence from the two chaps greeted my ears. In the background, I could still hear the banging away of several shotguns in the area and those damn .22s pinging away across Butte Creek and to my northwest as well!

I asked the question once again, and only got the sounds of rain pelting off my hunting coat as a response from my two now sick-looking lads. Then I began turning over more of the decoys from under the tarp. After about the tenth one turned over and identified as property of the Sacramento Outing Duck Club, I hit the jackpot! The next expensive, full-bodied duck decoy I turned over had painted on its keel the words "Butte Creek Farms Duck Club," another high-class duck club to our west!

"Well, well, well," I said. "If I didn't know any better, I would say you lads are taking advantage of the floodwaters and all the chaos it is causing. And if I also didn't know better, I would say you lads are helping yourselves to decoys from these nearby expensive duck clubs when their members are not out and about due to the flooding!"

Then I just stared hard at my two chaps as if waiting for some kind of a reasonable explanation. The lad in the bow, one Leander Jenkins said, "Officer, we were just duck hunting in these floodwaters when all these decoys came floating by. Figured we may as well take them instead of having someone else downstream helping themselves to them. So, we took them for ourselves for later use or sale back to the duck clubs."

"I would say you lads took more than a few and from two nearby duck clubs as well," I fired right back.

The sound of the rain pelting our rain gear was now deafening compared to my two lads' further explanations. "Let me ask you lads once again. Are either of you members of these clubs represented by these decoys, or are you acting on their behalf in picking up their decoys?"

"No, sir," answered Leander. "We was just hunting ducks in these here floodwaters and seen the decoys come floating by. Since they was just drifting by, we decided to take a few for ourselves since they was going to waste in the floodwaters anyways."

"Well, lads, the decoys belong to the duck clubs listed on their keels. Would both of you hand me your shotguns, butt first please?" I said. When both shotguns were in the bottom of my boat, I asked for and received their driver's licenses as well. Then I said over the almost constant pinging of .22-caliber shots coming from my northwest, "You two lads need to follow me. I wouldn't try to run or throw any decoys overboard because if you do, the law will just go tougher on the two of you."

Forty minutes later found the three of us back at my patrol truck on the levee. A quick radio call to the Colusa County Sheriff's Office soon brought Colusa County Deputy Sheriff Peter Grevie. Peter and I discussed what I had learned about the ownership of the decoys and who took them. With that information and my willingness to testify, he placed my lads under arrest for possession of stolen property. I loaded all the decoys into his trunk and front seat that I could with the rest going into the front seat and rear lockbox of my patrol truck. Then their boat and motor were loaded into the bed of my truck and chained down to prevent theft.

Some time later, both Butte and Colusa County District Attorneys (since the theft had occurred in both counties—Butte Creek Farms being in Colusa County and Sacramento Outing being in Butte County) filed charges. Each lad was later fined $500.00 in each county and placed on joint probation by each county since neither had a previous criminal record. The decoys were later returned to their rightful owners.

To all my readers, smell that U.S. Game Management Agent's "stew" now cooking, with the addition of green peppers, crookneck squash, and cubed potatoes as a "result" of this decoy stealing case. If I keep this up, we will soon have a "lumberjack's stew."

CLOSED-SEASON PHEASANTS BY THE GOB

Finished with my decoy thieves, I headed back upstream in the closing hours of the day with the "bit in my teeth!" I had pretty well pinpointed where my suspected .22 shooting was taking place, and Dog and I fairly well flew in that direction. As we plowed through the wind, rain, and debris-filled floodwaters, all I could think of was what these chaps had been shooting at all morning long. *Was it deer, quail, pheasants, muskrats, or just trapped feral cats on the high ground?* kept zipping through my memory banks. We probably went faster than common sense and safety allowed, but soon we were on station as to my ".22-caliber shooting" suspect's location to my way of figuring. Drifting back into a large bunch of willows, Dog and I waited for the sounds of shooting. Nothing but silence now greeted our ears in the way of light rifle shooting! Dad-burn it, I was too late to catch my shooters and whatever they had been shooting, I thought. Not satisfied with my current position, I shipped my outboard and began quietly paddling in the direction in which I had heard the last shots fired earlier in the day. Forty minutes of paddling resulted in nothing "being added" into my U.S. Game Management Agent's "stew pot." Boy, was I ever fuming! Now every type of illegality flew through my mind as a result of the earlier .22-caliber shooting escapades. Over limits of elephants, dead whooping cranes by the pile, endangered species piled up by the bucketfuls, over limits of spring run Chinook salmon, alligators, and everything else in between became suspect with all the shooting heard earlier while I was tangled up with my decoy thieves... Yeah, I was a little angry. I always figured that if I was going to abuse my body and family, I wanted to make my efforts pay. As it had now turned out, I just might as well have pissed into the wind...

Crossing over where Butte Creek had overflowed its banks, I kept paddling in the direction of Warren Davidson's Duck Club. That club was up on stilts because of the annual floodwater problems, and I scrambled up onto its upper deck for a better look around. I was rewarded with a big fat goose egg for my efforts! Crawling back down the steps, I paddled again to my north and several areas of known levees where various critters would hang out on the higher ground when the winter flood waters arrived.

Approaching the levee area just south of Putnam Road, I spotted it! Nestled up against a levee and partially covered with brush was a flat-bottomed boat. It had obviously been partially dragged up onto the levee and hidden from prying eyes. Well, I thought, that area was pretty far north from where I had heard the last barrage of "pings," but it was all I had so off I went like a house on fire.

Quietly paddling up to my suspect boat, I pulled alongside. Lying in the bottom of the boat lay about a dozen assorted ducks and four geese. No over limits there, I thought. Looking into the rest of the boat, I found nothing suspicious. A gas tank, an oar, several empty shotgun shell boxes, a box of tools, a gunnysack full of decoys and there it was! An empty box for Remington .22 shells floated in the bilge water. Then, there was more... Since when does a "sack full of decoys" ooze blood? Doing a double take, I moved my canoe in closer for a better look. Grabbing the "decoy sack," I found it to be full of a gob of freshly killed pheasants. And upon a closer look, they had all been shot with what appeared to be a .22!

Quickly looking all around to see if I had been discovered and finding myself still alone, I hustled my canoe out of sight under my camouflage parachute and into some nearby brush along a levee. Leaving Dog in the canoe, I hustled back to where I could stake out the boat with the "decoy sack" full of freshly killed pheasants and burrowed into the surroundings.

As I lay there in the rain and mud in the floodwaters along the levee, my mind raced. What I had heard earlier in the spaced shooting of a light rifle was the illegal killing of pheasants. Like turkeys in a roost, hapless pheasants will sit in treetops during times of floodwaters when there is nowhere else to go and they are soaked to the bone. They are so territorial they won 3t just fly elsewhere to stay dry. They will just stay within their small territory, even if it means roosting in trees while floodwaters race below, I thought as my memory flashed back over my upland game wildlife management training received in college and practical knowledge received during previous winter's floods.

Bottom line as I figured it, my shooters had discovered a ton of pheasants marooned by the flood waters like Christmas ornaments high up in the leafless trees and had begun popping them with .22s. Filling one gunnysack, I suspected they were now in the process of picking up and gutting the rest of their illegal kills just like before. However, this time like on a river in Africa, there was a hippo-sized lad lurking in the bushes like a Nile crocodile! And now being soaked to the skin, cold, muddy, and hungry, I was not to be denied.

As dusk approached, I, like all wet-as-a-muskrat lads skulking in the bushes, began thinking maybe the shooters had seen me earlier. Maybe they weren't coming and other like thoughts now stormed through my mind like the freshly falling rain around me. But I figured I was here for the duration because no one shoots a gob of my pheasants right under my very nose and gets away with it, if I had my druthers.

🙵

Then there it was! The smell of nicotine wafted past my nostrils for just a moment, but I caught it when it came by in the moist airwaves. Now, I would wait until hell froze over before I broke this stakeout. Well, as it turned out, I didn't have long to wait. In the darkness fast descending on me like a cold wet curtain, I heard footsteps in the muddy earth making slopping sounds as they came my way. All of a sudden, there were two darkened figures by the boat carrying another gunnysack of what appeared to be wet and bloody pheasants. Quietly and stiffly moving their way because of my long partial immersion in the cold floodwaters, I still moved every bit as stealthily as the Nile crocodile, and a big one at that! And to all my doubting readers, I was one hell of a lot prettier than that "croc" I was now emulating, and don't any of you forget it... "Hey!" yelled a scared voice, "there is someone crawling this way!" Well, maybe the Nile crocodile was a bit stealthier than I was... The sound of that voice of discovery was instantly cut short with the beam of a five-cell flashlight! "Hold it right there, lads. Federal agent!" I bellowed just to make sure God and everybody else within a mile heard me. Well, maybe not that loudly, but the incessant rains did stop for a moment and the nearby flood waters reversed themselves momentarily until the sound of my "somewhat loud" voice had drifted off into the wind...

"Don't shoot!" yelled a voice whose tenor was now reaching for the stars, if you get my drift.

I was alongside the boat and my two now-frozen in fear and very surprised lads. Reaching out, I disarmed one fellow holding two .22 rifles as his partner dropped a huge gunnysack he had been carrying with difficulty over his shoulder at my feet. Splashing my light across my two lads' eyes, I ordered both men to sit, which they did posthaste. Unloading their rifles, I placed them behind me on the levee, then I reached for the most recent gunnysack. It, too, was clear full of freshly killed pheasants and I do mean a "gob!"

Making sure I held command over the scene, I showed the lads my credentials in the light of my flashlight and then asked for their hunting and driver's licenses. Those were instantly forthcoming as the fear of surprise still manifested itself in my two young, stunned, stale nicotine-smelling shooters.

"You boys shoot all these pheasants?" I asked.

"Yes, sir," they responded in unison.

"Pheasant season is closed, lads," I advised.

My two lads said nothing, still getting over their fright at being ambushed when and where they had least expected it.

"Where did the two of you put your boat in?" I asked, now very cognizant of the fast-deepening darkness.

"At the south end of Putnam Road," said one Dale Roberts from the nearby Butte County Town of Gridley.

"Well then, I suggest one of you go and get your vehicle and back it down to where you launched. Then get your tail-end back here on the levee. In the meantime, I will count out all these pheasants and issue your partner a state citation. When you return, Dale, I will issue you a citation as well. As it now stands, both of you will be receiving citations for possession of pheasants taken during the closed season. You need to get cracking and make ready to load your boat because I need to do the same as well. Especially since I have such a long way to go in the dark," I continued.

I counted out 92 freshly killed pheasants from the two gunny sacks! As I later discovered, all had been shot out from their flooded roost trees by my two lads with their .22-caliber rifles with scopes. After issuing the lads citations for the pheasants, I issued seizure tags for the birds as well as their rifles. Both lads departed shortly thereafter, and I doubt either of them could pass an ounce of gas between the two of them, especially over the fright of being surprised and apprehended at the edge of dark by a rather large "thing" crawling around on the lip of the levee.

Now it was my turn to "head 'em out" and what a trip that would turn out to be. Have any of you ever tried paddling in floodwaters at night with a loaded canoe in a driving rain and windstorm? Well, unless you need the "time" of your life or it is on your "bucket list," you might pass on that one. Having enough close scares, I finally landed the canoe on Laux Road far from my patrol truck. Anchoring my canoe to a tree and leaving Dog in the boat in charge, I walked out to River Road and bummed a ride to the

Colusa County Sheriff's Office. From there, one of my buddies drove me back to my patrol truck, and I soon returned to the edge of the flood waters at Laux Road.

There I met my partner Shadow whom I had left guarding my evidence pheasants. Upon my return, boy, talk about a happy dog!

I guess she figured she was going to be left out all night in the rain with a couple of sacks of stinky dead pheasants. But she stayed right there as she had been told. Damn, I still miss that dog even to this day, some forty years later as these words are written. After being happily reunited, I loaded up my canoe, motor, gear, and gunnysacks of evidence, and headed home.

I finally arrived home around ten o'clock that evening to find a very worried wife. But guess what she had waiting for me for dinner? One of the best homemade and hearty beef stews I ever ate. Boy, did that woman ever have my number! In fact, Dog even got a large bowl of her homemade stew from my bride for bringing me home safely.

When I filed my upland game citations, the Colusa County Attorney decided to amend them. Since the pheasants were all freshly killed, he added the "taking" charges to the two lads' penalty as well, even though I had not observed the lads taking the illegal birds. He just figured there was enough evidence in their "taking" the birds as well as possessing them because of their freshness and body warmth exhibited by the dead birds.

Both lads later forfeited $1,000.00 each in fines and lost their .22-caliber rifles. A pretty expensive lesson for a couple of 19-year-olds to learn, I must say, for an afternoon's rainy shoot fest on a bunch of hapless, flooded out of their homes, sitting in the branches, pheasants.

But I wasn't done. My U.S. Game Management Agent's "stew" wasn't finished. For that pheasant escapade, I "added" beef stock and now the stew was almost complete. However, I still was lacking one needed ingredient to my way of thinking. That ingredient followed somewhat later...

THE ILLEGAL TAKING AND LOSS OF A GREAT "CRITTER"

A month later, the heavy winter rains had stopped and the mighty Sacramento River had once again returned to within its banks. However, because of that event and the one yet to come, I still considered what followed as part of my earlier U.S. Game Management Agent's "stew-making" escapade...

One day while walking the lower end of the Colusa Weir's deeply scoured grounds working my dog for crippled ducks, I discovered a deeply scoured-out pool in the ground. This pool had been cut deeply into the soil as a result of the earlier, violently flowing floodwaters. In that ten foot deep pool were a mess of fish now trapped because of the now receded floodwaters. One of those trapped fish in the deep pool was a massive, female white sturgeon! Just looking at the ancient creature from the bank of the pool, I estimated it weighed about four hundred pounds and was maybe ten feet in length! Damn, what a beauty and a tragedy-to-be if I didn't get my tail-end in gear before that great fish perished in the warming and rapidly becoming oxygen-deficient waters.

Looking all around to make sure "Fish" and I had not been discovered, I beat a hasty retreat. Once back to my patrol truck, I called the California Department of Fish and Game's Central Office in Sacramento. With that call, I made arrangements for the fisheries department to send a tank truck and fish rescue crew to trap and transplant the giant and genetically valuable sturgeon back into the nearby Sacramento River.

Then I made arrangements to borrow a D-7 bulldozer with a blade from a local farmer in which to plow a road across the rutted weir for the fish truck to travel. I figured I would do the road building since I had gained dozer operational experience in my high school and college days as a logger in the Sierra Nevada Mountains of Plumas County. That way, I would quietly build the road and the fish rescue crew could trap out the fish before anyone else was the wiser.

Since it would be a few more days before my fish crew arrived, I tried keeping an eye on my trapped sturgeon every time I was incountry. On one of those trips to the isolated pool out in the middle of the weir, I discovered it was empty of my sturgeon! There were .22 shell casings all around the now-shallow pool and bright red streaks of blood and deep drag marks along the sandy bank. Someone had discovered my great fish and had illegally killed it with .22 rifle fire. Man, was I pissed! Such a great fish, only to be trapped by receding floodwaters and then to be illegally taken by someone with only a half-ounce of sense! Cold-tracking the human footprints and drag marks of the fish, I came to the place where it had been loaded into a vehicle and there my leads ended once the tire tracks hit pavement.

Two days later, a newspaper article in a local Marysville newspaper bragged to high heaven the taking of a 433-pound white sturgeon by a couple of local "wonderfuls." In that article were the two chaps' tall tale of how they had been out looking for decoys that had washed away from the various duck clubs in the area during the flooding. They ran across the pool of water holding the great sturgeon. Then, according to the newspaper article, they had sped home, retrieved their fishing gear and returned. Once back at the pool, they had hooked the sturgeon and fought the fish for a long time before landing it. A friend of mine named Tom Yamamoto, who happened to be present during the weigh-in, saw the fish. He advised me that there were several small mysterious holes, like bullet holes, in the great fish's head and one in its body... At that point in time, there was little I could do legally. To try and get my two lads to confess would have been a lost cause because both of the men were experienced outlaws whom I had crossed swords with several times previously. That, plus the evidence was now long gone and in their freezers in the form of many dozens of soon-to-be fine-eating steaks.

To all you non-believers, there is a god who loves little kids, fools, and game wardens. That next fall while working duck hunters southwest of Colusa, I ran across my two "gallant sturgeon fishermen" mentioned in the earlier Marysville newspaper. They were duck hunting near the Colusa National Wildlife Refuge. Between them during one of our tule fog days, they had managed to kill 22 Northern pintail over the limit. To all my readers, the sturgeon group and Northern pintail, along with the golden eagle, are some of my favorite animal species. Neither Mother Nature nor I like anyone taking more than their fair share of any of the above species. Especially under unusual circumstances disallowing "fair chase" methods of capture (the golden eagle by state and federally permitted methods only). Suffice to say, my two "gallant sturgeon fishermen" paid fines of $1,000.00 each in Federal Magistrates Court in Sacramento for taking a gross over limit of pintail with the use and aid of shotguns capable of holding more than three shells and doing so without possessing valid federal duck stamps in their immediate possession... Gee, do you think the federal judge heard about the sturgeon loss and liked that species as much as I did and let that influence her high fine rulings...?

Being that the sturgeon find was more or less related to my original U.S. Game Management Agent's "stew" and the associated floodwater-related cases, I kind of figured that case was just an extension of my earlier stew making escapade. However, I found in the unfortunate loss of the female sturgeon, it sure didn't do anything for the ultimate good taste of my stew. With the failure relating to my sturgeon's survival, it now seemed my "stew" had "developed" a bitter taste. The bitter taste was similar to the one 1 developed when acting as a "Sword for Mother Nature" over my many years of conservation service to the American people trying to hold the line against that which was human induced wrong in the world of wildlife. One in which I wasn't able to catch all the bad guys before the damage to Mother Nature was done. A taste that I came to experience many times before my storied life and career would run its course. Damn, it is hell to be directly related, in a matter of speaking, to Custer while trying to protect those within the world of wildlife...

Chapter Four

THE STILLWATER MARSHES OF NEVADA

Sitting in my Colusa office one morning typing closed case reports (no computers in those days), my phone rang. Picking it up I said, "Good morning, U.S. Fish and Wildlife Service, Terry speaking."

"Tiny (my nickname in the agent squad), what is on your schedule for the next week?" asked my boss, Agent-in-Charge, Jack Downs, who resided in Sacramento.

"Morning, Chief. Just the usual, up to my last part over the fence in problems like nighttime "duck draggers," commercial market hunters, muddy roads which are impassable, rain every day, this damn crappy paperwork, and my boss probably calling me to heap more slop onto my head," I smartly replied with a grin, knowing what was coming next from the friend and supervisor I highly respected.

"You're fired, you big lug," Jack just as smartly replied, with a bit of mirth in his voice.

Jack and I both laughed over the easy friendship we shared. For me, the only man I respected more than this man was my dad, Otis Barnes. Jack Downs had been the Agent-in-Charge for the U.S. Fish and Wildlife Service for the Northern California District for as long as I could remember. In short, he was not only one hell of a fine officer but a great human being as well. He was extremely street-smart, a super catch dog when it came to apprehending human beings walking on the dark side in the world of wildlife, and was one of the "quickest" men I ever knew when it came to surviving on his "feet." Additionally, he was a tremendous supervisor and not afraid of any man, be it one with a gun or the high ranking bureaucrats in Washington. To my way of thinking, Jack was an agent's agent of the first degree!

"You making any money for the Service and earning your keep?" he asked.

"You 'cracker ass!' You know damn well I am more than 'paying for the gas and oil.'" Leave it to Jack to ask me that, I thought. He damned well knew I was working seven days a week and mostly 16-hour days. In the process, I was chasing those who were especially quick on their trigger fingers and poor in the counting department when it came to early shooting, late shooting, duck-dragging, market hunting or taking over limits of migratory game birds in the Northern Sacramento Valley of California.

"Yeah, I kind of figured you were out and about creating hate and discontent," he replied, with an "easy smile" in his voice. "Think that little gal you married would let you leave the state for a few days?" he asked in a more serious tone of voice

"That all depends. What do you have up your sleeve, Chief?" I asked.

"Our man in Reno is getting near the end of his string. He is close to retirement and I have a feeling a few things are not getting done in his area of responsibility. The "Big Boss" in Portland is also aware that our Reno man is slowing down a bit and asked me if you might be of service in that situation. Care to slide over to Nevada and work the marshes in and around the Stillwater National Wildlife Refuge these next few days?" he asked well aware of my long standing related waterfowl enforcement credentials.

"Never been there. What is it like and what are some of the problems they are having?" I asked with rising curiosity.

"Same as you have there in the Sacramento Valley only not in the same scope and degree.

Over limits, early and late shooting, violations by local Native Americans who feel they are not under the laws of the land, knotheads taking protected migratory game and nongame birds, folks taking closed season waterfowl species, and the like. I know it is a lot like the work you are currently doing, but I just feel that needed kind of work is not being done by our refuge people over there or by our man in Reno who is slowing down and is on the short list for retirement," he continued.

We only had two men in all of Nevada in those days and sadly it was true. John Wendler, our man in Reno, who is a good man, is getting on in years, I thought. As such, he is probably letting a few outlaws slip through the cracks and that was alright. First, it allowed for a "little outlaw seed to be spread around for future generations of catching," and second, John has probably earned some slack time in his life after all his good years in the Service. "You bet, Jack. Let me clear the slate here and I should be able to roll within a day or two," I replied.

"Ok," replied Jack, "I will let Wendler know you will be working the Stillwater area as part of your new agent training program. That should settle any ruffled feathers he might have over you working in his district. Besides, a little more adventure for a big bastard like you will do you some good. Maybe it will knock off some of those rough edges," he said, as he laughed easily at catching me not expecting him to make a playful "run" at me. "Just remember that when you finish, turn all your cases over to John so he can personally file them in Magistrates Court in Reno," he continued. We exchanged several more good-natured jabs at each other as close friends are wont to do and then we both got back to the needed work at hand after hanging the phones up.

Two days later, after leaving my home in Colusa around five in the morning, Dog and I pulled into my parents' yard in Quincy on my way to Reno which was still some eighty miles to the east. After a nice breakfast with my folks (their home was directly on my way), I once again loaded up into my patrol truck and headed for Reno, but not before loading all kinds of homemade sweet rolls, a pumpkin pie, homemade beer bun sandwiches, and a bread bag full of cookies. Boy, let me tell you, my mom sure could cook and bake! May she rest in peace as I fondly remember those days that went by all too quickly. Little did I realize my blessings in having those kinds of days and experiences as I grew into manhood... Those memories from my original family times are now long past into the musty pages of history. Thank God my bride is just as good a cook as my mother, if not better, and still occasionally caters to my sweet tooth for all things homemade.

Heading east on State Highway 70, I soon swung into the small Town of Blairsden and visited with one of the best men and fish and game officer I had ever known when I worked for the California Department of Fish and Game as a game warden myself. Clyde Shehorn was that man and a great officer and a truer gentlemen never lived! After a short visit, off I went on my way to what adventures lay before me at the Stillwater National Wildlife Refuge and the surrounding marsh areas in the State of Nevada.

"Stillwater," as it is locally called, is a large high desert-type of national wildlife refuge. It is located near Fallon, Nevada, just off Highway 116. The Stillwater Marshes are part of the Humboldt Sink area and are fed by the Humboldt River. Typical of Nevada, it is a cool, high desert marsh area that is home to many varied winged and other types of critters known to frequent that kind of ecology.

Waterfowl season was in full swing and I took my time in the area just getting acquainted with all the roads, members of some of the hunting public, the species of critters, and their favorite haunts and life histories. In fact, that early afternoon as I roamed the area getting acquainted, I feasted on some of my mom's homemade goodies as I eyed my "home" for the next several days. Passing many shallow desert wetlands on the south side of the refuge, I chanced upon a tremendous feeding area for black-necked stilts and avocets (both protected migratory shorebirds). Pulling off into a small nearby sagebrush flat overlooking the watered area, Dog and I got out and stretched our legs. Dog saw to it that she left several smelly things behind, while I also tended to the call of nature.

Gosh, what a great and stunning early afternoon it turned out to be. The fall air was crisp, the scent of sagebrush perfumed the air, the cerulean blue sky was as only God can make it, the pungent smell of the marsh was invigorating, and it was as quiet out as a goose feather floating gently down on an afternoon breath of wind. An almost imperceptible soft breeze was blowing from the northwest and the smell of alkali dust was faintly riding in the air from earlier hunters' passing vehicles. As such, those alkali and marsh smells kept greeting my senses. Standing there alongside my truck in such a moment of peace, I could actually hear and feel my heart quietly beating. In short, it was one of those rare moments of time burned into the soul of one of God's members of the Thin Green Line. A memory I still carry to this very day, 42 years later as these lines are written. To those readers who have never experienced such profound moments and wonders, I am truly saddened. For it is moments like that so long ago that clearly signaled there really is a Supreme Being...

NATIVE AMERICAN RIGHTS?

Boom boom boom boom went four shots in quick succession down the road from where I quietly stood lost in my senses that first afternoon! Quickly swinging my eyes in that direction to echolocate my shooters, I simultaneously blindly grabbed around in the front seat of my truck with my right hand for my binoculars. Finally feeling their cold steel in my hands, I quickly swung them to my eyes for a look-see for what that shooting was all about. Not seeing anything of interest out across the sagebrush or nearby marsh, I jumped up into the bed of my truck. From there, I scrambled up onto the lid of the large utility box in the back of my patrol truck. Standing a whole lot higher now, I had a clear view of almost the entire State of Nevada or so it seemed. About a quarter-mile away, I spied a four-door Buick sedan with the front and back doors swung wide open. Off to the vehicle's right front quarter near an open marshy area scrambled four individuals quickly gathering up something from the water's edge. Focusing in on my "gatherers," I spied the objects of their attention. They were gathering up a mess of just freshly killed shorebirds which, by the way, generally are pretty good eating! Pretty good in the eating department, but highly illegal to take or possess under state laws and the federal Migratory Bird Treaty Act!

The hell you say, I thought as I scrambled off the utility box and dropped onto the ground. "In the truck," I bellowed, as my dog, anticipating some kind of action because of my historically predictable fast movement, hurriedly became airborne. Into the back of my truck she sailed as I quickly closed the tailgate behind her. Giving her a pat on her big neck as I ran by, I swung my ample carcass into the truck's front seat. In seconds, the big 383-cubic engine with her four barrel carburetor roared to life and we were off in a swirling cloud of alkali dust, typically like the Road Runner did in the old Looney Tunes cartoons of the '60s on TV when it was running away from Wiley E. Coyote. The only thing missing was the "beep-beep"...

Turning off onto a dusty road that I figured would lead me to the Buick sedan, Dog and yours truly hammered right along. Soon the Buick came into view just as my four chaps, upon hearing my approaching vehicle, hurriedly closed the trunk to their car. Reducing my speed, I proceeded slowly right up to the front of their car on the narrow road on which they sat in such a manner that if they tried to flee, it would be a chore on their part. With that, I calmly shut "her" down. Then I swung my gorgeous frame out from the front seat, only to be immediately confronted by what appeared to be four rather large and not-too-happy looking, smelling faintly of whiskey, bellicose Native Americans. Remember that "profiling" thing the liberal Democrats are always bellowing about and I discussed with you readers in one of my earlier books titled, *Wildlife On The Edge?* Well, my four lads fit a profile... I quickly realized that four to one odds were really not wonderful. Especially when those odds tied in with their bellicosity. And there was that little thing that my lads were armed... So you see, my readers, many times different forms of profiling take place in the officer's mind even during what starts out to be a routine stop. And once again, I maintain as long as what you are doing is Constitutional, fits within The Bill of Rights and any other judicial guidance, what is the problem?

"What the hell you doing, white man?" said the driver of the Buick.

Walking up to their car where they all stood, I got out my badge from my shirt pocket for all the men to see (U.S. Game Management Agents were not field-uniformed in those days. As federal officers, we dressed just like everyone else did in the field.). That was followed with verbal instructions as to my official identity as a federal wildlife officer.

"I don't give a damn who the hell you say you are," said the driver as he started to get back into their vehicle. As if on cue, he was quickly followed by the rest of the sullen-looking men. When they did, their shotguns were carelessly pointed every which way as the men seated themselves rather abruptly into their vehicle, as they prepared to leave.

"Sir!" I said, "I am a federal agent. I just observed the four of you through my binoculars picking up a mess of protected black-necked stilts and avocets moments earlier. I would like to see those birds and your state and federal collection permits, if I may," I continued (the only way such birds could lawfully be taken was under a state and federally issued Scientific Collecting Permit).

"You have no right to check us, white man," said the driver. "This is Indian land and you have no authority to be here," he continued with an angry tone rising up in his voice.

"I beg to differ with you, sir," I replied. "As I told you earlier, I am a federal agent, not a state fish and game warden. As such, I have every right to check you or anyone else who is in this country. Especially when I observe you folks taking and possessing protected migratory non-game birds on these lands of the United States," I advised in a now-hardening tone of voice meant to match that of the tone of the moment.

Starting and putting his car into gear, my driver said, "And I told you, you have no authority here on Indian land." Then as an afterthought, instead of fleeing, he looked over at his front seat passenger saying, "Hand me that shotgun! I will blow a hole clear through this white son-of-a-bitch, badge or no badge!"

It was at that point that I had a gut full of my fellow American. When he reached for the shotgun sitting between himself and his passenger, he turned the "corner" as far as I was concerned. Reaching through the open window of his car, I grabbed his left hand which was still holding onto the steering wheel and I brought it violently out the window and down alongside his front door! That move was collaterally accompanied with my right hand grabbing the man's left elbow and shoving it quickly upward. You know, with that martial arts move, it was amazing just how fast a fat man with a big mouth can come out an open window of the vehicle in which he is sitting! Especially when you put such a twist on one's shoulder that to resist will result in a rather painful broken arm and shoulder...

"Yeow! I quit, I quit," he screamed, as his face violently slammed into and then flattened out on the hard Nevada alkali soil with a loud, dusty crump! A face that was mashed even flatter when his rather obese body smashed down on top of the rest of his miserable carcass.

Continuing my move, I twisted his left arm up behind his back and quickly brought him lurching upward to the tiptoes of his feet. Then once he was on his tiptoes with his arm twisted up behind his back, it was amazing just how cooperative he all of a sudden became...

"Now, the rest of you lads, if you know what is good for you, get out from the car and go and stand in front of the hood of this vehicle. And don't anyone touch any of those shotguns lying on the seats," I said in a tone and tenor of voice meant for everyone to clearly understand. I think at that point with my rather large fellow with the big mouth who had just "flown" out his front window, the remaining three lads more than got the message...

Once my three lads were out in front of the car, I had all of them sit down on the ground. Then releasing my lad I "had been holding hands with," I had him sit with the rest of his buddies. As my recently released chap started rubbing his sore arm and shoulder, I reached into his car, shut off the engine and pocketed the keys. With one eye still on my lads, I removed the two shotguns from the car and unloaded them. They were unplugged and full of five shells each. Another quick look inside the car produced a quart bottle half-full of Jim Beam whiskey. When I had "whisked" my lad out the front window earlier, I had detected the faint smell of "John Barleycorn" on his breath. I figured that was probably where he had gotten his false courage to square off with me when he should have thought better of making such a move.

Still keeping an eye on my Native Americans, I placed their shotguns into the front seat of my truck. With another short command, my rather large Labrador dog bailed out from the back of the truck and ran to my side. "Sit," I commanded and she did as told. It was at that point that I now had the undivided attention of my four new "friends." Especially when they had a chance to look at the size of the dog sitting there looking right at them...

"Gentlemen, as I said earlier, I am a federal agent. These credentials I am showing you once again will let all of you know I am a United States Game Management Agent with the U.S. Fish and Wildlife Service. As such, I am empowered to enforce the federal laws of the land and that includes those of the Migratory Bird Treaty Act. A federal act that protects those same kinds of birds I observed all of you collecting from the edge of that slough right behind us. Birds I suspect you folks shot since I didn't see anyone else in the immediate area other than you lads."

Before I could say anything else, the mouthy one said, "And I am telling you, you have no authority here. I am the chief on the Fallon Indian Reservation and we have every right to be here. You are the one, white man, who is trespassing, and I want your name and badge number so I can have our Indian Police arrest you for our false arrest," he continued belligerently.

"Well, first of all, I never saw any signs saying I was on an Indian Reservation. Second, that would not have made any difference because you folks are subject to the Migratory Bird Treaty Act same as any white man. And as such, you cannot have freshly killed migratory non-game birds like those I saw you picking up earlier in your possession without a permit. Do any of you have a Scientific Collecting Permit issued by the State of Nevada and the U.S. Fish and Wildlife Service allowing you to take protected migratory nongame birds?" I asked.

"We don't need one because we are Indians. And our reservation is just down the road a piece so you see, you are trespassing," said the man calling himself the chief.

"Well, if what you say is true, we are not on your reservation since it is "down the road a piece." Second, since none of you have a state and federal permit to collect such birds, that places all of you in violation of federal law." I said. "You are all United States citizens and this here piece of ground is firmly in the United States. Additionally, all of you are subject to the terms and conditions of the Migratory Bird Treaty Act when taking any migratory birds," I continued.

"What birds? We have no stinking birds. We was just shooting at a jack rabbit," advised another lad who had one of the prettiest shiners that you ever saw (probably from losing an earlier fight).

"Sorry, lads. With my binoculars, I observed all of you place your hands full of shorebirds into the trunk of your car. Those will be retrieved and all four of you will be cited into Federal Court in Reno for the illegal possession of protected migratory non-game birds," I continued.

"You can't look in our car," said the chief, "That is an illegal search."

"Not when I saw four of you gather up those protected migratory birds from the shoreline and place them into the trunk of your car," I said.

Those words were then met with sullen looks and silence from my Native American lads.

"Watch them, Shadow," I commanded as I headed for the trunk of their car. With those words of "command," I had the undivided attention of my Indian chaps as they carefully looked at the close- at-hand dog. Taking their car keys from my pocket, I popped open the trunk to their vehicle. Man, did I ever get a surprise! Therein lay four black-tailed jack rabbits, two sage grouse, 15 black-necked stilts, eight avocets, and an adult golden eagle!

Returning to my four lads, I said, "Well, lads, you have a mess of protected critters, both state and federal, in the trunk of your car. By the way, where did the golden eagle come from?" I asked.

"From off the highway," said the chief. "He got hit by another car while eating a dead jack rabbit and we found him (a common mortality factor in golden eagles). He is ours and you cannot take him from us because we are Indians and can have them. We can use him for religious purposes," he continued. "In fact, all those animals will be used for our religious purposes once we get back on the reservation."

"Afraid not, chief. In order for you to have that eagle you must first get it from our repository in Pocatello, Idaho, along with a permit allowing possession, or come by it in another lawful way while on your reservation."

Now my lads really got sullen and began grumbling among themselves. "Gentlemen, I will need some form of identification from each of you," I advised.

"What for?" asked the one with the rather large shiner.

"I am going to take down all your information

and seize the birds and your shotguns. Then all of that will be turned over to Agent John Wendler in Reno who will file the appropriate charges on the four of you in Magistrates Court. When he does that, he will advise all of you what you must do in order to settle up with the court. As for the eagle, I will see if Agent Wendler can fast track the paperwork so your folks can legally possess that bird since it does appear to have been hit by a vehicle. If that is the way Agent Wendler decides to go, then you will have a permit to lawfully possess that eagle. As for the state species, that will be up to the State of Nevada as to what they decide to do with you folks and those critters."

With those words about the eagle, there were instant smiles all around. By chance and pure dumb luck, I had found the key to settling that situation. Thereafter, with the help of a rather large dog looking all of them over trying to decide which one to eat first, the requested paperwork was soon forthcoming and the legal administrative work finished.

When finished up with all the paperwork, I gave the men evidence tags for the seized birds and their shotguns. Loading all the evidence into my rear lockbox on the truck, I paused and then changed my mind. Opening back up the lid, I removed the two freshly killed sage grouse and black-tailed jack rabbits and gave them to the men so they could have something to eat and show for their efforts. Now the men were all smiles as they thanked me for the critters. After all, sage grouse season was open and if they had killed them on their reservation, they could have lawfully possessed them.

Shortly thereafter, the five of us parted company. Me heading for the refuge to put my birds in their evidence freezers for safekeeping, and the Indians for who knew where. However, with their half quart of Jim Beam between them, it probably didn't matter after a while where they went or how they got there.

Each Indian later forfeited $100.00 for the illegal possession of the migratory non-game birds and their shotguns were returned. As for the golden eagle, Agent Wendler saw to it that the chief later received the bird and a permit to use such animal for religious purposes.

ONE CHUKAR FEATHER IN THE WRONG PLACE

Leaving my Indian lads, I headed for the main headquarters of the Stillwater National Wildlife Refuge. Once there, I met with the refuge manager and several members of his staff. He had received the news of my coming from Agent Wendler and was glad to have my help. He filled me in on the most commonly utilized areas by their local waterfowl hunters, migratory game bird locations, favorite early and late shooting spots, and where most of the redhead and canvasback ducks were concentrated (protected species that year).

While the two of us cared for my evidence seized from the Indians, I noticed the refuge had an airboat on-site. When asked, the refuge manager advised I was more than welcome to use it as I saw fit. It was then I began to sense that the refuge manager and his staff weren't too law enforcement-oriented and preferred if "hired guns" did the law enforcement thing on their refuge for them. That way the locals, pinched for wildlife violations by outsiders (like me), would not be so mad at the local refuge staff. That type of thinking was alright with me though. That just meant there would be less badge-carrying folks around to muck up the arena. I would find plenty of time to do that well enough by myself...

The rest of that day I continued familiarizing myself with the area. Since it was getting late and I had already put in a pretty long day, I returned to the Town of Fallon. There Dog and I rented a motel room and after a fair dinner we returned to our room in order to make ready for the morrow. What a great day that would start out to be...

Come an hour before daylight found Dog and yours truly eating the last of Mom's goodies sent with me earlier from home. Afterwards, the two of us sat on the north end of the refuge, overlooking a large shallow alkali pan full of ducks and shorebirds resting quietly. We had seen the concentrations of such birds the evening before, hence our location in that same country the following morning. And usually where there are game birds, one will find elements of humankind messing up especially during the hunting season.

Soon several vehicles rumbled into the area and "gorged" out several groups of expectant waterfowl hunters. Quickly our lads were ensconced in sagebrush blinds hastily made alongside the water's edge near several shallow water decoy sets. By daylight, our sports were having a fair shoot with a few ducks being taken. By ten in the morning, the morning's flight was over and our duck hunters began tramping their ways back to their vehicles. Several of the hunter's vehicles left, but one remained. The three members of that party began setting up a small campsite. Soon they had a fire going and were unloading sleeping gear and a tent from their camper truck. It was apparent they were staying for the weekend. Since they had taken several ducks and a Canada goose, I decided I would check my lads and then head off for greener pastures further west on the refuge where I had heard a fair amount of shooting earlier that morning.

Loading up Dog into the truck, we began our slow drive over to our hunters so as not to raise too much of an alkali dust cloud, cover their camp and as a result of the dust cloud, piss them off. Driving slowly into their camp site, I saw one of the lads hastily shut the lid of a large red ice chest once he noticed my arrival. Following that furtive move, he joined the other two men sitting around their campfire picking their morning's birds. Pulling up, I saw the men eyeing the unmarked California license plates on my patrol truck like a bunch of hungry robins eyeing a much wiggling, close-at-hand earthworm.

Stepping out from my truck, I said, "Good morning, lads. Federal agent. How was this morning's duck shoot (as if I didn't already know having watched them hunt all morning)?"

"We did alright," said a man I was soon to come to know as Brad Johnson. "We got a few mallards, pintail and a couple "blue bills." But Charlie there only killed a limit of "laughing mallards" (Northern shovelers, a medium-sized duck not known for their culinary appeal because of their eating habits which can make them rather strong tasting)."

With those words, all the men had a good laugh as I walked over to their campfire to check out their ducks and show them my law enforcement credentials. As I walked over to their pile of birds, I was particularly interested in the identification of the ducks they called "blue bills." Normally a blue bill is either a greater or lesser scaup. The greater scaup is normally a maritime species so I did not expect to find any of that species way out there in that part of Nevada that time of the year. Sometimes during severe winter storms, however, such species can be blown off their migration paths and end up in places like Nevada. In fact, they have been discovered by ex-Utah Fish and Game Officer Larry Davis as far away as in the marshes in and around the Great Salt Lake! Sure as God never makes a mistake, the ducks called blue bills by my chaps were none other than redheads! A diving duck that was protected that year in the State of Nevada, and as such, federally protected from taking during the waterfowl hunting season as well...

Like many other U. S. waterfowl hunters, my three lads didn't know their species of ducks from sour owl droppings. A factor not unusual in many sportsmen hunting in the world of waterfowl, though. Many sportsmen, as well as numerous conservation officers, really don't know all their ducks. That goes especially double for the diving duck species. That is unfortunate because states setting out their bag limits of ducks and geese do so by species. In short, mistakes happen if one does not know his or her species of waterfowl as they come zinging by at 45 miles per hour in fog, rain or the early morning pre-dawn. And when that happens, the species being protected, and many times the sportsman pulling the trigger, pays the price, if you get my drift.

Once again, a lesson on duck identification was given on the spot. And once again arguments were put forward by the shooters as to what species of birds they thought they had taken. Then I would go over my waterfowl credentials a second time so the offenders would know I was not pulling their legs in order just to write a citation. That bit of spent energy was then followed with the paperwork. Paperwork being a citation issued and evidence tags filled out for the offending shooter. Throughout the whole process, I tried keeping the situation as light-hearted as I could. There was no use rubbing one's nose in the mess he had made. I have found that everyone should be treated like they would like their family members treated. Enforce the laws of the land in that manner and one will have a better time at that "enforcement" thing...

Thin I noticed a "boo-boo." The lad named Brad receiving the citation for shooting three redheads during the closed season was also the same lad who had hastily closed the lid on the red ice chest when I had driven up. It was as if he had something to hide. What I had noticed earlier on the back side of his forearm was a wet chest feather from a chukar! An excellent-eating, grouse-like upland game bird found throughout many parts of Nevada. Trouble was, chukar season in that area was closed...!

"You boys been hunting anything else?" I casually asked noticing they were running California license plates on their vehicle.

A man named Dick Chester replied, "Sure were. We hunted deer during these last three days over in the Toyabe Mountains just southeast of here."

"Do any good?" I asked.

"Sure did. We all three filled our tags and they are now hanging in the locker plant in Fallon. Then we still had a few days left in our hunting trip so figured we would do a little duck hunting here at the Stillwater Marshes."

"Any big bucks killed?" I asked still trying to make light of the earlier citation issuance over the closed season redheads.

"Charlie there got a big five-point (western count of five points to a side), but the rest of us just got smaller three-points. They all had big bodies though, running 150 pounds or better field dressed." said Brad.

"Sounds like you boys, other than these redheads, all did pretty well," I said. Then I advised Brad what to expect in the way of notification from the court in Reno once I had handed the paperwork over to Agent Wendler and handed him a receipt for his three seized ducks.

"You boys hunting anything else?" I asked as I stood up from my kneeling ticket-writing position and looked Brad straight in the eyes. For just a quick moment, I thought I saw a flicker of doubt cross his eyes then, looking away, he said, "No. All we were hunting were deer, ducks, and some geese."

"Well, you boys won't mind if I check your ice chests then, will you?" I responded.

Man, you talk about funny looks swirling all around on the faces of my three duck hunters. It was as if a small gust of strong wind had just whipped all their heads around to where they were all looking in one direction. That direction was toward the suspect ice chest setting off to one side near their vehicle. For the longest moment no one moved or said anything, then Brad spoke. "There is nothing but our food, a lot of beer, and some ice in the ice chests, and maybe some cooked food in our camper truck. That is about all, officer."

"'That is about all?'" I asked. "What would be left?" I fired right back.

That question regarding his statement "That is about all" caught Brad flat-footed. "Well, that was just a manner of speaking," he finally said as he now looked nervously at me like an Eastern woodchuck would look at a hunter who had just outwitted him and was now in rifle range with his finger on the trigger...

"Then why don't I just start with that red ice chest?" I said still looking hard at Brad. By now, that poor chap had to feel like a cottontail rabbit run to ground by a mink.

"Why there?" stuttered Brad.

"Because when I drove up you had a guilty look on your face after you were digging around in it. Then upon seeing me, you hastily shut the lid on the red ice chest like what was in it was something you did not want me to see. Lastly, look on the back of your right forearm. There is a fresh chukar feather on it! I would say that is a wrong place for a chukar feather to normally be," I calmly advised, "unless you are part chukar."

Quickly looking at his forearm and spotting the chukar feather, Brad whipped it off like it was a female black widow spider about to bite...

For a long moment, Charlie and Dick just looked at Brad like, "Come on, Brad. Quick, find an answer to his question so that he won't look in that ice chest!"

No answer forthcoming, I strode over to the red ice chest and opened up the lid. Inside in ice cubes lay what were eventually to be counted 31 closed-season chukar! Inside their other ice chests was nothing but food as Brad had said. Then remembering the recent roadblock I had held on Interstate 80 on Donner Pass just a short ways out from Reno, I strode over to their camper.

Turning, I asked, "Who does this camper belong to?"

"It is mine," said Charlie.

"Mind if I look in it?" I asked.

"No, go ahead," said Charlie.

But just the way he gave me permission for a warrant-less search of his camper made me suspicious. Stepping up into the camper and looking around, I did not find any more hidden chukar or, as suspected, an extra deer. However, I was not through with my search. Remembering back to my recent roadblock on Donner Pass, I opened up the refrigerator's freezer. Inside were jammed four half gallon milk cartons. That is a lot of milk to drink for only three men, I thought as I reached in and grabbed one of them. It was obvious it had already been opened and then shut. Opening it once again, I discovered a dozen medium sized rainbow trout frozen in water inside! The other three milk containers also contained like numbers of trout all in ice water as had been the first. As I was soon to discover, the trout had been taken illegally from a small stream in the Arc Dome Wilderness Area where they had been camping and deer hunting earlier.

Later that afternoon, after turning my three trout and chukar chaps over to a Nevada Fish and Game Warden, I returned to the refuge headquarters to store my evidence ducks in their freezers. Dog and I later worked another part of the refuge's shooting area that evening for late shooters without finding any problems. That evening later, we returned to Fallon for rest and dinner. There I met another Nevada Game Warden. If my memory serves me correctly, that officer (his name escapes me) later went on to become their Chief or Deputy Chief of Law Enforcement a few years after our meeting in Fallon and a later session of working the outback together.

After dinner that evening in Fallon, it was decided we would work together the next day from my unmarked patrol truck. He suggested we work waterfowl hunters in the morning on the refuge. He needed some duck identification refreshing and, knowing of most Service agents' levels of expertise in that arena, wanted to avail himself of the learning opportunity. When the morning shoot had passed, he suggested we work some of his late season upland game bird and deer hunters in the outback where those seasons were open, and I agreed. That little venture was to bear fruit of the most memorable and unforeseen kind. Before the sun had set that day, our outing would end up embarrassing that officer to no end. But, he would get an excellent lesson in quail identification...

"THEM IS RING-NECKS" AND A LOCAL POLITICIAN FALLS FROM GRACE

Before dawn the next morning, the Nevada officer and yours truly were at the north end of the refuge overlooking the area's marshes. I had previously scouted out that area and discovered a large concentration of diving ducks of every make and model happily existing in several nearby lagoons. For the most part, the watered area on that part of the marsh was fairly shallow. As such, it was loaded with every emergent and submergent kind of vegetation happily known to those in the diving duck community. Included in that diverse feathered community were a hatful of wigeon and gadwall (puddle ducks).

Wigeon and gadwall were two species of puddle ducks who loved submergent types of vegetation. On top of that, the gadwall is one puddle duck who can easily dive in shallow waters for his dinner. The wigeon, on the other hand, was many times a "robber" duck. That species would many times watch diving ducks as they dove for the deeper, more succulent plants because they, the wigeon, were incapable of diving so deeply themselves. Then watching the diving duck coming to the surface, the wigeon would rob the dinner from the bill of the just-emerging hardworking diver in one quick swipe.

Reflecting on that type of behavior, I had to laugh. The wigeon was kind of like me. I would watch the outlaws reap their illegal and ill-gotten gains and then would swoop down and rob them of their "catch." But, I was somewhat different than the wigeon. First, I was better-looking and second, I would always leave the hardworking outlaw something for his ill-gotten gains. A citation and a trip to the local judge, if you will.

Being that the presence of a vegetable duck buffet was so close-at-hand, so was every kind of diver availing themselves of such a rich presentation. Nothing like have such rich grits on hand and in such abundance to fatten up the web-footed critters for their hard, southward migration still yet to come. However, when something of that event in nature occurs, man will usually discover such situations, realize the opportunities, and interject themselves into what was to soon become a violating three-ring circus of the worst kind.

Staking out the area from a safe distance away where we two "law-dogs" would not be seen but could see, the two of us set up shop. Unlimbering our 60x-power zoom spotting scopes and 7x50 binoculars, we waited for our portion of the day to begin. Soon across the desert floor to our southwest we began observing the bouncing headlights of what we suspected were arriving duck hunters heading for their favorite hunting spots on the marsh. A short time later, we had five vehicles parked below our stakeout point with their occupants identified by their waving flashlights heading out into the marsh. After a while the invasion of newly arriving duck hunters settled down. Soon their flashlights died out in the pre-dawn darkness and the alarmed ducks, previously frightened off with the flashlights, began quietly returning to their loafing and feeding sites from whence they had been disturbed earlier.

A half-hour before sunrise, we heard our first sounds of popping shotguns heralding the start of that day's hunt. Soon the marsh was alive with all the hunters shooting as the whistling wings of frightened waterfowl winged themselves every which way to get out from harm's way.

Each of us picked several groups of duck hunters and began counting the number of shots, times shots were fired, and the numbers of ducks as well as species killed. As our morning turned out, our shooters were not the best in the world, and only one set of shooters were able to kill over limits of ducks. That was just fine with the two of us though. It was always nicer for any conservation officer to find most subjects of his attention staying within the confines of the laws of the land.

But in every life's bucket of ointment there is at least one "fly." There was one group of five hunters off to one side in almost a blind slough. They had aligned themselves deeply into the taller rushes along one side of the slough. As such, we could not clearly see what each hunter was doing. We could hear lots of shooting and see the ducks flaring as they passed overhead, but many shots were also fired at low-flying ducks just skimming into their area over the water. Since that action occurred below our lines of sight in the taller marsh rushes, we were unable to accurately tally the toll. However, both of us kept that action in the backs of our minds for a later, more thorough examination when the time of field inspections came loping along.

As the morning's hunt quieted down and some of our hunters began picking up their decoys and leaving, we headed down to the makeshift parking lot to check them out. Driving into the mess of parked vehicles, I observed a brand-new Chevrolet Suburban sitting off to one side. All along one side window were plastered numerous decals announcing we had a real conservationist there. Ducks Unlimited, The Mule Deer Foundation, The Rocky Mountain Elk Foundation, Pheasants Forever, The Sierra Club, and several other decals announced to the world that here was a dyed-in-the-wool environmentalist. One of the "good guys" if you will. Perhaps a chap of the highest conservation ethics, eh?

Passing that vehicle temporarily from my mind, we made ready for the first group of hunters fast approaching our location. Soon that group of four hunters was upon us. Then we began checking their ducks, hunting licenses, duck stamps, shotguns for the required plugs making their guns capable of only holding a maximum of three shells, and basically "chewing the fat" over the day's events with our sports.

That group of lads were spot on and, after exchanging pleasantries, we moved on to the next group of fast-approaching hunters returning to the makeshift parking lot. That had been the group of shooters who we felt had possibly taken over limits. It took us a while to find their hidden over limits, but when I had them roll down their chest- high waders, out rolled those extra birds that placed our lads over the limit. I had the Nevada officer write up our two chaps for their over limits of ducks as I seized and tagged the birds with evidence tags. Those two shooters were so embarrassed over being apprehended, especially after having them roll down their chest-highs so we could find the over limits, that it was all they could do in leaving us behind in a cloud of dust when we finished. Before long, we had checked all the hunters except the group of five still banging away in that portion of the marsh hidden to our eyes. As it turned out, the remaining group still hunting in the marsh was our Suburban full of environmentalists. And with all their prolonged shooting, I was beginning to get a tad suspicious. With as much shooting as they were doing, they either had to be lousy shots or had gross over limits of ducks to my way of thinking.

However, wanting to get on with our day, the Nevada warden (not being as suspicious as I was) suggested we head out into his back country so he could proudly show me some of his district. Not altogether unreasonable thinking, in light of the fact that the remaining group of hunters represented by all the conservation organizations would more than likely be right with the laws of the land. I was tempted to leave as well, but something inside me told me to hang back and wait out our lads.

Suggesting we give our lads still out in the marsh another thirty minutes before leaving — remember Grosz's Rule: Wait a few more minutes before leaving — we headed back to my truck. There we dug out a couple of bottles of Coca Cola from my ice chest, some salami, cheese, and crackers. Then on the hood of my truck in the cool late morning breezes we had a picnic.

Gosh, it was a wonderful moment in time. The

air was cool and the skies blue as any Tanzanite gemstone going. The air had the smell of sage hanging heavy in it mixed in with the smells of alkali dust raised by our nearby hunters' vehicles. Out in the marsh, one could still see ducks moving to and fro, and the ice cold Coke "burned" our throats so good going down. Hard days to forget even as these words are written many years later.

Then we observed our "environmental" lads rounding the long line of dense rushes and starting out from the marsh. Putting away the remains of our picnic, we made ready. As we waited, I went over some of the duck identifiers I had shown my Nevada partner earlier in the day using the seized ducks recently removed from our shooters' chest-high waders as examples (I was also a duck identification specialist and waterfowl instructor for several state and federal academies).

As our lads approached, I told my Nevada partner to check out our duck hunters by himself, and I would oversee and quality control his methods. This he readily agreed to do since I would act as his backup. Now to some of my readers, you might think, "What the dickens? Game wardens should know their birds, fish, and animals as to identification." Well, you might think so and for the most part you would be right. However, duck identification can be problematic and accuracy eludes many an officer. Especially when the ducks are hard-to-identify hens, the birds are in the molt, the duck carcasses are all wet, muddy or chewed on by the hunter's retrievers, it is dark out, or the like. Plus, many wardens are so busy with all their other required activities that sometimes learning one's ducks can be left until the last moment. Lastly, officers may not have many types of ducks in their area, like say in New Mexico, compared to those found in the Texas Gulf region or the Central and Sacramento Valleys of California. As such, it is normal for an officer not to really know all their ducks if they work in an area where they just barely have enough water to drink much less float a duck... So for a variety of reasons, some game wardens may not really be up to snuff and dead-on in their duck identifications. And it was that way that day on the Stillwater Marsh. Bottom line, my Nevada officer was getting a refresher lesson on duck identification and I was helping him in the process.

Lastly for my non-duck hunting readers, duck regulations lay out what can and cannot be shot. Waterfowl biologists determine through many scientific methods, like surveys, nest counts, banding studies, brood counts, and the like, the numbers and health of each duck population (in theory, that is). Then federal and state outside season dates and bag limits are set for the American sportsmen to follow based on the above information and other sources as well (water, environment, nest success, etc.). Ducks which have low population numbers in any given year will have reduced limits that can be taken in the hunter's bag and restricted season dates. Ducks with expanding and healthy populations can be more liberally taken as to numbers, sexes and lengths of seasons. Through those methods, waterfowl populations, like other hunted animals, are managed and regulated in part through the sport of hunting. Bear in mind, however, the hardest thing for a biologist to do is to enumerate an animal population. For example, how many red-tailed hawks do you have in your county? How many mink do you have in your county? How many American black bear do you have in the woods nearest you? That is damn hard to accurately determine. I think you readers get my drift. So many times wildlife management agencies in your state, in addition to tried and true management actions based on good biology, are forced to use the SWAG Factor (Scientific Wild-Assed Guess). But, I digress.

Across the flats came our five "environmental" sports with their decoys and duck straps each carrying a mixed bag of ducks. I also noticed that each man sported several mysterious "bulges" in the game bags in the back of their hunting coats. Once they arrived, my Nevada partner identified the two of us and began checking out the lads. As he did, I noticed every lad took off his hunting jacket first and piled it into the back of their Suburban. Did they do so because the heat of the day was now being felt or for some other reason? All seemingly went well and my Nevada chap did a fine job in visiting with the sportsmen as he checked out their licenses, shotguns, and species of ducks on each man's duck straps.

That was when my partner hit a snag. That year in that part of the State of Nevada sportsmen could not have any redhead or canvasback ducks in their bags. Those duck species were having a hard year and their population numbers were below the biologically accepted norm. One reason was that the redhead duck is a poor "mom" and nester and many times lays her eggs in another duck's nest for that duck species to raise. When that happens, one has what is called a "dump nest" and many times the original nesting duck species whose nest is dumped in will abandon that nest. When that happens, predators will eat well for a while... That, plus there was an ongoing drought and heavy legal and illegal drainage being carried out by the "dirt farmers" on the prairies or "duck factories" (breeding grounds) of the United States and Canada which resulted in additional losses of habitat. So as a result of low population numbers, drought, and loss of prime duck breeding habitat, the wildlife management agencies had prohibited the take of any redhead or canvasback ducks that year in order to not further those population declines.

Checking out our lads' ducks, my partner correctly identified all the different species in our hunters' bags except one! He had misidentified a number of immature redheads as ring-necked ducks (a close like-looking species, especially in the female sexes). Probably the most common misidentification in the diving duck world, especially during the early fall when the birds are still in different stages of molting. Realizing an "explosion" of sorts was in the offing once that information came to light, I slipped into the ring of men looking on and gave my partner an unseen "high sign" suggesting I get involved.

My Nevadan was a quick one and catching my "look" said, "Gentlemen, this is Terry Grosz, a U.S. Game Management Agent from California. Since many of your birds are still in the molt, I would like to have him go over the birds' identifications with you so you can further enjoy your sport through better duck identification. Terry, care to give these men any pointers on duck identification especially with these dang gray and brown look-alike divers?"

"Hell, we don't need any damn fool federal parasite to identify our birds. We all are long-time duck hunters and members of Ducks Unlimited so we know our ducks. If you don't mind, we would like to get our ducks out of this damn Nevada heat and onto some ice so they will keep better," said a rather large fellow with a mouth to match.

Maintaining my cool and a little surprised over the lad's instant reaction to my introduction, I stepped closer into the ring of curious men. Having worked California in some of its finest duck hunting spots in the country, like the San Joaquin Delta, the Northern Sacramento Valley, and the Butte Sink, I had run across my share of know-it-all chaps like the "mouth" now flapping and jawboning at me in the parking lot. That went for numerous other run-ins with those fabled members of Ducks Unlimited. Now before you readers boil over, especially you members of D.U., let me finish. I have checked tens of thousands of bird hunters during my 32- year career as a state and federal officer. During that sojourn, I have run across many D.U. members who were outstanding sportsmen. Similarly, that organization has always been like Trout Unlimited putting its money where its mouth is. That is, boots and money on the ground where it is most needed. However, like in any group or culture in our society, there are those comprising the good, the bad, and the ugly. That also applies for the group known as Ducks Unlimited in California, especially in its earlier organizational days. I ran across more know-it-all hind-ends from that organization than I care to remember acting like they were entitled to more than their share when it came to the killing since they had previously helped the ducks with many of their on the ground projects. I also ran across numerous members of that august group that felt they were the only ones doing anything positive for the ducks and since that was the case, they were more than entitled to a larger share of the birds when afield!

Small case in point. I remember going to a D.U. banquet honoring the establishment of a new chapter in a major California city. The local game warden and I sneaked into the proceedings, at the invite of a damn fine and honorable Ducks Unlimited member, to enjoy the dinner and watch the following celebration. There was a list circulating around of all the founding members of that new club. On that list were 211 names. Between the local game warden and yours truly, we had caught 208 of the members on that list for such things as gross over limits of ducks and geese, shooting over baited areas, late and early shooting exceeding one hour, wanton waste, and the like!

Another small case in point. On one duck club comprised of only Ducks Unlimited members, I once seized and removed a 16-cubic-foot freezer from their clubhouse completely packed with over limits of picked and cleaned mallards and Northern pintail! All other species of ducks taken were considered junk ducks by those members and tossed into a ditch on the back side of that club as I later discovered! And walking through that club that morning checking its duck hunting members, I wrote every one of them for over limits of ducks and several more for taking protected species like canvasbacks! I could provide even more examples, but I think my readers get the message. As I said earlier, I have run across many thousands of some pretty damn-fine D.U. members. In fact, for years I have donated sets of my books to that club for their annual banquets. But I have also frequently run across that certain D.U. chap who is just a little heavy on the trigger finger, poor in the counting department, or loud in the mouth. And on that fine day in Nevada on the Stillwater Marsh it was no exception to that rule, and going to get better.

"Gentlemen, I have a Master of Science degree in Wildlife Management and have taught waterfowl identification to various fish and game agencies around the country for several years. I also taught waterfowl identification to several waterfowl classes over the years at Humboldt State College, one of the finest wildlife, higher learning educational institutions, in the nation. Now if you don't mind, I would like to go over some species' life histories and identifications on the ducks you have in your bag limits. That way when you are out hunting once again, you will be able to enjoy your sport even more and do a better job on your duck identifications."

"Screw that crap," said the big mouth as the rest of his buddies murmured their concurrence to his objections. "We have already been checked by a game warden and that is one time too many. Now if you don't mind, we would like to get our ducks on ice and leave," continued "big mouth."

Having had enough "lip" I said, "Yes, I do mind. The five of you have protected species violations in your bag limits and until we get that squared away, no one is leaving!" Man, what followed was pure shock on the faces of our five duck hunters.

"What the damn hell are you talking about? You don't know what the hell you are talking about—college degree or not, you haven't any idea as to what you are saying," flooded the airways from my circle of D.U. chaps with a collateral volume to match their collective indignation.

The hunters I ignored, but I almost burst out laughing at the reaction of and the effect my words had on my partner. He had the funniest look of surprise on his face when everyone erupted over my statement of illegality. He, too, didn't know what the hell I was talking about.

"If everyone will just cool down, I will explain," I said. Taking the following moment of silence for a go-ahead, I reached down and separated out their ducks into eight piles. Four piles of each man's legal ducks and an additional pile next to the legal ducks of nondescript, what turned out to be illegal, gray-looking ducks.

"Gentlemen, in these piles I have laid out each man's legal ducks. At the head of each of those legal piles lies each man's illegal ducks. Those illegal ducks laid out and off to one side are redheads. And as you lads should know, that is a protected species of duck and cannot be legally taken this year in Nevada."

"The hell you say," said the man with the mouth and attitude to match. "Them is ring-necks! Plain and simple, degree or not, you don't have the foggiest idea as to duck identification. Typical know-it-all federal bureaucrat. We all know our ducks and that is that. Now if you don't mind, we would like to take our ducks and head out. And lastly, I would like your badge number and name, so I can report your harassing actions to your boss and our local Congressman."

"As you were told earlier, my name is Terry

Grosz. I am stationed in Martinez, California, and my badge number is 82." Then I dug out my wallet and handed the "mouth" my business card containing my name, rank, and serial number for his edification.

"Now, gentlemen, before we waste any more of our time, let me show you what I am talking about. There are three diving ducks in North America that have gray speculum in their wings. Those ducks are the canvasback, the redhead, and the ring-necked duck. Two of those species are protected this year, those being the canvasback and the redhead. The ring-necked duck is lawful to take. Now if all of you will wait here, I have something to show you."

Walking back to my patrol truck, I retrieved the two bunches of ducks we had seized earlier from the two chaps who had tried hiding them in their chest-high waders. Laying those ducks in a pile central to the men, I sorted through them. Removing four of the evidence ducks from the pile, I laid them out for all the men to see.

"Now, gentlemen, this is what I am talking about when I talk about a duck having a gray speculum." With those words, I spread out the wings of my evidence birds for all the men to see that secondary portion of the wing in question. Then I did the same with all their ducks I had separated into their "illegal" piles. "Everyone understand about the gray speculum?" I asked. They all nodded except the loudmouth.

"You have got to be kidding. What do you think we are, children? Of course we can see the ducks have a gray speculum. So what does that prove?" he continued.

Reaching down to my previously seized evidence ducks, I spread all their wings to reveal the presence of green tertial feathers in the interior sections of their wings located next to their bodies. "Do all of you men see what I am calling green tertials?" I asked. All the men nodded, and at that point I realized none of them had ever looked and recognized before what I was showing them as an identifier. "This is what the wing of a ring-necked duck looks like, gentlemen, plus note that it is darker in color overall," I quietly advised.

"How the hell are we supposed to see those green feathers when the duck is flying by?" bellowed out the loudmouth.

Then I quickly continued before Loudmouth got another word in edgewise. "Now, look at these male ring-necks I brought over. Do all of you see that they have a white ring across the end of their bills?" Then reaching down, I picked up every duck in their "illegal" piles showing each man the absence of rings on the males in their piles. Then I flipped over each of their illegal ducks and showed each man the absence of any green tertial feathers on the underside of the wings. Pointing to the "evidence" ring-necked duck hens, I showed each man the prominent eye ring. I took each man's illegal ducks and showed all of them the absence of a prominent eye ring. I pointed out to the men that the evidence ring-necked ducks were smaller and darker than all of their illegal redhead ducks. Lastly, I showed them the differences in size, overall colors, and the bill differences between the canvasbacks and the other two similar species.

Standing up I said, "What all of you gentlemen have shot this fine day in your illegal piles are redheads and canvasbacks protected species. Now all of you can see why it is so incumbent upon each' of you that you know your ducks before you go duck hunting. Heck, gentlemen, even in the hand not a one of you was able to identify that all of you had shot some redheads and canvasbacks!"

Now even the loudmouth was as quiet as a mouse pissin' on a ball of cotton. In fact, my Nevada game warden had learned a thing or two about the basic differences between the species as well but, from the look on his face, he would never tell.

Then I switched gears. "Gentlemen, I am now going to check every one of your hunting coats lying in the back of that Suburban. When all of you came in, I noticed bulges in the game bag portions of those coats. Then every one of you quietly made sure you quickly removed your hunting jackets when you saw the two of us standing here, maybe figuring us for the law. Lastly, all of you placed them in the back of your vehicle and more or less out of sight. That little move has made me suspicious of those 'bulges,' and those I will now check as well."

With those words out front and center, the lad with the big mouth blew up. "You son-of-a-bitch. That is an illegal search. You cannot check in my vehicle without a warrant," he bellowed. When Big Mouth blew a fuse, I noticed none of the other men who had placed their hunting jackets in the Suburban said a thing. Almost as if hoping I would overlook their hunting jackets in the field inspection process.

"Well, sir, that is where you are wrong. Conservation officers have the right of inspection of any gear you use when hunting migratory game birds and that includes your hunting coats. Also, those coats are in plain view and under the 'Plain View Doctrine,' the Supreme Court has ruled as such they are also subject to warrantless inspections. Next, the 'mobility' of your vehicle and the 'ability to lose evidence due to that mobility,' legally enters into play here as well.

However, that will be explained to all of you if this case and the 'search' is contested in a court of law. Lastly, I observed mysterious bulges in each and every hunting coat in the game bag portion of your jackets. A place where many hunters will carry their game birds. However, since you folks brought your birds in on duck straps, that makes those bulges in the backs of those jackets even more suspicious. Therefore, before you folks leave today, because of that factor and the others I have explained to all of you, they will be searched for extra birds."

Without further ado, I walked over to the pile of hunting jackets piled up in the back of the Suburban. There I began going through the game bag sections of each jacket. As suspected, every jacket produced from three to five more ducks! And every extra duck was a redhead, a protected species! I also noticed every hunting jacket searched was of the "Redhead" brand... How was that for irony?

"Well, gentlemen, all of you not only have protected birds in your possession, but every one of you is also in possession of over limits of ducks as well," I quietly advised. For once, Big Mouth had nothing to say. "Gentlemen, I will need to see each man's driver's license since you will be cited into Federal Court for those waterfowl violations." Like in the first bunch of violators caught earlier that morning, the embarrassed lads quickly produced their driver's licenses.

Just in case my five Ducks Unlimited chaps who "knew their ducks" wanted to contest my identifications or "ability to count," I swung all those citations into Magistrates Court in Reno. That way, I avoided any suspected "hanky-panky" in the local court system by my "high-powered" D.U. members. That also took any potential political pressure off my Nevada officer if that was to subsequently rear its ugly head. However, my suspicions were unfounded. That group of men each later posted $150.00 in bail for taking redhead and canvasback ducks during the closed season and an additional $250.00 for their possession of waterfowl over limits in Federal Court.

Watching our five "conservation-oriented" duck hunters drive off in a spirited cloud of dust, I turned to my partner saying, "How about another Coke, some salami, cheese, and crackers, before we gut out all these birds to prevent spoilage? Then we can split for some of your backcountry to see what kind of devilment we can get into."

He just grinned saying, "Thanks for rescuing me back there. Hell, I didn't know the difference between those redheads, canvasbacks and ring-necked ducks either. I would have let them go if it hadn't been for you. Then catching those suspicious bulges was choice. I would have missed those as well because they were so casual about what they were doing. It is pretty obvious now to me that these chaps were really the cheating types. I will remember to check all those fellows from Ducks Unlimited more closely in the future. Yeah, I think it is time for another Coke and something to eat before I take you off into doing what I know and do best and leave the duck identification to you."

That ice cold Coke when guzzled, like the first one earlier, "burned" so good once again going down. But probably not as much as the loudmouth was "burning," as he thundered down the road in his gaily decked-out and highly decal-covered Suburban announcing to the unsuspecting world his prowess in duck identification and "excellent" hunter ethics.

Finishing our repast, we boarded up and headed out into another adventure, only this time one not adjacent to the Stillwater Marshes. Heading east into the Stillwater Mountains, the two of us rattled down the many four-wheel-drive dirt roads leading to and fro in that mountain range. As we did, we kept our eyes peeled for anyone hunting deer. There were a goodly number of those chaps out and about so we spent most of the afternoon checking suspicious hunting vehicles or deer camps. Additionally, we ran across several sets of chukar hunters and managed to "scratch" a few over limit citations in that arena as well. By evening, we had run out of our supply of Cokes, salami, cheese, and crackers, and were heading back towards civilization for a well-anticipated steak dinner in Fallon.

Rattling down another four-wheel-drive road from our work area, we chanced upon a new black Ford three-quarter-ton pickup with a white camper shell. It was parked on the back side of a long canyon. Then, off in a distance we spotted two men hunting a series of rolling sagebrush-coated hills.

"Chukar hunters! Stop the truck and let's take a look," said my partner. Pulling off into a small stand of mountain mahogany, we got out our optics and took a look. For the longest time we took a gander at our two hunters as they hunted the rolling hills. Both men appeared to be carrying shotguns and one was carrying a couple dark-looking birds in one of his hands.

Rustling around in the cab of my truck, my partner took out his spotting scope and affixed it to his now rolled half-down window. For the longest time he said nothing as he examined our two hunters closely. Then he blurted out, "Damn! That is my County Commissioner. Now there is one hell of a man. He is not only an excellent sportsman, but one of the best supporters of the fish and game department we have ever had."

Removing his eye from the spotting scope, he turned and continued extolling the virtues of his commissioner and, as I soon discovered, close friend. "Come on, Terry, let's move on down there, and I will introduce you to one hell of a man and conservationist," he excitedly continued.

Putting my truck into gear, we slowly worked our way towards the Ford truck and the two men who were obviously hunting chukar partridge. Getting down from the mountain, we moved across the sagebrush flat until we arrived at the parked Ford truck. Getting out, we stretched our tired frames as we waited for the two men coming from a short distance away to arrive.

Finally the two men arrived, and my partner went over to his commissioner and warmly shook his hand. Then the commissioner introduced my warden friend to his hunting partner. Finally, the three men walked over to where I stood and introductions were made all around. It was then the commissioner walked back to the rear of his truck and opened up the camper door. Soon all of us were sharing some soda pop, crackers, and deer jerky from the commissioner's supplies. As we feasted on the repast, talk soon turned to local fish and game matters as I listened. Then the commissioner posed numerous questions for me about the Service, some of our problems, manpower shortages, and law enforcement in general. It soon became very apparent to me that here truly was a man who was a dyed-in-the-wool supporter of the highest degree for the Nevada Fish and Game Department.

As the two men began cleaning and picking their two freshly killed chukar, I turned to my partner. I mentioned that tomorrow would soon be fast upon us and we needed to get back to Fallon because daylight came early the next day. Additionally, I mentioned I still had several days' work and numerous areas I wanted to cover on the Stillwater Marsh before returning to California so we needed to get moving.

With that my partner advised he was ready to go, but before we did, he would do a courtesy check on the two hunters' hunting licenses and their birds. This the commissioner happily consented to as he dug out his wallet and produced a valid hunting license.

"Terry, how about checking the commissioner and his friend's birds, while I finish checking hunting licenses?" he asked.

Nodding, I headed for the back of the Ford, opened up the ice chest, and extracted a large plastic bag of completely picked and cleaned dove (season was still on) and chukar partridge.

Counting the dove, I could see the men were far short of the limit of 15 birds each and returned those carcasses to the bag of cubed ice. Then I counted out the chukar bodies and as I did, I noticed something out of the ordinary. Mixed in with the chukar were the bodies of six completely picked and cleaned, large, fat mountain quail! If I hadn't been on my toes, I would have missed them because of their similarities in size. But I did catch them and laid them out on the tailgate for my partner to see. He was still busy happily chatting with his commissioner and when he finally looked back at me and the birds laid out on the tailgate, his face hit the ground! Quail season was closed! Yet, here were six very obvious mountain quail bodies cleverly mixed in with all the rest of the bird bodies. However, the meat of the quail was lighter in color and their body sizes were different...

With my discovery and the following revelation, the commissioner just melted. "Damn. We got into that covey of quail earlier this morning and before you knew it, we had killed six of them. We didn't want to waste them so we brought them back, cleaned, and placed them in with the chukar and dove hoping no one would notice them. You got us, we are wrong," he sickly admitted, obviously embarrassed to the high heavens.

Suffice to say, we had a surprised and now highly embarrassed state game warden as well. Sure as God made smelt from Lake Superior great eating, I had one highly perplexed officer in my midst. Then after a long awkward period of silence, as we all stood around after the revelation, I had to give him credit.

"I need to see a couple of driver's licenses, if you please," said my still-highly embarrassed partner. Once proffered, he quietly wrote up the two men for illegal possession of quail during the closed season while I quietly bagged the evidence and threw it into our cooler.

We parted that sad scene a short time later and for the longest time my highly embarrassed partner had nothing to say. Finally he said, "Damn, Terry. I sure hated to write him up because he has done a lot of good for our department and has been a sure-fire supporter for law enforcement and our wardens. Then I have to go and pinch him over a few quail. I guarantee most wardens would have missed those picked and cleaned quail all mixed up with those other birds. I just had to pick one of those damn sharp-eyed federal officers to upset my apple cart," he said with a grin. "But he was wrong and I did what I had to do," he said with finality of the right purpose rising in his voice.

Arriving back in Fallon somewhat later, we

went to dinner together. Since I had been the one to cause him a lot of embarrassment through my search of the commissioner's ice chest, I bought dinner. If I recall, he had two double whiskeys with that dinner... Since he had other duties in his district to attend to, we separated that evening and I worked by myself during the remainder of my assignment. I never again had the opportunity to work with that officer in the field because I was stationed a state away. However, as I said earlier, he later made either Chief or Deputy Chief of the Nevada Fish and Game Department's Division of Law Enforcement. In his particular case, that was the mark of a damn fine officer to my way of thinking. And I always knew that whoever crossed swords with an officer of that caliber had better bring a lunch. "Bring a lunch" because when all was said and done, that Nevada officer would be hungry, if you get my drift...

"JOHNNIE LAW" AND SIX TUNDRA SWANS

For the next several days, I worked throughout the waterfowl hunting area surrounding the Stillwater National Wildlife Refuge. On several of those days, Agent-in-Charge John Wendler came over from Reno and the two of us worked the area together. I enjoyed those days we had working together. He was the typical U.S. Game Management Agent of old that I had come to know since joining the U.S. Fish and Wildlife Service in the spring of 1970. Considerably older than me, quiet as a mouse pissin' on cotton, smooth as a "school marm's thigh," when dealing with people and one whose eyes were that of an eagle and never missed anything going on in the world of wildlife.

Boy, I will tell you, I had met a number of unique old-time U.S. Game Management Agents in my short time with the Service. If I had to catagorize most of those I had met, it would be of the old gunfighter school and style. Quiet, quick as all get-out, totally dedicated to the moment and the wildlife resources at hand, and once they got on your trail, the only way to shake them off was to kill them... If there was something smelly going on in the wildlife world, John was a "Man-Tracker" pure and simple. Those two days we worked together, I don't think he said twenty words. But through his actions, he sure as hell showed me many ways to trap someone walking on the "dark side." Techniques I used until the day I retired and only after I had passed on many of those traits to my two, working in law enforcement sons.

Then John had to get back to his office and once again I worked the waterfowl hunting scene by myself. But that was no problem. I always enjoyed working by myself and at my own pace.

Plus, it gave me every opportunity to investigate every nook and cranny of the environment in which I found myself. It was really great being a person of the soil and a student of history, both of which allowed me to revel throughout the surroundings in which I found myself in the historical State of Nevada during those heady days so long ago. That included hunting for arrowheads, checking out old mines, and observing the varied wildlife found around every spring and wet spot I discovered within my high cool Nevada desert surroundings as I worked throughout the wildlife law enforcement arena.

On one particular morning, I found myself sitting on a small knoll overlooking a shallow end of the refuge's marshlands. Below me were several parked cars and out in the marsh duck hunters plied their trade. It was one of those typically "soft" days of fall when it was not too cold, and the sky was as blue as the Old Boy upstairs could make it. There wasn't a cloud in the sky and, if one listened carefully, he could hear a world of bird calls "ghosting" throughout the area.

The shoreline of the marsh was riddled with many small groups of shorebirds of every make and model known to "seeing" man probing the muddy flats looking for swampy delectable bits of chow. Collaterally during the morning, ducks quietly moved throughout the watered areas as if they had not a worry or care in the world. Talk about idyllic! It was one of those perfect moments in time that I had come to appreciate so much. In those special moments that day, I discovered the perfect day has a voice. One just has to learn how to listen... Then as if almost on cue, the crap hit the fan in big smelly gobs!

Moving out across the shallow pans of water and marsh came a small flock of Arctic or tundra swans flying not twenty feet off the water's surface. Their soft, happy family group calls came echoing across the water as they noisily dropped their feet and landed at the edge of a set of duck and goose decoys near a large patch of rushes. Then like migratory birds will do just after landing in a new area, the family group held their heads high looking all around for any signs of danger. In the process, the group of swans gathered closely together as another safety precaution until they were satisfied all was well.

Boom boom boom boom quickly echoed four shots into the family unit of swans! Even from where I stood on a knoll, I could see the swaths of deadly shot streams spewing across the closely packed heads and necks of the swans like a scythe through a wheat field! In an instant, the deadly shot streams had killed all six closely packed swans where they sat in the water! That avian disaster quickly brought me out from my early morning daydreaming into pangs of dismay and then into retributive action.

Reaching through the opened front window of my truck, I grabbed the binoculars from my dash and fastened them onto that patch of rushes from whence had come those deadly shots. For the longest time nothing suspicious moved to catch my eyes. Then the dense patch of rushes parted and two lads exited their blind and began quickly walking out into their decoys towards the "still kicking their last" family group of swans.

At first there was excitement shown as the two men noisily splashed across the shallow water towards their "kill." Then, even clear over to where I stood watching the sad scene, I could sense the men's changing moods. Expecting snow geese lying in their decoys, I could see through my binoculars amazement and then questioning looks spreading across the men's faces. Especially when they began lifting up the huge-bodied swans by their long necks and feeling the weight of their large sizes. The shooters' moods began turning to wonderment. After a few moments, through my binoculars I could see their wonderment readily turned to a degree of panic with the realization over what they had done. Next, the two men hurriedly conferred over their unusual kills. Having second thoughts over what they had done, they began looking all around like an early Nevada settler would as if expecting to see a horde of Paiute Indians rapidly swooping down on his family. That was followed with more conferencing out in the pond among their decoys. Finally both men gathered up a couple of swans apiece and hurriedly dragged them back into their patch of dense rushes and out of sight. Then one of the men quickly reemerged without his shotgun, grabbed the remaining two swans, and took them to their blind in the rushes as well. As if in remembrance of this moment of shame, for the longest time nothing moved. Not even any number of the commonly found yellow-headed blackbirds in the area.

It was then I observed another duck hunter, one hundred or so yards distant, emerge from his duck blind and, as if on a mission, begin splashing his way through the shallow waters towards my two swan shooters. Finally arriving at the swan shooters' dense patch of rushes, he stopped and shouted something I could not hear because I was too far away. Soon I saw two heads pop up in the patch of rushes and the three men were obviously having a very animated conversation. Quite a conversation it had to be, if the wild gestures from my lone man standing out in front of the swan shooters' blind meant anything. Then my singleton out in front of the blind stomped off back towards his distant duck blind. As he walked away, the two heads once again quickly popped out of sight into the patch of rushes. Then nothing moved other than the stream of fall spider webs slowly drifting on the breeze through the rushes along the shores of the marsh.

Knowing I had the high ground and could cut off my illegal swan shooters when the time came with their parked vehicle below me, I held my position. Using the hood of my patrol truck, I kept my binoculars on my suspect patch of rushes and cattails for any other information they would yield. Some time later the two heads popped up from the rushes and carefully looked all around once again. Then the two men quickly emerged without their shotguns and carrying gunnysacks. With sacks in hand, my two lads began picking up their floating duck and goose decoys and bagged them. Once finished, the two men returned to their blind and soon one emerged dragging a floating sled-like device behind him.

Onto the floating device they loaded the two large bags of decoys. Following that action, one lad returned to and then emerged from their blind carrying their shotguns, duck straps with ducks killed previously, and a couple of stools used for sitting. With that, and no swans, my two lads began walking across the shallow water pans towards the parked cars below my hidden observation point.

Just before they arrived, I headed down the knoll with my truck and drove for the makeshift parking lot near the marsh. Arriving a short time later, I pulled up to my two lads as they were loading up their car making ready to leave. Exiting my unmarked patrol truck, I walked over to my two lads who were eyeballing me like a mink does a fresh, flopping carp on the bank within reach.

"Morning, gentlemen. My name is Terry Grosz and I am a federal agent. I would like to check your hunting licenses, ducks, shotguns, and federal duck stamps if I may, please."

"Yes, sir," replied the taller of the two men. Taking out his wallet and opening it, I immediately saw a law enforcement officer's badge conveniently placed on one side of the open wallet for easy viewing... Then the man dug out his hunting license from the wallet with the federal duck stamp attached according to law and handed it to me. As I examined the man's hunting license, his partner also produced the same for my inspection. He, too, conveniently opened his wallet to display a law enforcement officer's badge on one side of the open wallet. Suffice to say, that kind of unprofessional behavior pissed me off. I resented any officer's behavior such as wallet badge placement in such a manner as to advertise an official position for any "officer courtesies" it might bring. I made a point of ignoring their little display of intimidation as my lovely morning was now getting "browner" by the moment, if you readers get and can smell the drift my day was taking...

"May I now check any birds you gentlemen have as well as your shotguns for plugs?" I asked with a still well-concealed "browned-off" feeling in my gut.

That they did with a minimum of discussion. It was clear to me that the two officers would be happy to be rid of me and get the heck out of Dodge if they had their druthers. However, we still had the little matter of six dead swans left back in their blind...

"Well, lads, everything checks out except for that small matter of what the two of you left back in your duck blind," I quietly said as I stared intently first at one man then the other.

Man, you talk about a "thunderclap" of attitude change with those words. Both men were on me verbally like a Rhode Island Red rooster on the first June bug spotted in the morning scurrying across the ground within grabbing range!

"What the hell you talking about, man? We showed you our few birds and our gear. It all checked out if you will remember, and now we have to get back to work. Our patrol shifts start in another hour and we need to get back to our office, shower, and dress for roll call," said the taller man. I guess he had to say that about his patrol shift since I had not paid any attention to his earlier badge-in-the-wallet-display-meant-to-garner-attention. The other man just grunted his support for what the first officer had to say.

"As I said earlier, we still have the matter of the six dead swans the two of you killed and left back in the blind," I continued quietly. Man, with that second accusation, you could sure tell who was the chap dropping the turd into the senior class prom punch bowl. Once again, there was instant denial all around as to any wrongdoing from my two law-dog chaps.

"Well, I guess we have nothing else to do then but return to your blind and retrieve the evidence," I said.

"Well, maybe you can, but the two of us just told you we have our law enforcement patrol shifts to accomplish in a short period of time from now. If you want to return to our blind and look around for something we didn't shoot, be our guest. But we aren't going back with you on such a foolish endeavor. We have our patrol shifts to accomplish and that is what we are going to do," said the taller one who appeared to be the senior officer of the pair and ringleader to my way of thinking.

"Well, here is the drill, gentlemen. Since I observed the two of you kill six tundra swans at 8:39 this morning and hide them in your blind, you fellas crossed the line. That is a state and federal violation because those swans are migratory birds protected under the Migratory Bird Treaty Act and state law. So here are your two choices. All three of us can return to the blind and retrieve the dead swans, or I can arrest the two of you on the spot for killing them. After I book the two of you into the nearest federally approved lock-up, which is probably Reno, I will return for the swans. Then the two of you will be expected to appear in Federal Court in Reno at a later date to contest the charges if you so desire. That is the bottom line, men, and now it is your call," I said in a tone of voice not to be misunderstood.

"What if we don't let you arrest us?" said the taller one.

"I will arrest the both of you and, rest assured, I will get that done. And if either of the two of you decides to resist that arrest, that is an extra five years in a federal lock-up for such a stupid move," I said in a tone of voice now really meant not to be misunderstood...

"Come on, Charlie. Let's do as he says and be done with it," said the other officer in the mix realizing their little act of swan shooting was now escalating into something he personally did not want to experience.

For the longest time, the only sound I heard or movement seen was that from a nearby yellow-headed blackbird swinging and singing on a cattail at the edge of the nearby marsh.

"If you want to go back out there with this son-of-a-bitch, that is your call, John. But I am not going to help this son-of-a-bitch try and hang a violation on us. Besides, it is his word against the two of us, and that will get him nothing but "jack" in any court of law in this state, especially against sitting state officers in good standing," uttered the tall one named Charlie.

"Charlie, I am going back out with him and, since I have the car keys, that means you will have to wait. Besides, other people have recently used that blind and anything he finds out there he can't hang on us anyway. So to avoid any further so-called federal entanglements, I will go back with him. You can wait if you want or start walking, but I will be back soon," said the other man named John Boothe.

With that, I hiked up my hip boots and the two of us headed for the blind in question. I figured no use in pushing the issue of address identification from Charlie since I had his partner with me. If Charlie wanted to bolt, so be it. I still had the means to track him down through his partner so I let the identification issue on that chap slide for the moment to avoid further altercation. But to my way of thinking, "hell was coming on a black horse" and Charlie had better have a "carrot" for the devil's horse when "it" arrived. If not, he was about to reap the whirlwind he had started both in the marsh and on the shore...

John and I splashed noisily back to the patch of rushes they had earlier claimed as their blind. Once there, he remained outside the blind standing in the water, as if that move would save his carcass, while I entered the tangle of marsh plants. It took me a while to find where they had hidden the swan carcasses but when I did, I started dragging them out. But not before I took each bird's temperature with my ever-present thermometer. And as it turned out, each bird's rectal temperature was within five degrees of each other. Dragging them out, I laid them at John's feet in the water and then returned for the remaining swans. Emerging from the rushes the second time, I was surprised as I looked across the water to see two duck hunters hurriedly splashing my way. Seeing they were headed for the two of us, I waited to see what they wanted. Soon the two men were upon us and they were hot!

"Are you some kind of game warden or such?" asked a ruddy-faced, heavyset man.

"Sure am, gentlemen. My name is Terry Grosz and I am a United States Game Management Agent or federal game warden," I responded.

"Great," said the ruddy-faced man's partner. "We observed this man and his taller partner kill these six swans earlier this morning. Jack here came over and ate their hind-ends off for killing those protected swans, and they told him to go eat crap and bark at the moon," he angrily exclaimed. "Now, since you are here, me and my partner would like to testify in a court of law as to what we saw when these idiots killed those swans," he continued. "We will just see who is going to 'eat crap and bark at the moon,'" he growled. Just the way the man uttered those words made me smile inside. It is not often the public wants to get involved, but when they do, "Katy bar the door." Their actions in such circumstances can be like "a woman scorned."

"No use in calling anyone names or getting carried away," I cautioned, not wanting this to turn into a full-blown "hell-raising" in the marsh.

"Why not? That is how my partner and I feel. Anyone who kills swans thinking they are snow geese is a knothead and deserves to get caught," said the man called Jack.

Still trying to avoid a "hoo-rah" out there in the marsh, I finally got things settled down. Then I took the information down in my notebook as to what they had seen and what they could testify to. I made sure I knew where my two incensed duck hunters, who had fortunately observed the whole thing and were more than willing to step forward and be heard, could be reached. As for my guilty Nevada Highway Patrol Officer, he said nothing because doing otherwise was only going to get him and his partner "in even deeper."

Thanking my two honest sportsmen, with difficulty I gathered up the six swans by their long necks and headed back to my patrol truck where Charlie stood waiting. Back at the parking lot, John immediately told Charlie about the other two duck hunters and their agreement to testify against the two of them for shooting the swans. That quickly put a plug in his partner's mouth, now that he saw the Scales of Justice tipped in my favor with the addition of my two surprise duck hunting witnesses.

Some time later, I finished up with the paperwork associated with this case. Both officers had little further to say as I instructed them on the anticipated Federal Court proceedings in Reno and their options. Two weeks later both men chose to forfeit $500.00 each (the maximum fine under the Migratory Bird Treaty Act in those days) for taking protected migratory non-game birds during the closed season (today, in some states like Utah, they can be now be legally hunted and are technically considered "game birds"). I also had Agent-in-Charge John Wendler write the two sportsmen who were willing to testify against the officers a nice thank-you letter for their sportsmanship and assistance.

After my two Nevada Highway Patrol Officers had left the scene, I tossed the swans back into the bed of my truck. Moving up a short distance into the sagebrush, I gutted the six birds to avoid spoilage in case they were donated to a college teaching collection or to a needy family somewhere for the good eats they would provide. Then I hustled the birds over to the refuge headquarters where they could be put into their evidence freezer for safekeeping in case this issue went to trial. Finishing up with those duties and remembering the refuge manager's earlier offer, I hooked up the refuge airboat to my patrol truck for the afternoon's use out on the marsh.

All my readers need to know when another officer breaks the law, no matter what law, they need to understand that it is to be adjudicated correctly and professionally. I always stuck by that ethic and when I became a supervisor years later, I advised my subordinate officers to do the same. That is, if you get caught doing something wrong, take your medicine and settle the issue. Then grow up and move on. I also told my officers don't ever flash your badges and try to get off from whatever infraction you were tangled up in. If they ever did, they were told best not let me find out unless they wanted a damn good sandpapering on "their last part over the fence!"

You can bet after that episode, I obeyed every speed limit when I left Nevada that fine fall period after my Stillwater National Wildlife Refuge detail was completed. Especially since my two Nevada Highway Patrol Officers had by that time discovered their minimum bail was going to be $500.00 per offense... That doesn't sound like much in today's dollars but, in those days, that was about a month's wages for anyone holding a good job...

LATE SHOOTERS AND LIGHTNING STORMS

Leaving the refuge headquarters trailing the airboat, I sped for the nearest commercial boat-launching ramp on the Stillwater Marsh. After checking my airboat for an extra fully charged battery, full fuel tanks, and a loaded tool box, "she" was launched. Parking my truck and trailer off to one side in the parking lot, Dog and I boarded our latest "steed" for an afternoon's work. Digging around in the tool box produced a spray can of ether (made the cold aircraft engine start more easily) which I liberally sprayed into the exposed airboat carburetor. Then I stepped up onto my elevated seat, switched on the engine, and hit the starter. The 165- horsepower Lycoming aircraft engine sputtered once, then roared to life. Adjusting my rather large "Fatty Arbuckle" hind-end onto the seat, I checked the gauges. The fuel tanks indicated full; the amp gauge read normal; the temperature gauge read cold; and when both magnetos were checked, they were fully operational. Still getting used to the individual peculiarities of that particular airboat, I let it idle a short ways across the marsh as my aircraft engine heated up. When the temperature gauge read normal, I reversed my baseball cap so it wouldn't blow off into the whirling prop to the rear of where I sat and advanced the throttle. Leveling off at 2,300 rpm on the throttle as we sped out across the expansive Stillwater Marsh, we were soon up and on step.

God, what a great feeling that was. The airboat was up on step; the engine ran like a Swiss watch, and the marsh ran under the boat like I was running across a piece of glass. The warm fall air caressed my face (as did the multitudes of floating cobwebs); the controls were finger-light to the touch, and the feeling of power was one of extreme exhilaration. Out in front of me ducks, geese, coots, and flocks of shorebirds frightened by the roaring apparition "flying" across the water rose into the air in living clouds. To my way of thinking, flying across the water that afternoon had to be as close to Heaven as a mortal can get. The only other time I felt such energies coursing through my body was when, as a young man, I operated a D-8 bulldozer on a logging show in Plumas County. Folks, let me tell you, there is nothing quite like the power one feels from operating an airboat in the marsh, or "skinning" a 25-ton D-8 bulldozer in the rugged high Sierra Mountains on a stunning, late summer day... It is times like that, that God lets us mere mortals have a peek into what awaits each and every one of us when "summer is gone."

For those few of you who wonder, Nature has two faces. One that "she" lets you see and the other you must look for. That beautiful day, I was looking for that second "face." Namely, the face of man doing evil things among God's natural creations. And knowing "The Old Boy's" penchant for protecting his creations, He was more than apt to let me cross swords with those He considered doing evil things to His handiworks behind that "second face."

Steaming around a long point covered with tall rushes in the Stillwater Marsh, I observed a large decoy set looming on the glassy water's surface in the distance. Bearing down on that decoy set at 2,300 rpm with my 165-horsepower Lycoming aircraft engine howling like a flock of banshees, I soon observed three chaps slowly standing up in amazement in the makeshift reed-and-Phragmites duck blind they were currently calling home. Standing up, I was sure they were trying to see what the hell was bearing down on them from out of the lake's haze like an airplane that had missed the runway. I had to grin at what I surmised the thoughts were going through my three chaps' minds at that moment in time.

Closing the distance, I reduced the throttle until I was just idling up onto my three still-surprised duck hunters. Sticking the nose of the airboat into a dense stand of Phragmites to hold it in place and the whirling prop away from my duck hunters, I held up my badge for all to see. Then I told them I was a federal game warden there to check their hunting licenses, shotguns for plugs, federal duck stamps, and their birds. My lads never moved an inch over that transfer of information. It was obvious they were still getting over the roaring demon that had just exploded into their heretofore quiet and enjoyable lives as duck hunters alone and out on the duck marsh.

Finally realizing I wasn't doing their duck hunting any good sitting there, my three lads moved quickly responding to my requests. However, when it came to checking their bags, I discovered some wrongs. In their collective duck bags were four illegal birds. My chaps had killed four protected species, namely redheads. Once again, duck identification gone wrong by the American Sportsman.

Knowing that I was now going to be tied up for a while, I turned off the engine on my airboat to save fuel and reduce the noise. Pointing out the error of their ways on the duck identification issue, I finally untangled who had shot what and issued citations to two sports for killing the wrong species. Throughout the ticket-writing process, I could still tell my lads were in shell shock over the noisy and surprising entrance of "Johnnie Law" and his trusty steed, the airboat. They finally told me they had been hunting in that area for four years and that was the very first time they had ever been checked by the law or had seen the airboat. Those comments did nothing to change my earlier assessments regarding the current refuge staff not really being into this "law enforcement thing." Now I was beginning to see why my boss had sent me over to work this particular area. One can have all the fish and game laws he or she wants on the books but if they aren't enforced, bad things will happen to those in the World of Wildlife. And, this country's past history of animal kingdom destructive excesses is mute evidence to the validity of that statement of fact... That is, unless you can't remember what happened to the bison, passenger pigeons, Carolina parakeet, ivory-billed woodpecker, Atlantic salmon and dozens of other unfortunates.

Finishing up with my redhead-shooting lads, I thanked them for their patience, crawled back into my seat, flipped on the ignition, and hit the starter. The airboat engine, now warm and not needing the shot of ether, quickly roared to life. Cranking over the steering rudders and turning on the power, I soon plowed my way out from the dense stand of Phragmites and onto the open water. Realizing my noisy craft was letting everyone in that end of the marsh know there may be some law afoot, I headed deeper into the reaches at the northern end of the vast marsh.

Roaring out into deeper water and becoming more cautious because of those conditions (some airboats are unstable in deeper water if they have a narrow beam), I backed off on the power and made wider, slower turns. Soon another set of decoys came into view on the eastern side of the marsh and I now headed in that direction. As I neared my duck hunters, I again observed two hunters standing up looking out across the haze in the marsh to see what the hell was bearing down on them making such a racket.

This time my two chaps were out on a shallow point in a makeshift, brushed-up duck blind. As I neared those chaps, I could see their blind had been made rather flimsily. It consisted of a small frame made from sticks and chicken wire. Then my duck-hunting chaps had a mess of

Phragmites woven therein and loosely placed thereon. Behind that blind knelt my two chaps in the mud, out of sight and mind of the ducks. When the ducks swept into their decoys, my lads would raise up and shoot. No big fancy deal of a duck blind for this group of hunters, I thought. And from the pile of dead ducks lying behind my two shooters in the mud, their flimsy little blind and decoy set had worked very well.

Reducing my power, I slid the airboat up onto the mud flat they occupied, shut off the engine, and stepped out so I could check my pair of hunters. I identified myself and proceeded checking their licenses and ducks. As it turned out, these two hunters knew their ducks and did not have any illegal birds in their bag. After a short conversation on the quality of hunting and operation of the airboat, I headed back for my "ship." Back on board, I switched on the ignition, hit the start button, and my warm engine once again roared to life. Waving good-bye to my lads, I hit the power and turned the craft in order to get off the muddy shelf on which she now lay heavily stuck in the suction of the sticky mud.

Now to my readers who have never operated an airboat, they are a different kind of craft to manage. They are stern-heavy, due to the extreme weight of the full sized aircraft engine located thereon. So when one slides one of those heavy crafts up onto a mud flat, they settle deeply into the mud. No big deal, though, as long as the operator is skilled. All the operator has to do is gun the engine and turn the rudders behind the whirling propeller from side to side until the boat works itself loose. Then, off you go. Well, not quite. It depends just how deeply one is stuck in the mud. If one is deeply stuck in the mud, you need to use lots of power in order to break the mud's suction on the keel of the boat. Then off you go. Well, not quite. In my particular case, I was stuck pretty well and deeply into the gooey mud flat.

That necessitated me really gunning my engine and swinging my rudders (vertical blades located behind the engine which act as steerage for the boat. Steerage being accomplished as the wind created by propeller flows through the rudders located behind the engine, thereby directing the path of the craft with the stream of air depending on which direction the rudders are turned).

Well, I was damn-well stuck in the marsh's sticky mud comprised of ten thousand years of goose shit and tule roots. Lost in what I was doing, I put the hammer down to 2,600 rpm and swung the boat back and forth from side to side trying to break the mud's suction on the keel of the boat. Once again nothing happened! No problem, just give the powerful engine more gas.

Putting the hammer down even more, I ran the engine up to 3,000 rpm! Now with the increased power, the airboat was swinging rapidly from side to side. However, I was still stuck tighter than a Western wood tick on the side of a fat mule deer in the spring of the year! That did it! Being German and liking power, I put the hammer down on the throttle! With that last bit of action, I ran the engine up to 3,500 rpm! With that almost-red-lined power surge, the heavy craft burst free, and once again I was sailing footloose and fancy free down the marsh's lake like a big grinning bullfrog on a fast moving lily pad.

Looking back to wave goodbye to my duck hunters, I got a major surprise! In my energy of the moment and lack of common sense trying to get my airboat unstuck, I had forgotten my duck- hunting lads in their blind located off at a safe distance. In those efforts to bust the boat free from the mud's suction, I had neglected to consider the direction in which my furiously whirling aircraft engine was pointing. When I hit 3,500 rpm, that wall of air from my madly howling engine had blown my two chaps' duck blind asunder! Asunder hell, it had blown their flimsily built little duck blind into the next county along with their duck hats! As for my two duck hunters, they were covered from head to toe in a dripping wall of mud and ten thousand years of goose shit and tule roots... In fact, their mud-covered shotguns looked like slime-covered tree roots! Man, what a dumb ass I had been in neglecting the welfare of my what I had thought were off in a safe distance, duck hunters... By then I was so damn embarrassed over what I had done as an air head that I didn't dare go back and apologize. I just hoped they didn't remembered my name so they couldn't write a Congressional letter complaining about my lack of brains and common sense...

That was one time I was glad I was flying away from my latest contacts at a high rate of speed... Then I got to laughing at what I had just done to my two unfortunate duck hunters. Soon, I was roaring with laughter over my just-created duck hunter muddy apparitions. That was until a rather large dragon fly flattened itself out into my open mouth and onto my exposed teeth with a stinging *kersplat!* Who says God doesn't always have the last laugh when someone gets a bad case of the big head and does something stupid? I sure hoped those two lads would end up blaming the refuge lads for such a thoughtless action...

Cleaning a dead bug, and a rather large one at that, from my teeth, I headed further north into the great marsh. Finally getting the bitter bug taste out of my mouth, I noticed another small set of decoys off to my northeast. Heading in that direction at 2,400 rpm, I covered the lake's surface to my next bunch of hunters at a flying clip. Approaching, I noticed this time no one stood up to see what the hell was bearing down on them at a screaming clip. Getting closer and mindful of the decoys and their hunters, this time I reduced my speed. Suffice to say, it is not nice to suck up one's decoys into the prop and have them come out the back of the prop wash as bits and pieces. Finally, mindful of the "ever-clutching marsh mud," I wedged the airboat into a small bunch of Phragmites and killed my engine. It was then my three duck hunters emerged deep from within the dense stand of Phragmites on the edge of which they had built into their duck blind.

Dang, I thought, that is strange. Normally most lads would have stood up to see what was coming their way, especially as noisy as I was in the airboat.

Walking out to the bow of my airboat, I stepped off into the shallow water and mud. Then I walked over to the duck blind just as my three lads stepped out from the dense stand of Phragmites in which they had been hiding.

"Afternoon, lads. My name is Terry Grosz and I am a federal game warden. I would like to check your hunting licenses, ducks stamps, shotguns, and birds, if I might," I said. I noticed with those words, my duck-hunting lads' faces turned from one of surprise over my quick appearance to one of slightly cautious and then to almost sullen in appearance.

To my readers, being able to "read" people and their attitudes is to remain alive throughout one's career, especially if you are a badge carrier. And those officers that are able to correctly "scent the winds of change," will not only live longer but make many more cases than most other "also-rans" during their tenures as badge carriers.

The "scent in the wind" that afternoon had really changed once I had identified myself. They were quieter than all get-out and had less questions for me than normally would have been asked of someone in my position. In fact, it was almost as if they wished I would soon be on my way. Keeping that "suspicious scent" in the back of my mind, I got about the business at hand.

Checking my hunters, I looked for what I felt might have been wrong. At first nothing "ugly" showed itself on the "winds of change." Then, there it was! On one man's hip boot, I spied a single fluffy gray feather and a swipe of blood like one would make when wiping off his hands after gutting out a critter. Saying nothing of my curious discovery, I continued my examination of the lads' hunting licenses, duck stamps, and shotguns for conformance with the laws of the land. Only this time after I checked for the plugs in their shotguns, instead of using a plug checker and then reloading their shotguns, I handed the shotguns back to each man empty. One does that when he is suspicious of what might be coming next...

"You lads have any birds?" I asked.

"We have a few," said a man I was soon to know as David Betts.

"I would like to check those as well, if I could," I said.

"They are back in our blind," he replied.

"That is fine," I said, "I will just walk back there and check them." With that, I walked out to their blind at the edge of the Phragmites patch and began checking their birds laid out in a pile behind them. It was then I realized that none of the men accompanied me like most duck hunters normally would... They just continued standing in the Phragmites where I had first met them. Getting on with the business at hand, I finished checking out the birds the men had killed. There were no two ways about it. These men were duck hunters. They had killed only mallards and Northern pintail, some of the largest and best-eating ducks going.

Standing up from my checking activities, I looked out over their decoys. Then something floating on the water caught my eye. Walking back out into their decoys, I picked up several floating feathers. Feathers like those left behind when a bird is killed in the air and then in its fall, violently hits the water. And in that collision with the water, the critter leaves a few feathers behind. That is when it hit me! The feathers on the water were not from any duck I knew. They were solid gray and very fluffy, like a non-water swimming bird. And the feathers picked up matched the one feather I had seen earlier on the man's hip boot as he had emerged from the dense Phragmites patch.

Walking back to my three "deaf mutes" at the Phragmites patch, I said, "Is that all the birds you lads have?"

"That is it," said David.

"Then you boys won't have any trouble if I check the Phragmites patch from where all of you first emerged when I approached, will you?" I asked.

For the faintest moment of time, I saw a "look" fly across the collective faces on my chaps. A look that slightly spoke to panic. Remember what I told all you readers about "scenting the wind" and being alert to behavioral changes? My eyes went to the man I was soon to come to know as Robert West who had the unusual fluffy gray feather still on his hip boot with the bloody swipe. Before he could do anything, I reached across from where I stood and picked the unusual feather off his hip boot.

When I reached for the feather on Robert's boot, he had jumped back like a bug on a hot rock. "What in the Sam Hill are you doing?" he blurted out.

"Just looking at this unusual feather," I said. Then comparing it to the few feathers I had picked up in their decoys, I saw they were the same kind. Gray, ultra-light body feathers of some sort, unlike those from any duck I had ever seen... And, I knew my species of ducks and geese as well as the best of them.

"What were all you lads doing back in the Phragmites when I arrived?" I quietly asked.

"We were gathering up more reeds for our blind," said a now- recovering-his-composure Robert West.

"Then none of you will mind if I go back and take a look for myself?" I asked again.

None of the men answered and, with that, I began following their muddy hip boot tracks back deep into the Phragmites. A few minutes later, I discovered their dark little secret. A secret that matched the unusual soft gray body feathers I had discovered earlier. Lying in a pile were four adult sandhill cranes! Birds that were totally protected during that day and age! All were in various stages of having their breast muscles removed for easier and secret transport home for eating. To you readers unfamiliar with the sandhill crane, they are basically seed eaters. As such, they are excellent eating. Standing there looking at the mess of freshly killed birds, I surmised this small flock had probably decoyed into the three men's decoys and had all been killed outright. Gathering up my crane bodies and as much meat as I could carry, I headed back to confront my duck hunters.

Arriving back where I had left them standing, I got the surprise of my life! My three duck hunters were nowhere to be seen! Dropping the crane bodies, I quickly looked all around. Finally I spotted my three chaps hotfooting it across the shallow-panned marsh as they heading for a parked vehicle at the edge of the marsh some hundred yards distant! They had left in such a hurry that they had even abandoned their small decoy set. I guess they felt it best to lose a few decoys rather than a large part of their wallet's contents due to a hefty fine being levied for illegally taking a mess of totally protected sandhill cranes (today they can be lawfully hunted in many states as a migratory game bird).

Running for my airboat, I "jumped" up onto my seat (as only a 320-pounder can). Flipping on my ignition switch and hitting my start button, the engine coughed once and then spun noisily to life. Putting the hammer down, I cranked the airboat out from the Phragmites. When I did, I left a bunch of the tall plants mowed like grass in the wake from my whirling propeller as I headed for my fleeing chaps. They had a rather good head start since it had taken me so long to find the crane bodies in the dense Phragmites, but I was now up on step and "flying!"

Ahead of me, I could see my chaps had made the shore and were now sprinting for a vehicle parked a short distance away. That really pissed me off! With that observation, I put the hammer down and at 3,200 rpm, I was almost airborne! Quickly making shore, I didn't even brake the throttle. Up onto the grass-covered ground airboat and I hurtled heading towards my fleeing runners and their vehicle! Meanwhile, Dog, who had gone along for the ride did as she always did when I "hit the hammer," just laid down out of the way and waited for the action to subside. Damn, what a great dog! She knew what was coming next from her half-crazy master... Seconds later, I skidded the airboat directly in front of their car just as my chaps reached it. Cutting the power and throwing my shut-off switches, I stepped off the still now-slowly sliding airboat.

"Going somewhere, lads?" I bellowed.

It was as if someone had let out all of the sand from their bodies as they collectively slid to a stop just feet from their last hope of escape. With heads hanging in embarrassment and abject surrender, one man said, "Not now."

"You got that right," I continued, bellowing like a bull moose in rut, still in surprise that they had chosen to run from me over a few cranes. Needless to say, my three lads were tagged into the Federal Court system in Reno for illegally possessing four closed-season sandhill cranes. Especially since the three of them under questioning later admitted the birds had swung into their decoys and, since the hunting had slowed that morning, they figured they would take some cranes home as well to see how they "ate."

Finishing up with the paperwork, I asked if they had any questions. They had none, so I asked Robert to move his car away from my airboat so I could leave (I had slid to within two feet of the front of his vehicle). This they did and then they stood around to see how I could make my airboat move on dry land. And since I was forty yards from water, I supposed they figured I had a long walk ahead of me in order to get home. And if they had their say, I wouldn't be riding in their vehicle any time soon if it came to me walking home because of a now land-stuck airboat...

Crawling back up onto my seat, I flipped up the ignition switch and hit the start button. My good old airboat engine coughed, then whirled to life, as I sat there letting her warm up for a minute. Checking both magnetos to make sure I had full power and telling the men to stand back (remembering my earlier blown-away duck blind experience), I kicked over my rudder and then slowly advanced the throttle. Slowly the airboat began to spin in circles. Continuing to increase the throttle until the airboat was rapidly spinning in a tight circle to the right, I checked all around me for my next move. Then feeling the time and momentum was right, I hit the left full turn rudder. Breaking my spin, the airboat flew off the crazy spin in the other direction and we headed full speed for the marsh's waters. Hitting the marsh with a splash, I headed back to the Phragmites patch where I had left the crane carcasses. Looking back, I saw my three men staring in disbelief at how the airboat had successfully flown off dry land, down a dirt road, over a small bank, and back into the water. Hell, boys, I thought with a grin, this is nothing more than an air sled. Nothing like blowing the smoke off the end of your revolver after making a great shot and then placing it back into your holster like nothing out of the ordinary had just occurred...

Back at the Phragmites patch, I retrieved the crane carcasses and the removed breast meat. The breast meat I threw into my ice chest so it wouldn't spoil, and then the airboat, Dog, and yours truly headed further north. As for my three errant shooters, I just left their decoys for them to retrieve. As I sped along, I noticed many duck blinds scattered along the northeastern shore with a few hunters therein. I also observed several cars driving into the area on the landward side as if coming in for the evening hunt.

It was then that I noticed heavy dark, low-based storm clouds scudding ominously into the area from the northwest. The wind picked up putting a short chop on the marsh waters advertising more was sure to come. Gliding to a stop out in the marsh, I realized being out on the water in a high-profile boat with a rare, late fall oncoming thunderstorm was not the smartest idea in the book. Especially if lightning was to accompany the oncoming storm. Having been raised in a similar-type area in northeastern California, I knew lightning was a coming attraction from such a late summer thunderstorm. Plus an airboat becomes dangerous in strong winds. That is because you lose some if not all of your steerage, especially if the winds are strong. With those thoughts in mind, I turned her nose back towards the launch site and added more power to my flight from the marsh and the ominous storm clouds slowly flooding in behind me from the northwest.

Sometime later, I had the airboat on the trailer and was heading for the refuge headquarters. There I returned the refuge's airboat and put my evidence birds in their freezer.

Then remembering the late afternoon vehicular traffic coming into the northeastern end of the marsh for the evening duck shoot, I fired up my truck and Dog and yours truly headed that way. If nothing else, I figured there would be some late shooting of waterfowl if the oncoming thunderstorm stirred up the birds with its wind and subsequent wave action. The birds would move to quieter waters and, to my way of thinking, that would be along the marsh's leeward shoreline and inlets. And if that happened, that would give my land-based gunners reason to shoot ducks after legal hours. Man, was I ever to find out about that Nevada thunderstorm happening and big time in short order!

Slowly gliding into a well-used parking lot out on a sagebrush flat alongside the Stillwater Marsh, I shut her down. Realizing just how tired and hungry I was, I headed for the back of my truck and its ever-ready and filled with "game warden goodies" ice chest. Removing some salami, cheese, hot jalapeno peppers, and two large Cokes, I headed for the hood of my truck. Out from the cab came a box of crackers and Shadow and I had a full-blown game warden's picnic off the hood of my truck. Plus, the appearance of a picnic gave me some cover. Standing there eating off the hood of my truck, I looked like any ordinary rube. That is, any incoming duck hunters would not feel concerned that I was the law and continue doing what they did best. Taking my time with lunch, I observed a number of vehicles lumbering into the dusty parking area. Once there, their occupants hastily grabbed their hunting gear and headed out to the marsh edge into the face of the now-threatening black and forbidding rolling and scudding, low-based thunderheads.

Then the sun finally shone on the manure pile behind the barn. These duck hunters had been here before during such violent weather events! They must have had some experience with bad weather and winds kicking up tremendous evening flights of ducks. If that were the case and from the looks of the oncoming storm, they were in for one hell of a shoot. And what better cover to use to break the law than bad weather with lots of thunder to cover the sounds of their late shooting. Brother, you talk about a hunting method that would work slicker than cow slobbers. Those signs of oncoming weather and all the arriving sportsmen sure posted all the indicators of a furious late-shooting event in the making.

Soon legal waterfowl shooting hours came and went, and not one soul on "my side of the ranch" left the marsh! Looking around from my truck, I counted 13 vehicles parked in the area and still no one appeared willing to leave the area, especially in light of the freshening winds and increasing movement of the flocks of ducks off the big water heading shoreward.

By now the popping of shotguns could be heard all up and down the eastern side of the marsh by my late shooters. Giving all my lads a ten-minute leeway for their watches being off, I then swung into action. Grabbing my Starlight Scope, binoculars, and a five-cell flashlight, I commanded my dog to remain in the back of the truck and then headed for that part of the marsh where it sounded like a second Pickett's charge at Gettysburg was taking place.

By now, I had a twenty-knot wind howling and raindrops the size of duck eggs starting to fall sideways. Just my kind of weather, I thought with a grin. Then it turned ugly! I could smell the ozone in the air, and now the lightning was crackling across the heavens in such volume and frequency that even tall ol' me was getting a little concerned. Sometimes in such weather being 6 foot 4 inch tall in three-foot tall sagebrush when lightning is whacking everything over four feet high has a tendency to give one pause! Especially when the hair on my arms began to stand up from all the static electricity in the air... But my late shooters had been here before so I took solace in that fact. It was as I had earlier thought when I saw the lads streaming into the shooting area almost at the end of legal shooting hours. It was almost as if the shooters over years hunting in that area had discovered during such violent storms, if they had enough "sand" and stayed with it, that they were assured of having a good shoot along the edge of the Stillwater Marshes as the birds fled the violent open water and sought shelter along the inlets. And boy, I sure couldn't agree more. The mallards were dropping into secluded coves along the shoreline as the various species of diving ducks made like cannon shot sailing into the Phragmites looking for hiding spots until the storm subsided. And my gunners, well, they were having a field day during this Great Basin thunder storm and light show. My move off the airboat and onto shank's mare sure was a good one, I thought, as a nearby bolt of lightning splattered a tall clump of sagebrush into smoking ruins some fifty yards distant!

By now, I was running at a bent-over trot towards my closest group of four late shooters. They were banging away at every flying thing that moved. I swore I could see St. Elmo's fire glistening blue off their now-dangerously upraised gun barrels. Yet still they chanced Mother

Nature and all her wrath as the ducks flew and dropped as the winds howled and they continued shooting.

"Say, lads, don't you think we ought to stop shooting and head for our cars before this storm gets any the worse," I said as I slid into a thick bunch of Phragmites along the shoreline alongside my targeted four late shooters.

"What the hell for?" said one man as he was hurriedly reloading. "Can you believe this duck shoot we are having?" he continued as he dropped a hen mallard with one shot on the land behind his place of concealment and nearly at my feet.

"Well, first of all, it is after legal shooting hours and dangerous as hell if any of this lightning around us means anything," I continued, dropping to my knees alongside him.

"Nah," he said. "With shooting and the false light a storm like this provides, why the hell stop?" he hollered back over the howling winds.

Showing him my badge in the light of my flashlight, I said, "Because if you don't stop this late shooting, you will be arrested."

With that revelation in the eerie light produced by the violent thunderstorm, he thankfully lowered his lightning-attracting shotgun barrel. If he hadn't, sure as feral cats make fine rifle targets, I could just see the two of us blasted off the edge of the marsh by the next of many lightning bolts flying through the area. In fact, the storm had reached such an unholy intensity that I could feel the hair on my arms standing up even higher now because of all the static electricity in the air! Asking for and receiving his driver's license, I recorded the time of his last shot and then hustled over to his three nearby partners.

It was amazing that in all the storm's fury those three guys were banging away like they owned a piece of the Remington Arms Ammunition plants. I could certainly see why they had gotten so carried away. If it hadn't been illegal, the storm was creating a living duck-shooting gallery of the greatest kind. The violence of the storm and winds were such that the birds were just trying to get the hell off the big water and out of the howling winds. And if that meant getting a face full of killing lead shot from my late shooters, then so be it! Stopping those three shooters, I repeated the procedure like on the first, and then made ready to move on to my next set of late shooting gunners.

However, in my shirt pocket I now held the driver's licenses from my four previous shooters along with my notebook of their shooting times. I also left them with instructions to quit shooting and began gathering up their freshly killed birds before they were lost in the now-violently frothing, shallow marsh waters. Then off I went after my next bunch of late shooters in the rain and lightning further down the shoreline.

My next three shooters were all in one clump and that made my catching easier. However, this bunch was into the killing mode so much that I actually had to grab one guy's gun barrel after I had told him who I was and to stop shooting! It was amazing. The shooting was so fast and furious that the fellow had gotten himself into such a killing trance that he just ignored me and continued shooting until I finally physically took his shotgun away from him! Gathering up those three men's licenses and leaving them with instructions to pick up their birds and wait there for my return, I hustled down the shoreline after my next group of hunters.

It was now getting darker than all get-out and I was forced to use my Starlight Scope. But that was problematic as well. Keep in mind the scope magnified all visible light by a factor of 50,000. Imagine what that was like when a nearby bolt of lightning showed itself. A flash and then instant darkness in the scope as it shut down with the extreme light overload. Even under those conditions, I was able to bag four more late shooters.

Wildlife's Quiet War | 363

Fierce lightning or not, I was now in a trance as much as were my late shooters, but mine was human-catching in an attempt to collapse their little illegal and dangerous duck-shooting event down around their collective ears before we all got blown to hell in a hand basket!

By now my late shooting duck shooters down the line were sensing something was wrong as the shooting went silent along the shoreline below them. There were still a few diehards and I managed to grab off four more of them but, the rest sensing "danger" if they continued shooting, picked up their ill-gotten gains and headed back to their vehicles.

Then it was over. It had gotten so black, except for the flashes of lightning followed by a deluge of rain that only a Great Basin thunderstorm can produce, that everyone headed for their vehicles. Holding the line in case someone got trigger happy once again, I let the lads file by me in the dark as they finally headed in. Their little illegal duck shoot was now over for either natural or unnatural man-made reasons.

But before Mother Nature and one of her minions put an end to this Stillwater Marsh "turkey shoot," I had managed to bag 15 illegal late shooters. Their late shooting times ran from 23 minutes after legal shooting hours (sunset) to one hour and 45 minutes late!

With Mother Nature and all her fury soaring to the Heavens all around me, I finally headed back to the parking lot and a nest of long-faced chaps who had run afoul of "Johnnie Law." Two hours later I had finished up with all the paperwork. I would write up one lad in the front seat of my truck while the rest of my late shooters sat in their own vehicles in the driving rains. When finished, I would shout out another name from the driver's licenses in my pocket and another wet-as-a-muskrat late-shooter would appear out from the dark, sit in my truck, and pay back Mother Nature for the error of his ways. All the time this was going on, the howling winds and pelting rains hammered my truck like God's wrath was trying to get in and extract an even greater toll from the duck-killing miscreants... In the light of the lightning flashes, I could see my dog in the back of the truck. She was loving the wind and howling rain adventures! Her head was in the air and she ran from side to side in the back of the truck as if taking in all of Mother Nature's fury. What a goofy dog...

I spent the next hour in the wind and lessening rains drawing all the ducks I had seized from all my late-shooting lads (the birds were taken after legal shooting hours and, as such, could not be legally possessed). However, that made my duck-gut-eating dog happy as a razor clam on a sandy flat in the Pacific Ocean as she polished off stream after stream of warm duck intestines. When I had finished, the storm's wrath had moved on. The next morning at daylight, I found myself parked in the same spot. No late or early shooters and lightning that time. Only the silence and soft breezes that follows one of Mother Nature's "Wrath of God" storms. The air was light, clean smelling and fresh with just a touch of late summer-early fall to come floating around in it. Finishing up my salami and crackers breakfast, I went back out into the marsh backtracking my steps from the previous evening. Scouring the marsh where my late shooters had such a field day, Dog and I found 26 more ducks that had been killed the evening before but lost in the storm's intensity and the dark of night. And that didn't account for all the lost ducks the night critters had discovered and eaten in my absence. This is another reason there is a time limit on every given day of hunting season. Nature is limited and to waste it is to want it later on in life. By then, you can want it with all your heart for all the good it will do. It that case, you can forget it! It is now long gone like the snowflakes in the first November snowstorm with your children and theirs being the ultimate losers in the varied richness of much of the life that Mother Nature had to offer...

Since I could not tie them to any of my cited late shooters, those ducks I picked up that morning went back to the refuge staff for their consumption. Because their salaries consisted of "all the hatchery trout they could eat and a dollar a day," I figured they deserved a few meals on their menus with meat in them, same as anyone else. That way, the ducks didn't go to waste but went for the greater good.

That day concluded my "training assignment" in the Stillwater Marshes of Nevada. I had a great time, saw a lot of nature and the glorious Nevada countryside in which she resided. I also managed to "turn" a few heads, if you get my drift. While still in Nevada, I observed all the speed limits on the way home back to my duty station in California. I didn't figure my earlier-captured "law-dog swan shooters" were still looking for me, but I wasn't going to give them a "shot" at me like they had taken on the tundra swans days earlier. As for Mother Nature, she had put on quite a light show during that typically violent Great Basin thunderstorm. During the height of the storm and the lightning, I once again had a chance to reaffirm my mortality as I kept my head down, but not so low that I still couldn't appreciate the wrath of God in one of His finer moments of fury.

Chapter Five

**DUCK CLUB FUNNIES
ONE "RED HOT" DUCK BLIND**

BY THREE O'CLOCK in the morning, Dog and I were located on the commercial duck club in the Butte Sink that I had targeted and where I wanted to be for that morning's hunt. For the last two shoot days (Wednesdays, Saturdays and Sundays were normal shoot days in the Butte Sink area so they wouldn't "burn out" the birds), that particular duck club had been shooting up a storm. Hence Dog and me locating ourselves in a convenient spot so we could watch that hunting club's activities that fine morning. Opening up my heavy jacket in order to cool off from an hour's hard-paddling efforts, I sat there in my Grumman Sport boat listening to the hundreds of ducks flying to and fro. Man, it was great to be alive! I was out in the middle of one of the greatest duck hunting areas in the country, namely the fabled Butte Sink in the Northern Sacramento Valley of California. A historic waterfowl hunting area located just adjacent to the Sutter Buttes, the smallest mountain range in all of North America.

The noise of hundreds of thousands of happy ducks and geese resting on the bean field just to my west was as thrilling a sound as any the Good Lord could have created for me that morning. Especially if one was a conservation officer, a lover of wildlife, and one who counted on the great outdoors as his personal "church."

It was cool out and, to a fat man like me, that was a touch of heaven in and of itself. Then there was an orange-colored half-moon caused by all the rice straw burning in the valley by the farmers accompanied by the faint smell of burned rice straw on the morning's breezes. A sight and smell germane to the Northern Sacramento Valley in the fall heralding the annual migration of great hordes of migratory waterfowl. Lastly, ducks were constantly streaming by me in whistling singles, paired doubles, and smaller groups, many of which were identifiable by their calls. And to my front, the worried but beautiful calls from nearby disturbed wood ducks just added to the "mustard of the moment!" Like I said, it was great to be alive and in the middle of such wonders knowing you were there to help those who had little or no voice. Help in the sense that those who were heavy on their trigger fingers that grand day would soon pay the price for such foolish behavior in God's beautiful house surrounded by the world of wildlife. And if one looked carefully off in the distance, he could see the wispy figure of Mother Nature standing there with a proud grin on her mug as she surveyed her minions as well.

Getting back to the work at hand, I continued my paddling towards a duck blind which I had located and targeted several days earlier after the fact. A suspect duck blind from where the heaviest waterfowl shooting on that particular duck club had been emanating. To all you conservation types out there reading these lines, remember Grosz's Rule. That being if a wildlife out law is able to have his way illegally with Mother Nature without any interference from the long arm of the law, he will often return for "bloody seconds." Hence my beautiful presence with Dog in the Grumman Sport Boat in the area that fine fall day so long ago... Paddling around until I found a satisfactory spot located off to one side and slightly behind the suspect decoy set and duck blind of interest, I buried myself into the dense covering vegetation. Then taking out my camouflage parachute, I covered up the Grumman in such a way that I could see but not be seen by the shooter or ducks flying directly overhead once daylight arrived.

Satisfied with my hidden location, Dog and I sat back and had a Terry Grosz standard early morning game warden breakfast. Me, a hard Italian dry salami with a Coke and Dog, her usual giant can of Alpo dog food. Finishing breakfast, I lay back in the Grumman while Shadow, my Labrador retriever, began "perfuming" the air with the remains of her rich, "all-the-duck-guts-she-could-eat" dinner from the evening before. Man, it was amazing what that dog's digestive system could do towards "enriching" the environment. Especially in a small, covered canoe out in the middle of a marsh or in the heated confines of the cab of a pickup on a cold winter morning. To all of my outdoor readers out there who are large dog owners, especially of a Labrador, you know of the very essence of what I speak.

Soon all the ducks I had scared off with my earlier arrival began filtering back into the decoy set and areas surrounding my duck blind of interest. That's good, I thought. When my duck hunters would eventually arrive and see all the ducks in the area they would think that there wasn't a federal agent around. And in so thinking, I would be able to see and experience my sports' true colors, if you get my drift.

To all my "law dog" conservation officer readers out there, that is the beauty of getting into your selected stakeout area very early. That allows for mistakes, vehicle breakdowns, and you getting lost in the dark when coming into your targeted area in question. That is also when your club members are sleeping their soundest so they won't hear your arrival or suspect your miserable carcass is incountry. Lastly, by arriving so damn early, it allows for the wildlife to reenter the area and settle down after being disturbed and makes all things natural on-site appear normal. The way I figured it, if I was to neglect my health and family because of the profession's demands, I damn sure wanted it to pay off. Hence my early arrival and the best chance to catch someone doing what he or she shouldn't have been doing to Mother Nature. After all, extinction is forever...

Retreating further into the warmth of my heavy jacket, I lay back against the outboard motor, closed my eyes and listened to the wonderful world of waterfowl waking up around me. Since the wealthy Butte Sink duck clubs did not have any competition, their shooters usually didn't come out to hunt until just at daylight. Hell, they didn't have to come out any earlier. Their duck club was private; many times their decoys were left out all night; and they had already drawn lots for a given duck blind so there was no other human competition. So why hurry?

Snapping open one eye somewhat later, I heard the soft uhrr sounds of an outboard motor coming my way. No problem, I thought as I closed my eye once again. It would take my shooters a while to arrive and get up into their blind before my "services" would be needed. As soon as the outboard motor sound got louder, I could hear the ducks and geese which had returned to the immediate area noisily lifting off in alarm. That was my cue. Sitting up and taking one last look at my hidden position in the pre-dawn light, I grabbed my 7x50 binoculars and made ready to do what a conservation officer does best. Soon I saw part of a boat and the head of a hunter moving swiftly along above the rushes approaching the blind I had selected. Good, I thought. The boat only had one individual in it and that made my job of counting "drops" (shots fired, times noted, dead ducks counted) easier. My hunter slowed his boat and let its forward motion carry it under the stilted duck blind in question and out of sight. Then my lad scrambled up into the duck blind with his shotgun. For a few minutes I saw him eagerly looking around at the ducks flying overhead in the early morning's dawn skies.

My chap disappeared altogether for a few minutes, then reappeared. Only this time in his mouth he had one of those long and expensive cigars like Winston Churchill used to smoke.

You know, those big fat ones that are at least a foot long. Liking cigars myself, I wondered what a cigar of such proportions, quality, and value had cost my wealthy duck hunting chap. Me, all I could afford to smoke were those cheap old Italian crappers that ran .25 cents per box of five. But their acrid smoke was always good for killing the ever-present mosquitoes when I was out and about, so I guess I shouldn't complain.

Then a pair of mallards whistled into the decoys from behind me and my shooter killed both birds cleanly with two shots. Taking out my notebook, I recorded the time my lad had shot, number of shots fired, and numbers and species of birds shot. The sounds of those shots set the rest of the "wings" in the marsh in his immediate area into the air in alarm. Soon the air was filled with confused waterfowl flying about reminding me of what an overturned hive of bees must look like. A small family group of white-fronted geese swung into my shooter's blind's decoys and, just as they had dropped their feet to splash down, my shooter rose from his place of concealment firing three quick shots. Three white-fronts dropped deader than a stone as the remainder of the flock frantically "clawed" for the air to get away from the danger below. Again, I recorded the needed evidentiary information in my notebook. I also recorded the fact that my shooter now had a daily bag limit of dark geese or white-fronts (in those days three dark geese per person per day was the limit).

I just stared at my shooter. He had done all that shooting without removing his cigar of monstrous proportions. How the hell he could shoulder a shotgun and shoot so accurately with such a huge cigar still stuck in his mouth amazed me. I thought I had seen it all, but no. The Good Lord had seen to it that I now had another chapter added to my book of world of wildlife law enforcement experiences. Or at least a chapter of renown soon to come.

Then five of North America's most beautiful little ducks, the wood duck, flew into view. In those days the limit on such birds was one per day because of their low population numbers. Having been shot at before, that little flock warily circled the blind's set of decoys. Finally they decided all was right, set their wings, and dropped in like winged rockets. My chap with his huge cigar "in mouth," rose again and shot three times with his Browning AL- 5. Two of "my" little wood ducks dropped deader than a brace of hammers giving my shooter an over limit on that species! I thought about stopping my lad right then and there, but the next blind over from my shooter was killing ducks like mad as well. Getting greedy, I settled back down into my

Grumman. No use just grabbing one knothead when I could grab all three of my shooters in one fell swoop, I figured (there were two shooters in the adjacent blind). That way when my just-cited and chastised chaps returned to the clubhouse, they would have embellished stories to tell about the marsh being overrun with and full of "feds." Their embarrassment at being apprehended by a "horde" of federal agents would be somewhat lessened in the eyes of their compatriots because of the odds stacked against their fellow, just cited, club members. I figured that would also go a long ways towards soothing their savaged egos in the eyes of other club members. I guess it is tough to "man up" when one is a millionaire many times over and is caught doing something stupid by some lowly chap making just $13,000 per year (my government salary during that period of time in my career)...

Next to tempt fate was a small flock of Northern pintail ducks. Eight birds circled my lad's decoys and, removing his cigar, he blew his pintail whistle like all get-out. That siren call enticed "my" pintails back for a closer look and, once again, three ducks fell to the straight shooter in the blind with the huge cigar back in his mouth. No two ways about it. I had chosen the "hot" duck blind for my stakeout if the previous shootings were any example of what the day was to become. Now my lad had a total of seven ducks and a limit of three dark geese still floating in his decoys. So far, my lad was just one shy of a limit on his ducks and could only kill three lesser snow geese in order to remain legal. I was beginning to get the feeling that my cigar-chomping shooter was a real killer if I was to consider his straight-shooting abilities exhibited up to that moment in time. And if I was correct, I was just the medicine the doctor ordered for such a "kill everything in the air that flies" illness!

Then a flock of mallards numbering about twenty sailed straight away into my lad's decoys and landed before he could even get going on his duck call. *Boom boom boom* went three quick shots into the flock of just-landed mallards as they sat bunched-up on the water! Only eleven ducks fled from their most recently selected death trap and, of that bunch, three had their legs hanging down signaling "seriously wounded" and who would more than likely die a lingering death later on somewhere in the Butte Sink.

That did it! I thought. Here this chap with the cigar had some of the finest duck-shooting in the world on a private duck club in the Butte Sink. Then he goes and shoots a flock of ducks on the water. Some sportsman, I grimaced. Now my lad had 16 ducks and three dark geese lying scattered about in his decoys. And all of that damage to

Mother Nature in just twenty minutes! For sure, I had probably picked the "hottest" duck blind on that particular duck club. However, the adjacent blind was still shooting like ammunition was free and now I faced a dilemma.

Wait a little longer so I could catch them as well, or let this chap continue killing like there was no tomorrow? Then my shooter settled that dilemma for me. Standing up and looking all around like he was looking to see if a game warden had seen what he had just done to the flock of swimming mallards, he exited his blind. Getting into his boat, he began slowly paddling around in the marsh picking up his dead ducks and geese. This time I noticed that he was without his huge cigar. Fastening my binoculars on my lad as he picked up his dead birds, I double-checked my duck identifications to make sure the actual kill and my notes jibed. Then I had another worry. Several of his ducks had fallen near my place of concealment. That being the case, when he came into my area to pick up his birds, I might be discovered. However, I was so well hidden and my lad was so heavily concentrating on retrieving every bird he had killed that he did not notice a rather large but "handsome" fellow closely eyeballing him from his camouflaged place of hiding. To all you budding game warden types, remember another of Grosz's Rules: that being, if they aren't looking for you they won't see you. However, that time I did not get the chance to see if that rule worked as predicted...

Then my lad looked over his shoulder, stood up, and began screaming, No! No! No! He was looking back towards his blind in disbelief.

What the hell11 thought as I watched him going nuts in his boat. Then I, too, swung my eyes towards his duck blind trying to figure out what was so severely vexing my chap. I instantly saw what he was seeing! His duck blind was ablaze like a Roman candle! And I mean like a full torched inferno.

Then it dawned on me. My duck-killing chap was without his cigar. With that realization, the sun finally shone on the steaming manure pile behind the barn. My chap must have laid that huge cigar down on the wooden-framed lip of his blind and crawled into his boat to retrieve the dead ducks and geese in his decoys. Well, his blind had been heavily covered with willows and Phragmites to cover the wooden duck blind frame. During that period of time from early summer when the blind had been brushed up until the late fall the vegetation had dried and was now dryer than a popcorn fart. When my chap had laid down his cigar on the wooden railing lip of the blind, it must have rolled onto the dry vegetation and set my lad's blind afire.

All I could do was look on in wonderment and with just a tad bit of glee in my heart. For all you reader nonbelievers, there is a Duck God... And from the looks of it, he was a cigar smoker, too!

My shooter began paddling furiously back towards his "torch" of a blind. It was then I realized why there was such paddling urgency on his part. His new Browning AL-5 shotgun with the ventilated rib was still in the blind! Now I really began smiling... Just as my chap got to his burning blind, his extra ammunition began cooking off. *Bam! Boom! Slam! Boom!* went the live rounds as they rebelled against the blazing heat from the madly burning duck blind. Ducking his head, my shooter began furiously paddling away from the now wonderfully burning torch of a duck blind.

Then came the icing on the cake. *Uhrr-uhrr-uhrr* came the sweet sounds of three adjacent duck club members in their boats motoring towards the burning duck blind. Since my shooters had yet to look in my direction, I quickly rolled up the camouflage parachute, dropped my outboard motor's propeller shaft into the water, and primed the motor with one slow pull on the starter rope (an old game warden's trick. With just a slow pull on the starter rope, one puts fuel up into the cylinders of the motor. Then with a later abrupt pull on the starter rope, the motor would quickly spring to life and off one could go with a minimum of delay.).

Around the corner of the duck pond came three duck club members' boats, including the club's gamekeeper, all heading "hell-bent" towards the smoking and burning duck blind. As all three boats converged with my shooter's boat, I gave a quick pull on my starter rope. *Uhrr*, my motor snapped to life as I headed for my "not believing what they were observing" duck club chaps sitting together in a clump of boats. In short, it was kind of like ground sluicing that mess of mallards by my shooter earlier, only this time it would be a bunch of duck club shooters being ground, eh, water sluiced by the local federal agent...

That burning duck blind surprise was soon followed with the arrival of the world's largest and most beautiful, happy-as-a-clam federal agent. To those lads, my arrival was at probably the worst time in their lives. For you see, the gamekeeper had been removing all the extra birds from his other duck club members' blinds earlier so they could keep shooting as he had moved through the area. In illegally doing that, that gave the duck club's gamekeeper a super over limit! All the present and accounted for duck club members in the "boat clump" who had raced to the fire in the burning blind also had their over limits on board. Talk about a "ground sluicing" of chaps needing a "face full of federal agent!" That was one that by the grace of God was custom-made for yours truly. And, who was I to mess with the helping hand of God?

⁂

"Morning, gents. Terry Grosz, federal agent. I saw the blazing duck blind and thought I would come over and see if I could help (I lied but it was a great and professional introduction). But since we all are here, I might just as well as check your hunting licenses, shotguns, and birds if you don't mind," I said with a big, no, huge gotcha smile. One that was so richly deserved by all the lads in my clump of boats.

Suffice to say, as Rome, eh, the duck blind finished burning to the waterline behind me, I availed myself of providing a public service to all my gathered chaps. Christmas came early that year! Before the morning was done, I wrote all five of my boat chaps (which included my shooter) citations for over limits of ducks. As for my personal shooter, he also received an extra citation for shooting an over limit of wood ducks. Most of my duck club chaps that morning were from four to seven ducks over, with the club's gamekeeper leading the charge with 15 over! Before it was all said and done, my Grumman rode considerably lower in the water than it had earlier in the morning when I had arrived. It was amazing how much lower it rode, especially with a total of 93 evidence ducks tucked inside! As for my chap with the "burning bush," eh, blind, all he retrieved from the remains of his duck blind was a burned and now-rusting piece of steel resembling a brand new and expensive Browning shotgun, with a ventilated rib, of course.

Paddling my Grumman back to my hidden patrol truck with my evidence ducks, I started grinning and then laughing out loud like an idiot. Yes, I guess one could say I had picked out the "hottest" blind that fine day on the Butte Sink Duck Club that had been doing so much shooting several days before. No two ways about it, that was one hell of an expensive cigar...

SCRATCH ONE SET OF FALSE TEETH

Over my years as a California State Fish and Game Warden and later as a U.S. Game Management Agent the White Mallard Duck Club located in the Butte Sink always "paid for my gas and oil" when I officially visited it. That is, I wrote so many tickets while on that club that they more or less paid for all my daily expenses including my gas and oil costs while out and about. It just never seemed to fail. I don't know what it was for certain other than maybe the abject arrogance of many of its members. But no matter how one looked at it, those impacted never seemed able to obey the laws of the land when it came to the sport of hunting. And once again on a fine windy and rainy December day, the "Great and Beautiful Grosz" (that's me) tangled with the "good doctor" from San Francisco (an old nemesis of mine who couldn't accurately count the numbers of birds he killed on any given day) on the White Mallard Duck Club.

Pulling my Grumman into a thick stand of willows and young cottonwoods on the back side of the White Mallard Duck Club early one morning (is there any other time to be out and about?), I tied her off. Then I draped my camouflage parachute over the Grumman so I wouldn't be so easily seen by the ducks and any of the club's shooters who happened my way. Opening up the front of my heavy hunting coat to let out my body heat from the exertion of paddling there, I lay back against the outboard motor and placed the strap holding my binoculars around my neck. It had taken me longer than anticipated to get where I wanted to go that morning (see why I usually left so early on stakeouts?), and shooting time was just minutes away. I had purposely located myself between several likely looking, known duck blinds to increase my chances of catching someone with an over limit.

I didn't have to wait for long. Off to my west, I could hear several outboard motors coming my way. Burrowing further into my cover hoping not to be observed, I saw two boats slowly moving my way as they headed down the White Mallard's main boat channel. One boat headed for one of the blinds I was staking out and the other headed for the back side of the duck club. Then I heard several more outboard motors coming my way. They, too, bypassed my hiding place moving to the back side of the duck club as well.

Oh well, I thought, I still have one blind to watch and if they can hit their backsides with the amount of ducks that are flying today, I should be able to catch them with over limits. And as for the other shooters on the back side of the duck club, well, they had to return my way and I would be waiting. Swiveling around on the seat of my Grumman Sport Canoe, I began watching my two shooters in the now-occupied blind I had staked out for the morning's shoot.

As the mornings shooting began to crescendo on all the duck clubs throughout the Butte Sink, the air filled with thousands of ducks and geese. They were confused because for the previous two non-shoot days they had a safe haven in which to loaf and rest from the ever-pounding shotguns outside the area. However, today was a shoot day in the sink, and it was now all the many thousands of ducks and geese could do to find a safe haven instead of a face full of lead shot (legal in those days, however, one must use steel shot when hunting waterfowl today to reduce the mortalities caused from the inadvertent ingestion of lethal lead shot by feeding waterfowl). In short, those looking for that safe "sweet spot" had to run the gauntlet of at least one hundred duck blinds and their decoy sets laid out for the birds' review and consideration within the Butte Sink. And if they made a mistake and fell to those clever blind and decoy deceptions, it was for many their last "shoot day" on the planet.

Soon my blind's shooters began making hay on the feathered manna from heaven. In the space of thirty minutes, my two shooters had limits and showed no signs of leaving if the sounds of their barking shotguns and blaring off-key duck calls spoke to reality. Rolling up my camouflage netting before my shooters killed every avian heartbeat over their area, Dog and I began our quiet trip to my two still unsuspecting shooters' duck blind from their blind side.

Rounding the turn in the boat lane to their blind, I heard someone say, "What the hell? Chet, is that the big federal son-of-a-bitch from Colusa?"

With those words, my shooters quickly disappeared from sight within their blind. Figuring they were trying to put the plugs back into their shotguns, I sped up my paddling until I arrived at the blind. Looking inside the open doorway into the blind, I saw my two lads sitting on the raised floor hurriedly trying to replace their plugs back into their shotguns so they would be legal in the eyes of the law.

"Too late, lads," I said. "Leave those shotguns as they are, or I will seize them as evidence and they won't be returned until after the trial which means the end of duck season." With those words, my two would be "gunsmiths" lay down the pieces of their disassembled shotguns and stood up with grumpy looks on their faces.

Twenty minutes later, as other shotguns from nearby unseen duck blinds hammered around me, I finished the paperwork at hand. Both of my shooters were cited for taking over limits of ducks and the use and aid of shotguns capable of holding more than three shells. Since I had ticketed one of those lads twice and the other three times before for waterfowl violations, they had no questions on the Federal Magistrates Court process in Sacramento soon to follow. Thanking the lads for their patience, I shoved off in my Grumman with all their over limits (now my evidence) and headed due west knowing that my two lads would pull a "Paul Revere" on the rest of the White Mallard's nearest occupied duck blinds as soon as I was out of sight. You know, speed around and spread the word the British, eh, actually I was German, were coming. That was alright with me though because I had a Plan B.

Just as soon as I was out of sight, I turned my Grumman to the northwest and quickly headed for the lower boat landing on the White Mallard Duck Club. I figured my two just-cited lads would let everyone else know I was on-site and that would scramble the rest of the rats into doing what "rats" did best. Namely, gather up their gear and leave the shooting area with all their birds taken that morning in tow. And, they would be heading right into a trap set by yours truly.

Paddling like the devil was on my tail, I finally arrived at the last boat narrows leading to the White Mallard's lower boat dock. There I pulled my Grumman into the cattails so that just the bow was barely sticking out into the boat channel. That way when one of the "rats leaving the ship" came roaring back into the duck club proper to dump off their extra birds, I would be in a great position to intercept them and "make" their day.

In the past, I had never found any of the members who had taken too many ducks leaving them behind. In every case, they had stubbornly brought their illegal ducks back into the duck club proper with them figuring that once they were back at the duck club hanging facility, they could hide their ill-gotten gains, I guess. However, on the way in, the extra birds would be hidden in decoy bags, military ammo boxes holding tools on board their boats, or on their persons. But they always brought them in, and I was depending on that historical behavior in order to work my "magic" that fine windy and rainy day so long ago.

About twenty minutes after my two recently cited "Paul Revere" type duck club members had done their thing, I could hear outboards buzzing around on the duck club like cars on a San Francisco freeway during rush hour. Soon I could hear one coming my way like a large alligator was hot on his tail. Timing my "surprise" just right, I waited until I could hear the boat slowing as it hit what I called the "narrows" on the boat trail through the tall reeds. When I heard the expected sound getting closer, I took my oar and shoved my Grumman across the boat trail in the canal so any oncoming boats would have to stop. Where I had positioned my boat across the canal was still a good twenty feet from any approaching boat as they rounded the channel turn. That way, they had more than enough time to stop, but yet be so close to the "long arm of the law" that they couldn't escape or toss their illegal birds.

Sure as God made cows a slobbering affair, here came a duck club member I called "the good doctor." He had to be in his early seventies at that time and just as cranky as a one-legged owl in a room full of razor blades and pissed-off hungry feral cats. And as I was to find out that day, his basic attitude would be no different. I had cited him several times before for over limits of ducks and he had no love for my miserable carcass. And once again, that "love affair" would manifest itself that fine day in all its "glory" once we were together once again.

"Ho! Ho! Ho!" he yelled in surprise when he saw me sitting in my Grumman blocking the canal some twenty feet distant. Refusing to yield to the inevitable, he shut down his outboard to a crawl to avoid a collision. Then standing up in his boat, he turned, grabbed his throttle handle with his right hand, leaned heavily on it and, using his left hand, shifted his outboard into reverse. I guess he figured he could still escape if he moved fast since his outboard was more powerful and thereby faster than mine.

That was when the crap hit the fan. The huge following wave he had created caught up to the stern of his boat and lifted it high into the air. That lift, plus the good, heavyset doctor leaning heavily on his throttle handle as he put his motor in reverse, set the free- flowing crap following such a hair-brained action into motion.

Snap went the throttle handle on his motor as it broke off in his right hand from the combined weight of our rather ample-sized doctor pushing down and the lifting action of the earlier, following wave. Snap went the throttle handle in his hand as it broke off cleaner than a hound's tooth! Bam went the now falling good doctor's head as it slammed off the engine housing and then glanced downward onto part of the now-broken throttle handle still dangerously exposed and attached to the outboard engine. *Whoomp* violently went the doctor's rather rotund face onto the broken end of the throttle handle as his eyeglasses spun wildly off his head into six feet of murky swamp water with a quiet *ker-plush.* Then the still off-balance good doctor decided to take a cold December bath in the waters of the duck club... With all his falling energy, *ker-plush* went the good doctor head first over the stern of his boat! In a split second, the good doctor's rather rotund carcass disappeared from sight over the side of his boat. If I hadn't been so surprised at all the rapid turn of events, I would have been laughing at this Laurel and Hardy "duck club funny."

However, figuring the good doctor's usual temper and attitude had been quickly "cooled off" in the cold December waters, I shoved my Grumman alongside his boat. Once alongside the good doctor, who by then was spewing water into the air like a gray whale off the coast of California, I went into reflex action. Reaching over the side of my boat as he started going under once again because he was being dragged under by his now full hip waders, I grabbed the top of his full head of hair and lifted him up.

Well... not quite. Unknown to me, the good doctor was wearing a toupee. In my Herculean effort to keep him from drowning and only having his fast-disappearing head of hair to grab hold of, I made my move and jerked it clean off his head! Surprised at my powering effort that produced naught in the way of resistance, I stumbled backward in my boat. Then I lost it, literally and figuratively! The toupee sailed out of my hand as I let it go realizing I was falling and tried to break my fall with that hand. Once I had landed in the bottom of my boat, I quickly turned only to see the toupee sitting all askew on the top of my Labrador retriever's head who was patiently sitting in the bow of my canoe! Seeing that and the stupid look on my dog's face, I totally lost it! Roaring with laughter, I almost forgot about my good doctor going down for the third time in the deep boat canal's waters.

Then realizing he was still floundering in the icy cold December waters, I quickly got to my feet, stepped back and once again looked over the side of my boat. By now the good doctor was holding onto the side of his boat and again I had to stifle a huge laugh. First of all, his front lip was bloody as all get-out from hitting the broken throttle handle on his boat when he initially fell overboard. But that wasn't the best part. His mouth looked like that from a 100-year-old man! It was all pouched in like that of a big carp! Then I realized why he had such a funny look. His teeth were gone! All of them! As I later discovered, he had a full set of false teeth. When his head had hit the engine casing or when his mouth had struck the broken throttle handle, his teeth had shot out of his mouth and gone into six foot of muddy canal water never to be seen again! Well, at least his eyeglasses that he had lost earlier had company, I thought...

By then, the good doctor had settled down and cooled off enough in the winter waters. At that point in the "duck club funnies," he had enough of the Laurel and Hardy episode. Reaching for my outstretched hand, I pulled him up into my Grumman. While I grabbed the lead rope on his boat, there sat one wet, bedraggled, hairless, toothless, bloodied, and contrite doctor. Then I spied it! The toupee that had once resided on my dog's head was now gone! Where it went I never discovered, and you can bet I never said anything about it to the doctor either... However, one had to give my dog credit. She had recognized a good head of hair when presented with one at birth. And as for any bad ones, like the good doctors', she had chucked it somewhere...

Towing the good doctor's boat to his boat dock, I tied it up. Then I noticed he only had one limit of mallards laid out on the middle seat of his boat. That just didn't make sense, I thought. With only a legal limit of ducks, why had he made all that fuss? As the good doctor just sat there trying to regain his composure and stem the flowing blood from his badly split lip, I emptied out his decoy bag. Lying hidden in among his duck decoys were 13 more ducks! Between his legal limit and those discovered in the decoy bag, the good doctor had a very nice over limit. That made me feel one hell of a lot better.

The ending of this event could have gone rather badly politically if the good doctor only had one limit of ducks. Especially after breaking his motor, losing his teeth, dropping his eyeglasses into the canal, getting whanged on the lip by the throttle handle, and losing his beautiful Robert Redford hair piece. And that did not include his unintentional rather cold dip in the waters of his duck club.

"Well, Doc, you know who I am or do I need to show you my badge and credentials?" I asked upon discovering his rather large over limit of ducks in the decoy bag.

"No. I know who the hell you are, and you are still a son-of-a- bitch. I suppose after surprising me like that and causing me such problems, you are now going to issue me a citation for a lousy 13 ducks over the limit. If you do, that is a travesty. I have bought duck stamps since 1934, and I would have thought that has more than paid at least ten times over for the lousy few ducks I take over the limit," he grumbled. However, now as he spoke, I really had to listen carefully to his words. He now sounded like he had mush in his mouth because it was hard for him to speak with no teeth and a badly cut and now hugely swollen lip. But regardless of the cold bath and all, the good doctor got a citation for possessing an over limit of ducks.

In fact, my ticket writing presence worked out better than I ever could have planned it. Two more duck club members came in early because of my two earlier cited for over limits "Paul Reveres." As they did, they boated right up to the boat dock like they owned it. They had spied the doctor and had looked right passed me. In they came figuring with the outlaw doctor on the boat dock, it was safe to come in. Well, they were safe until I surprised them with my magnificent Robert Redford self and cited both of them for over limits of ducks as well!

The good doctor never said anything to me or my superiors about losing his teeth, eyeglasses or toupee over that incident. I never could figure what happened to that toupee though. It looked good on my dog, but I guess she didn't think so and somehow had gotten rid of it. I suppose some muskrat found it floating later in the marsh and took it home for a rug or bed. Who knows? I do know that the good doctor, after paying for a new set of eyeglasses, toupee, and set of teeth, plus a $350.00 fine for his over limit, had to think twice about ever taking too many ducks again. But then...

As an aside, my son and then-Special Agent Rich Grosz pinched the good doctor for the use of lead shot on the White Mallard Duck Club some years later. The good doctor was still just as full of it then as ever and had some fine things to say about Rich's dad when pinched by his son. Letting my son work as I stood off to one side and out of sight so he could learn the ropes, I just listened to the conversation between the two men. But for my readers, you will have to wait to see where that episode took them and read that in Chapter 8, "Rocky Mountain Reflections" of my book titled *Wildlife on the Edge.*

You know, something just came to mind. I have often wondered how the good doctor could tell the difference between a gall bladder and a "gizzard" during an operation, when he couldn't even correctly count the numbers of ducks he killed?

BEATEN UP BY A SWAN

Checking duck hunters on the Butte Creek Farms Duck Club one December Saturday, I heard nothing but a ton of shooting coming from the east on the Sacramento Outing Duck Club. Figuring that would be where I would work the next shoot day because of such gunning action, I finished up my citation business on the Butte Creek Farms Duck Club. Then waiting for the shooting to subside and for everyone to be back in their clubhouses drinking and watching the football games, I slipped by shank's mare into the Sacramento Outing Duck Club's suspect blind's location from where I had heard all the previous shooting (an easy thing to do when one knows his district so well that he can more or less pinpoint such suspect shooting locations).

Looking into the suspect blind, I saw the floor was littered with empty, freshly fired shotgun shells. That went double for the numerous empties floating in the water around the duck blind and in the decoys as well. Suspicious over the numbers of ducks I had surprised still feeding in the decoys when I arrived, I turned and walked back to my hidden patrol truck. Soon I returned with a bait scoop (steel-netted rectangular device designed to be dragged on the bottoms of ponds to ascertain if the area is illegally baited). Upon my return, I scared off several dozen ducks feeding in the decoys around the blind in question. That was just not normal to my way of thinking. Especially since the birds had been shot at previously from that same blind. Walking in among the decoy set dragging my bait scoop, I immediately discovered why the ducks had found this blind so appealing. It was baited to the "nines" with fresh barley! Grabbing a quick sample, I hotfooted it out of there before I was discovered and then "the cat would be out of the bag before the mice could play" if that was to occur.

But before I left, I also discovered a necessity that I had been looking for. Looking the area over quickly as I left, I found a small copse of trees just to the west of the blind in which I could conceal myself while watching the shooting action when the time came. With that information tucked away for future reference, I slipped out from the area unseen and made ready for the next day's shoot at my baited blind.

Later that Saturday afternoon, I received a phone call from an informant about the Tennessee Ernie Ford Duck Club shooting over bait and taking over limits of ducks when Ford was not present. Boy, when it rained it poured. Having two active baited duck clubs in the district made for a real "swarm of bees" when it came to getting the job done and the outlaws captured. But, I happily knew just the "bee keeper" for such a duality of jobs... Not changing horses midstream with the two duck clubs now in question being baited, the next shoot day found me addressing my earlier-discovered baited duck club problem on the Sacramento Outing Duck Club. That Sunday shoot day found me hidden in the small copse of trees way before daylight waiting for the arrival of shooting time and my hoped-for shooters taking advantage of my recently discovered baited area. Since my previous shooters hadn't been disturbed by the law when I had first heard all the earlier shooting, I was hoping that maybe they would be the same ones returning that current shoot day as I lurked in the trees. And if they were and continued shooting the "lights" out on my ducks over a baited area, guess who would see to it that Christmas came early that year to my "naughty and not nice" violating chaps?

Glassing the Sacramento Outing Duck Club clubhouse from my hiding place, I failed to see any lights indicating the possible presence of shooters residing therein for that day's shoot. Disappointed, I still held my ground figuring I would do so until "the last dog was hung." That is one distinct difference about good wildlife officers. The really good ones have the "patience of Job." You need to be a patient son-of-a-gun if you are going to be successful in the wildlife law enforcement trade when "hunting the lawless."

And on that particular shoot day, my patience was soon to pay off in spades. As it turned out, I chanced seeing a wildlife violator cross swords with one of Mother Nature's minions and come off an embarrassing second best...

Right at daylight I observed a vehicle slowly driving down the road in front of the Sacramento Outing Duck Club Clubhouse as if casing the joint. Then the vehicle drifted out of sight down the road. Ten minutes later that same vehicle came back repeating the earlier procedure. It again drifted out of sight down the road towards the nearby Sutter Buttes. Ten minutes later, that same vehicle drifted back into the area and this time it stopped alongside the road by the farm trail leading into the blind on which I was staked out. Shortly thereafter in the early morning dark, I observed a lone figure hustling down the road leading to the baited blind in question. As he did, numerous ducks enjoying the "barley buffet" rose in alarm and left the baited area in and around the decoys. Then as if he owned the place, my lone figure entered the duck blind and disappeared quickly from sight.

With the approach of legal shooting hours, the other Butte Sink duck clubs began their "dance of death" with the ducks and geese. The popping of shotguns announced the start of another shoot day, and soon the volume of shooting approximated the first day of battle at Gettysburg many years earlier by Union Cavalry General John Buford and the clashing Rebel forces. In the soft morning light, I observed numerous skeins of ducks and geese heading towards the duck blind and decoys that I was watching.

Within moments, the soft trilling calls and sounds of whistling wings foretold of an approaching flock of Northern pintail. Into the decoys in front of my suspect blind plunged a dozen unsuspecting ducks. It was all too apparent that they were happy as a clam in a tidal pool to find a safe place to land. To their great surprise, my lone figure stood up and killed five ducks in the bunched up formation of close-at-hand ducks with just three quick shots!

Back down into the blind my lone shooter disappeared like he had done this before. That same procedure was carried out four more times until 21 dead ducks littered the decoy set! Figuring I would let my lad shoot one more flock and then drop the hammer on his miserable carcass for a gross over limit (the legal daily bag limit was eight ducks) and shooting over a baited area, I got one hell of a surprise that fine day because I had waited.

All at once a lone adult tundra swan silently hammering along from the west appeared. The fully adult bird majestically circled my shooter's blind and decoy set several times and then made up its mind to land. Slowing its wing beat and dropping its jet black feet, my swan made a final approach as it headed into the edge of the decoys. Hauling back at the last moment with its wings, my swan flared upward and "water-skied" into the decoys with a swish of water from its paddle-like, large webbed feet.

Then it immediately started running across the water to gain speed as if something "out of place" had caught its eyes. Taking that as his cue, my lone shooter rose in his blind and coldly shot the swan, a totally protected species! Ker-plush went my swan in a massive, wing-flailing wreck into the duck pond. Then, not willing to give up its life so easily, the great bird gathered itself up and tried to fly once again. However, it had been wing-tipped by my shooter and could not lift its great weight off the water. With that realization, it settled down and began swimming quietly away from the offending blind. My shooter stood up in the blind again and raised his shotgun to shoot the swan one more time before it was out of range. Then he changed his mind, probably not wanting to draw any unwanted attention to his evil deed. Lowering his shotgun, my shooter looked all around as if to see if anyone had observed his patently illegal action. Satisfied at seeing no one looking on at what he had done, he grabbed his shotgun and started off after the crippled swan before it disappeared into the flooded brush of the Butte Sink and onto adjacent duck clubs.

Across the shallow duck pond my shooter went as the gentle swan continued looking at and swimming away from his pursuer. But my shooter could move faster than the crippled swan and quickly closed the distance between man and bird. Soon my shooter was upon the wounded bird. Swinging his shotgun barrel at the swan's head, he "clomped" the bird a good one. In so doing, he knocked the swan silly as a mess of kittens in a knitting basket. Once again, my shooter paused and looked all around as if looking to see if anyone had witnessed his dastardly act. That turned out to be a capital error and a major mistake in judgment...

As he reached down for the dazed swan's long neck to wring the life from the wounded bird, the tables instantly turned. Recovering from being struck on the head, pissed off and unwilling to be captured or give up its life so easily, the great bird rose up out from the water on its great wings and turned. As my shooter reached down, the swan (later determined to be a cob, or large male swan) shot its great bill upward like the strike of a snake. In that instant, the swan had latched squarely onto the nose of my shooter! Then the crap hit the fan! Pulling hard downward, the swan jerked his heavy body out from the water and using the hold on my shooter's nose as twisting leverage, it brought forth its great, bony hard wings in a rush. In the next moment, the hard bony wing bones smashed into the downward pointing face of my shooter. That not only happened once but several times in rapid succession. "Yeow!" screamed my deeply injured shooter as he tried to recoil from his feathered attacker. That was to no avail. The swan hung on to the shooter's proboscis like his life depended on it as he continued pummeling the shooter's face rapidly with its hard, wing bones. Stumbling backwards in surprise and agony, my shooter fell into the duck pond flat on his back. It was then the swan let loose of the man's nose and grabbed his right ear. Trying to get up out of two feet of water, my shooter found the swan standing on his chest pummeling away once again at the man's head with the bony edges of his wings, all the while tearing and jerking on his ear.

During those moments of combat between my shooter and the swan, I just knelt there in hiding looking on in amazement. I had never seen a swan take it to a human being out in the field. To me in the cab of my patrol truck earlier in my career when I was trying to help a crippled swan, yes, but never in the open field. Canada geese, yes, at the drop of a hat and with a fury, but never a gentle swan. But I was seeing it now! Then my shooter rolled over face down in the water in an attempt to get away by pushing off and rising. But the swan was having nothing of that maneuver. The swan had let go of the man's ear and was now tearing out great gobs of the shooter's beautiful, long hippy hair-do. And each time the swan pulled out a gob of hair, what followed was a deadly flailing forward of those long wing bones from the leading edges of the wings on the shooter's back, side of the face, and head. In fact, that swan wasn't particular. He took hold of any body part offered and beat the hell out of it!

By now, I figured my shooter was almost drowned and had enough of the beating he was taking from the swan. Finally scrambling from my place of hiding, I ran to the shooter's rescue. Splashing across the pond, I got to my still-face down in the water shooter. The swan, seeing me approaching in a threatening manner, turned his wrath on me. The swan must have figured if the man's partner wanted a good "ass-whuppin'," he was just the bird to administer such treatment no matter how big I was.

In a half-second, the swan was on me like stink on a striped skunk with a bad case of attitude. However, the swan was not aware that as a previous wildlife student and later as an officer, I was familiar on how to handle many species of crazed animals. And for a pissed-off swan, it was a piece of cake. Reaching out, I gently grabbed the great bird's head and just steered its smashing, frantically beating wings off to one side of my legs. You see, the swan had to go where I led its head. That is unless it wanted a broken neck. After about two minutes of flailing away at me all to no avail, the bird settled down. However, his head never left my hand and I watched his body movements in case there was more violent action to come. Especially when I could feel him pulling in my hand as he tried once again to launch his body and wings in my direction.

With the swan under control, I looked over at my shooter. He was sitting in two feet of water holding his head in both hands. And he had good reason for such a holding posture. His nose was bleeding like a stuck hog and it was broken! One of his eyebrows was completely pulled off and a bloody rag of what was left of it limply hung down. His left ear was a bloody mess and his forehead was a purple mass of marble-sized knots where the swan's wing bones had beaten the drumbeat of the "wild" on it. But that wasn't the best part. The shooter's right eye was closed and full of blood where several blows from the wing bones had done a beautiful number on my lad. As for his other eye, it was the prettiest black, blue, yellow, brown, and purple mixture of color you ever saw. In short, the score was swan one, illegal shooter zero...

Holding the swan off to one side by his head, I used my other hand to help the badly beaten shooter up from his sitting position in the duck pond. All my shooter could do was moan and spit blood from his upper split lip (did I forget to mention that one as well? It had been split clear to the bottom of his nose!). As for the swan, he was still pissed. If he could have gotten a fair shot at me, he was fully well-prepared to do the same to me before I did it to him. Man, you never saw such a pissed-off bird.

"Come on, lad," I said. "Let's get you over there onto some dry ground." The shooter just mumbled something through his split lip, as the blood from his broken nose continued gushing down the front of his shooting jacket and camouflage hunting pants.

Then he said, "Wait. My shotgun. Where is my shotgun?"

Standing there looking at a muddy duck pond, I didn't have the foggiest idea where the man had dropped his shotgun when the battle royale started. As it turned out, I had been so fascinated at the swan giving my shooter a great ass-whuppin', that I had not paid any attention to the disposition of his shotgun... So for the next twenty minutes, the two of us shuffled our feet across the bottom of the muddy duck pond hoping to find the weapon with our feet. One, the bloody one, staying way clear of the swan as he did so, and the other chap still dragging the swan by its head as he shuffled along searching for the shotgun with his feet as well. Well, we never found the man's shotgun. I just hadn't been watching where or what he had done with it when his battle with the swan had started. As for my shooter, it would have been almost impossible to see where he had thrown his shotgun with a swan's bill twisting his nose until it broke and hard, bony wings beating the hell out of his face...

Finally giving up the shotgun hunt, the three of us shuffled through the duck pond's mud back to the blind. Once on dry ground, I tied my handkerchief over the swan's eyes so he couldn't see. Then taking some parachute cord from my gear bag, I tied its feet together so it couldn't stand. Finally, I lifted up its wings and tied them together at the junction between its primary and secondary wing feathers to avoid having the bird destroy its flight feathers in any further struggles before laying it down. That done, I tended to my other charge who was still sitting there on the ground mournfully holding his swollen and bleeding head. Looking him over once again, I could see that the marble-sized welts on his head and face were now the size of small chicken eggs. Man, he sure was a mess. Like many folks, myself included, have said previously, it is not nice to mess with Mother Nature!

Getting out my citation book, I ticketed our chap for taking an over limit of ducks, to wit, 13 over the limit. He was also cited for shooting over a baited area and taking a protected migratory nongame bird, to wit, one tundra swan. Then as my lad sat there at my instruction, I went out into the decoys with my bait scoop. One pass with the bait scoop in the decoys produced several handfuls of fresh barley which I displayed to my shooter. That way, he damn sure knew he was shooting over a baited area in case the issue ever came up in a court of law. Then that bait sample went into a plastic bag as my evidence.

Come to find out, our shooter was also a trespasser. He did not belong to the club and as he later advised, he would check out the club on the shoot days. If no one showed up to shoot the Sacramento Outing Duck Club, he would sneak into the area and shoot it himself. That admission also got him a state citation for trespassing.

Some time later, my lad forfeited $1,250.00 in Federal Court for the federal violations and an additional $250.00 in state court for the trespassing violation. I had no idea what his doctor bills cost him. As for my rather aggressive swan, he was released in a licensed zoological aviary in San Francisco to live out the rest of his life (no, my swan wasn't a San Francisco liberal; it was just a good home...). That was because after a veterinarian had looked at the bird's damaged wing, he had determined the bird would never fly again.

That tough old swan, along with many other species of waterfowl, died two years later when a case of fowl cholera broke out in that aviary. He now "resides" in the Fish and Wildlife Service's waterfowl identification teaching collection at the National Academy in Glynco, Georgia.

However, to this day, whenever I hear swans calling or flying over, I have to chuckle. Never again during my career did I see a swan take it to someone in such a manner as I did that day (in my truck, yes, but never again in the field). Canada geese, yes. But swans, never after that day. In fact, the smaller Canada goose has historically been credited with killing a man when the horse the man was riding accidentally stepped into the bird's nest. That bird was so pissed off that it dive-bombed the man off his horse, killing him and the bird alike. Who would have thought it?

A "DUMP" AND A DUMP

Coming in off Butte Creek via a small drainage ditch heading easterly early one morning during waterfowl season, I soon found myself in the area of numerous Butte Sink wealthy duck clubs. The Butte Sink's natural geological depression in the Northern Sacramento Valley, has been the ancestral home to millions of waterfowl for eons. That particular day at 2:30 in the morning was no different. Quietly trying to cool out from the long drag of my Grumman Sport Boat through the shallow, overgrown drainage ditch, Dog and I sat there listening in wonder. Even at that time in the morning, the sink was abuzz with the sounds thousands of calling ducks, geese and swans make as they awoke to a new day. The harsh quacking of female mallards, the beautiful fluting calls of the Northern pintail, the always worried-sounding calls from the ever-present, beautiful little wood ducks, and the lilting calls of Pacific white-fronted geese filled the air. As if those weren't enough heaven-sent sounds to a wildlife officer's ears, above that din came the clarion calls of the lordly Canada geese and the sing-song sounds of lesser snow geese. Man, you talk about a great morning to be alive under the light of a half-moon and in among thousands of nature's whistling wings, this was it. Man "ain't never lived" until he can experience the very essence and close-at-hand heartbeat of God and Mother Nature up close and personal-like. And that morning so long ago, I could clearly hear all three of our heartbeats!

Wildlife's Quiet War

Finally cooling down from my early morning canoe-dragging exercises, I zipped up my heavy jacket and now in deeper water, began paddling towards the northeastern side of the Butte Sink. Crossing duck club boundary after boundary, I finally arrived at Bob Stack's Duck Club. It wasn't a particularly large club but one I hadn't worked for some time. In fact, the last time I worked that particular duck club, I had pinched the gamekeeper for killing his and his wife's limit of ducks. Working my way into the specific area in which I wanted to hide, I grounded the Grumman alongside a small, old, abandoned rice field levee. There I let my dog Shadow out to smell and scent mark the area while I prepared our breakfast. Dog got a can of Alpo dog food and one of her favorites, a thickly spread PB&J sandwich. Me, I got the usual dry, hard Italian salami and a Coke for breakfast.

Sitting in the moonlight, I looked upward into a tall cottonwood a fair distance away. There, cut into the top of that tree, was an aerial duck blind. Then about twenty feet below the floor of that duck blind was a small built-out area holding a stove, a few shelves, some plates, utensils, and the like. Then another ten feet below the small "kitchen" area sat another built-out over the water below structure holding an outdoor "crapper," proper toilet seat and all. Then below that and off to one side to miss the "crapper" droppings as they fell into the duck pond was a boat slip in which to hide the duck boat. All in all, a pretty neat set-up.

The current duck club owner, as I mentioned earlier, was none other than Robert Stack. In real life, besides being a movie star, Bob Stack was always one hell of a duck shooter to watch. Whenever his shotgun barrel went up, a duck dropped. He was one of the finest wing-shooters I had ever seen and a real pleasure to watch because sometimes he had a little problem in counting the number of ducks he had killed, if you readers understand the gist of my drift...

That was why I was there that morning. My boss, Jack Downs, had written Bob Stack a citation for killing an over limit of ducks earlier (Stack was also known as "Elliot Ness" of early TV fame on The Untouchables). Now I figured it was my turn to do the same. That was, if Mr. Stack cooperated. However, as it turned out that fine day, I was to be disappointed. No one showed up that morning come daylight to shoot the club. Not an uncommon happenstance in the world of wildlife law enforcement. The officer can lay the best plans to catch someone and many times will find the targeted chap will never, for whatever reason, show up. In fact, the ordinary wildlife officer will also find many times he or she will set up on bad guys who are willing to break the law of the land, and the critters won't show up and cooperate either. But that is nothing more than the spice of life in the wildlife law enforcement profession when "hunting the lawless." Many times when that happened, the Old Boy upstairs would throw the wildlife officer another "bone" on which to chew. And that is what happened that outstanding day in the Butte Sink as the world of wildlife whirled around me in all its magnificence and noisy, winged glory.

Waiting until long after legal shooting hours had begun, I finally decided no one was coming to shoot Bob Stack's blind that day. Switching to Plan B, I figured I would just cast about within the many Butte Sink duck clubs and see if I could snare off an unsuspecting gamekeeper. You know, the ones who liked to "patrol" looking for game warden-types on their duck clubs and then give the warnings to all their other unsuspecting members, acting like "Paul Revere" of old in the process. Or the other kind who liked to visit their various club members' duck blinds during the morning's shoot and remove the extra ducks from them for safekeeping so the illegal shooters didn't get cited for having an over limit. That way the members could keep shooting ducks as the gamekeepers ran the extra ducks back to the clubhouse for the members to pick up at a later time and thereby thwarting the game warden. Many times for doing the members such favors, the gamekeepers pick up a little extra spending money in the form of "thankful" tips ultimately gathered up at the critters' expense. Damn, I sure am a suspicious type...

Rousting up dog from her now noisy sleep on the levee, I pulled the Grumman from its hiding place and headed out into the Butte Sink duck clubs to see what I could scare up. Quietly paddling my Grumman, I was soon up onto a blind of unsuspecting chaps having one hell of a duck shoot on what I called the Millionaire's Duck Club. The blind's two shooters were only shooting green-winged teal and what a shoot-off they were having. The winter air was full of the migrating little speedsters (North America's smallest duck, about ten ounces in weight), and a hell of a target they made. But for once, the teal had met their match. Both shooters were dead on, and when one of the fast-flying little ducks was killed and hit the water, it inevitably skipped across the water like a rock skipped by all of us when we were bored youngsters with nothing else to do. For you non-duck hunters' edification, any one of the three species of teal commonly found in North America is considered very fine eating by the gunning public. That is because teal ducks are rather particular as to where they swim and what they eat. They mostly are found in clean, fresh water and eat primarily seeds. Any time you kill and eat a species of wildlife that is a seed eater, you are in for an epicurean treat. They make a perfect sized dish for a wife or child who is not used to eating game birds and I would recommend them highly to all my readers.

Glassing the decoy-littered pond area in which my two lads were shooting, I counted 19 teal bodies silently floating thereon. Since the limit was only eight ducks per day per shooter and they were over the limit, I figured I would put an end to their little game. However, before I could paddle my way over to my very accurate shooters, they had three more of the little ducks down for the count.

Not saying a word when I came into their views, I just kept paddling towards their blind like I knew what I was doing. I figured the little teal had to have a voice in what had just happened, and now they had one that could be heard clear to where God sat if necessary. Or at least to and into the Federal Court in Sacramento...

"Hey! This is a private duck club. Get your ass off our property or I will call our gamekeeper on the handy-talkie and have him run you in for trespassing," said the tall one with a long necklace of duck and goose bands (from banded birds taken during previous kills) hanging proudly around his neck.

You do that, I thought, and I probably will end up with your gamekeeper in "my" game bag as well.

Just then five more teal hove into sight and started to land in their decoys. Both of my shooters (note I didn't call them hunters) quickly emptied their Browning shotguns into the birds, before I could stop them. Not a single bird escaped that fusillade, and that did it to my way of thinking!

"Federal game warden," I boomed out over the marsh as I held up my badge. Man, you talk about getting one's attention. Both shooters just dropped out from sight as if hiding in the blind would allow them to escape. Fat chance of that happening, I thought, as I began picking up the 27 teal floating in the decoy-littered pond.

Disgustedly throwing the last bird into the bottom of my Grumman, I turned and began paddling my way towards my still-hidden in the blind, "tough guy" shooters. "Morning, gentlemen. Federal game warden, I would like to check your hunting licenses, duck stamps, and shotguns for plugs, if you don't mind," I said in such a way that my chaps knew hiding in the blind was now not an option.

"We thought you were a trespasser," said the one with all the duck bands strung around his neck on a necklace as if that would settle the issue of an over limit of ducks.

"Well, as you can plainly see, I am not a trespasser. Now I would like to see the items I requested earlier," I said.

With that, both men handed me their shotguns barrel first! Pushing the ends of the barrels aside so I didn't get blown out of the Grumman by accident, I never said a word about the unsafe manner of handling a firearm. Somehow I thought if I had said anything to those chaps about the careless handling of a firearm, it wouldn't have registered. Especially with the heavy smell of stale whiskey wafting through the air...

The lads checked out within the confines of the law except for the dead teal. "Who shot what when it came to these birds?" I asked pointing to all the broken bodies lying in the bottom of the Grumman.

"We don't know who shot what, officer," said the older of the two men. As I later discovered, they were father and son having a shoot-off to see who was the better shot. And since both of them were California skeet shooting champions, I think it was pretty much a draw as to who was the better shooter. However, since neither could or would claim any number of the birds taken over the limit, I just wrote the both of them for joint over the possession limit, to wit, eleven birds over the daily bag and possession limit (the daily bag limit in those days was eight ducks per person per day).

After finishing with the paperwork, I asked the man with the duck band necklace if he had sent the band numbers into the Fish and Wildlife Service for their biological and banding records (records showing when, where banded, and the name of the bander).

"Hell no! Do you think I am stupid or something? If I was to send those band numbers into you people, you would do nothing but send someone out to pinch me once you found out where I hunted and shot those birds," he blurted out.

"Mr. Stevens," I said. "All we use that data for is for biological purposes. It in no way is used to track someone down and write them a citation. If all those birds were taken lawfully, you have nothing to fear from the government. That banding information is very valuable to our banding folks back in Washington, D.C., and it sure would be nice if you would send those band numbers in with the kill data."

"Take this citation back and I might consider it," he replied arrogantly as he handed his citation back towards me with a leer on his face...

One month later through their attorney, both Stevens men forfeited $500.00 each in Federal Court in Sacramento. The Service never did get that valuable band information from Mr. Stevens. From then on, every time while I was in the Butte

Sink checking duck hunters, I managed to swing by that particular blind just in case someone was having another contest to see who could kill the most ducks. I subsequently made a lot of money for the government because of that blind and its caliber of shooters over the many years I patrolled the Northern Sacramento Valley. For some reason, it always seemed to draw the worst of the shooting kind and one rather large but beautiful-looking (of course...) federal agent when the leaves turned, the ducks were migrating, and the popping of shotguns and whistling wings could be heard...

Leaving my two shooters, neither of whom had won the duck shooting contest that fine day, I had to chuckle because both of them had not only lost the duck shooting contest but ultimately had won the "award" for attracting the ugliest federal agent in the valley. In fact, I was the only federal agent working that day in the Northern Sacramento Valley. The rest of my fellow officers were getting ready for court. How is that for the odds against ever getting caught? Even more so, slowing down or stopping the illegal slaughter of wildlife?

Paddling away from that blind with my Grumman load of dead teal, I turned back towards Bob Stack's duck club. While at my teal shooter's blind, I had heard the occasional shot coming from that area. Perhaps someone had come to shoot on that club after all. Paddling back towards that area, I heard two more shots from two different guns, then nothing. Putting on my "sneak" mode, Dog and I quietly paddled our ways through the plant cover towards Stack's club. Rounding a brushy turn, I slammed my paddle deeper into the water to stop my forward progress. Then a quick paddle backwards hid me and the Grumman behind a large brush pile and copse of young cottonwoods.

To my front about forty yards distant was a small canoe. In it were two, obvious from their garb, duck hunters. They were in the progress of picking up a dead duck and I grabbed my binoculars for a closer look. Neither duck hunter appeared to be the type of hunter found on the wealthy Butte Sink duck clubs. Both men were bearded, looked a bit ragged, in need of a meal, and their small canoe had certainly seen better days. I suspected both men were trespassers and hunting in a "catch as catch can" mode. Since folks like that were usually good bets for game violations, I held my ground and just watched.

Then the goofiest damn thing I had seen in a long time happened. The man in the stern of their canoe grabbed some nearby bushes and held on for all he was worth. The chap in the bow stood up in the canoe and looked carefully all around.

Then without a moment's hesitation brought on by an internal emergency, he dropped his chest-high waders, jeans, and underpants down around his ankles! Through my binoculars, the man was so scrawny he looked like a plucked and hairy turkey vulture. Then he very carefully hoisted his last part over the fence over the side of their very unsteady, narrow-beamed canoe.

At that point, I was beginning to laugh silently to myself. It was obvious the man had a serious problem! Why else would one drop his britches and everything else in front of God, the ducks, geese, and muskrats, and then hump his hind-end over the side of a very tippy canoe. He had to be in severe distress and, clear over to where I sat out of sight, I could hear why.

At first I heard the most God-awful sounds coming from the man hanging his hind-end over the side of the canoe. It had to be gas of the worst magnitude. Then came what was bothering the man's insides. And I do mean "came!" The water shot into the air under his bare bottom as what was bothering the man's insides came forth into our world. And it wasn't pretty! The volume of sound and liquid material from the man in obvious pain over his last night's banquet was more than just a bouquet of smells.

By now, the man in the stern of the boat was gagging and laughing all at the same time. Our bow man continued blessing the world by blowing out his liver, gizzard, and maybe even his lips for all I knew. I was silently laughing so hard that I had to put down my binoculars and let my worried dog know through a series of head- petting strokes that I was alright...

Then it really happened! The stern man was laughing so hard that he let go of the bushes he was holding onto to steady the canoe. When he did, the canoe quickly rolled clean over in a flash! When that unfortunate event happened, I lost it. I was now kneeling in the bottom of my Grumman laughing like all get-out! Hell, even the dead ducks collected in the bottom of my Grumman were laughing. You talk about a raw Laurel and Hardy comic moment. Sure as God made pissants, below me in the area of the other canoe one hell of an event was in the making.

Then realizing their danger, especially in the cold water, I got back up onto my seat and began paddling furiously towards my two now-floundering men by the overturned canoe. As I got closer, I saw dozens of dead and floating ducks that had been dumped out when their canoe had overturned. Damn, Terry, I thought, in addition to the swim they are now taking, these lads have what appears to be an over limit to boot. Then I realized my two lads were now standing in neck-deep water trying to right their canoe. The water they were in was only about five-and-a-half feet deep so there was no danger of them drowning at that juncture. But there was that other "danger." Both men were in an oily, smelly, greenish slick that sure as hell didn't come from a blow-out on a nearby oil well. Maybe from an intestinal "blow-out," but not an oil slick...

Slowing, I moved over to my two lads just as they got their canoe righted and had crawled back into it. Both men looked like a couple of storm-soaked muskrats from their little ordeal. Around them floated two paddles, thermoses, several duck decoys, and a boatload of dead ducks.

Being careful to avoid the "green slick" in the water near their canoe, I identified myself. Then without a word, I began picking up the dead ducks until they numbered twenty lying in the bottom of my boat! By now, my lad who had looked like a plucked turkey vulture as he hung his backside over the side of the canoe had his chest-highs pulled up and did he ever present a sorry sight! He was totally covered with something "green" that smelled pretty putrid. As for his partner, he wasn't much better off. Both looked like drowned muskrats and smelled like spotted skunks!

As they bailed out their canoe with an old coffee can, I gave them the bad news. "Boys, if all these ducks are yours, you have a few too many,"

I said, barely able to suppress my laughter over how the two looked...and...smelled. By now, they had bailed out their canoe to where it would float without any difficulty, but as for the green color on its insides and covering their seats, well, they had a ways to go in order to be featured in any Fourth of July Parade...

Then it dawned on my two lads. Their two shotguns were gone! When the canoe had rolled over, the guns had flipped out and gone to the bottom. Soon both men had stripped naked (remember, this is December), and were diving for their shotguns. One, an old J. C. Higgins pump was found, but alas, the other could not be located. And by then with all the cold and the green smelly oily substance in the water, both were far from eager to return to the Butte Sink's "water world."

Realizing these lads had best get back to their vehicle and warm up, I added more grief to their misery. "Lads, I need your hunting and driver's licenses, if you please. Both of you are in possession of over limits of ducks and, as such, will be receiving citations for those violations."

At that point, I doubted if either man cared if they were cited or not. Both men were shaking like dogs passing peach pits from the cold and wet trips they had taken and just wanted to get my business over with so they could head for home.

Being careful when I handled their licenses so as not to come away smelling like that bedraggled pair, I got my paperwork done. Then giving them an evidence tag for their ducks, I bid my pair good-bye. Hell, I didn't even have the gall to give the lads a state citation for trespassing. I figured they had enough of the outdoor world so why heap more misery on their collective heads. But, boy, did they make a pair as they paddled their way out of the Butte Sink. One chap was wearing chest highs waders that were still oily green-in-color on the outside and inside. The man in the stern, well, he was just plain damn smelly.

When I got up to the Sacramento National Wildlife Refuge later in that day to clean my seized ducks and put them in the freezer, they all had a distinct non-duck smell. In fact every time I opened my freezers after that incident, I gathered in a slight smell of rotting human insides. I don't know what that guy had been eating, but I sure could tell why his body was trying so hard to expel it. I guess that was one time when a chap went to take a "dump" in more than one way of speaking.

"QUICK, HIDE IN THE BLACKBERRY BUSHES!"

Driving the last mile of a muddy farm road without lights in the pre-dawn, I finally arrived to where I wanted to park my patrol vehicle.

Turning, I said to Deputy Sheriff Glenn Ragon, "Well, Partner, here we are. A half-mile walk across that harvested sunflower field to our south, and we will be at the back side of the duck club we need to work. Once there, we can change into our chest-high waders, cross the canal-like moat surrounding the flooded duck club, and then the work begins. Just for your information, the duck club owner has planted the sides of the berm around his club with stinging nettle. It is rumored that he does so to discourage game wardens from creeping onto his duck club. The last time I was here with Warden Buck Del Nero those stinging damn plants were about four feet high. So we need to be careful with our eyes when walking through them. To do so, I suggest we put on our heavy hunting coats, put our hoods up, and glove our hands. When walking up the berm onto the club after we have waded the moat, we need to keep our heads down as we plow through the nettles. Surrounding the top of the berm running around the external boundaries of the duck club is nothing but a continuous ring of dense blackberry bushes. Once in those damn things, we will have to be careful so we don't hole our chest-high waders with their thorns when we are trying to hide in them," I continued.

"Why do I allow myself to be dragged into these kinds of adventures with you?" said Glenn with a bit of eager anticipation registering in his voice over the morning's potential of "catching-a-mess-of-bad-guys" events.

"Ah, because you love it and you know it. Just think, if you were still back in Colusa County on your vacation you would be hunting ducks and having a grand time. This way you can get rained on, cussed out by those 'hombres' we catch with too many ducks, stung all to hell with the stinging nettle, poked with blackberry thorns, and then we turn around tomorrow and do it all over again somewhere else," I said with an easy laugh.

Glenn was a Humboldt County Sheriff's Deputy that I had met in 1966 as a rookie game warden. He was a little ol' short, fireplug-sized son-of-a-gun who was tougher than horseshoe nails. He had been a Navy diver during World War II and had seen many things he never cared much to talk about. In his early years after the war, he had been a logger in the redwood forests and later a commercial salmon, halibut and Dungeness crab fisherman off the north coast of California. To be quite frank, Glenn had been a bit of an outlaw in those early days and now he was nothing short of a fierce warrior for all things conservation-related. In fact, I used to tease him all the time that he was now doing penance for all the earlier wildlife wrongs he had committed as a younger man... Come to think of it, I was kind of in the same boat. As a youngster growing up and being raised without a dad, I had taken to the world of hunting and fishing. I did so partly out of necessity because with just a now divorced mother trying to make ends meet, we found ourselves short rations many a day. Knowing that and always hungry as a kid, I made sure my mother had lots of pink-meated trout and mountain quail (her favorites) to grace the table. If that meant over limits of trout or closed season quail, so be it. Never did I ever realize that the Old Boy upstairs would get my services back in spades for the resource wrongs I committed in my earlier days. Who says He is not all knowing and seeing?

Being that Glenn was a peace officer for the State of California, I always made use of his legal talents when he was on a hunting vacation near my home in Colusa. That went especially double with helping me chasing wildlife outlaws in the Sacramento and San Joaquin Valleys. He was damned good at what he did, never flagged, and was always there for me when the going got tough or dangerous. It always seemed that when we were working together, the bad guys and the evil things they were doing flocked to our presence and within our "kill zone." And when they did, "Christmas came early" that year for those walking on the "dark side." Especially to those who had trouble in the resources illegal taking, possessing, and counting departments when it came to Mother Nature's pantry...

I just talked to Glenn two days ago as these words are written. He is now over ninety years old, and all the hard years he had during his early life are coming home to roost. His beloved wife of over 65 years has recently passed, and just last week, the doctors sent Glenn home because they could do no more for him. His valiant warrior's heart is on a downhill slide and the end is near. However in that recent telephonic discussion, he said he is ready. He told me he now says his prayers every night like he used to when he was just a small child. Only this time, he is now asking the Good Lord to take him for he has nothing further to live for and is so tired... I sit here crying as I write these words because, Lord, Glenn is a warrior and dear friend. One now with a bowed head and a broken body which he "earned" while helping to build this great country of ours. When it is his time, Lord, please put him in a marsh full of ducks so he can hunt his beloved waterfowl one more time. And when you turn out the lights forever in this warrior's eyes, Lord, please forgive him for his sins and let him rest in peace, all the while understanding the wisdom of Your ways. Damn, as I sit here, it is sure not enjoyable being one of the last in a long line of friends and now, as of late, family...

But for now on that cold winter day so long ago, we had work to do otherwise the ducks and geese would pay the price. Trudging our ways across that muddy harvested sunflower field, we constantly stumbled and labored as the woody plant stalks tangled in our feet in the darkness. Finally arriving at the berm surrounding the backside of the duck club of choice that morning, we rested. As we did, we could hear thousands of "happy voices" of the waterfowl world on the other side of the berm happily feeding in the standing and flooded unharvested corn and "discussing" the day's events in their lives yet to come...

"Well, we won't have to worry about the birds showing up for today's shoot," I said as I struggled into my cold chest-high waders. Glenn just grunted as he stood up in his chest-highs and pulled the straps tightly up over his shoulders.

"Let's hide our walking boots here in this clump of grass," I said. Together we shoved our footwear under the tall grasses so they wouldn't be discovered and removed by the Mexican laborers walking the outside of the duck club boundary looking for wildlife officers. A routine they regularly followed at the owner's insistence anytime he or his cronies shot over their duck club. Note I didn't say "hunted" because that denotes fair chase, and "fair chase" was not on the menu for the chaps Glenn and yours truly now hunted that fair morning so long ago.

Mexican farmhands were just the last level of "protective" barriers the crooked duck club owner placed in the ways of wildlife officers on the prowl. First was the deep canal circling the exterior of the duck club proper. That moat was about twenty feet wide and plenty deep. In fact, it was all Glenn could do, short-legged as he was, to get across without the cold wintery waters flooding down inside the front of his chest-high waders. Once on the other side came the stinging nettle. The duck club owner had gotten a good crop to grow all along the steep sides of the berm surrounding his flooded shooting area that year. Shrouding our bare skins as best as we could, the two of us crawled up the steep bank leading to the duck club's flooded shooting area. Arriving at the top of the berm, the two of us rubbed those burning places we had not covered well enough to avoid the stinging glass-like hairs from the troublesome stinging nettle plants.

To our front in the pre-dawn dark lay a dirt road running all around the top of the berm encircling the flooded unharvested corn. That road that was regularly patrolled as a final protective measure by the owner's Mexican farm laborers looking for any sign of concealed wildlife officers or their footprints left in the soft mud. If discovered, each of the Mexicans carrying a single-shot twenty-gauge shotgun had been instructed to fire one shot into the air announcing to the club's shooters the presence of wildlife officers. That early warning would then give the club's shooters time to stomp their extra ducks into the mud, plug their shotguns, or sprint for their nearby hidden jeeps to convey the ducks to the clubhouse to hide them in its cavernous insides before we could make contact. Make contact and "do unto them as they had done to the ducks and geese" as the "Good Book" says to do...

Looking into the shooting area proper, it was a shooter's paradise. The duck club was nothing more than a man-made berm surrounding a twenty-acre flooded cornfield. Into the standing corn before it had been flooded, a harvester had cut out boat paths and areas in which to place the decoy spreads around sunken battery blinds. Then the rest of the corn had been left standing for the ducks (legal under the baiting laws of the day) and flooded to such a depth that all a duck had to do was swim to a hanging cob of corn and feast. And let me tell you, there had to be ten thousand ducks and geese there that morning helping themselves to the free-breakfast "corn buffet!"

Looking all around in the dark with my binoculars, I was satisfied that no one had witnessed our arrival. Walking in, Glenn and I were careful to avoid the dew-covered grass alongside the berm's muddy road (when walking in the silvery wet grasses, one will leave a dark green trail where he has knocked off all the dew from the wet grass. Any driver arriving in the dark driving with headlights will be watching the road so he does not have a wreck and provides his guests the smoothest ride possible. In so doing, he will spot your dark green walking trails in the silvery wet grasses if you aren't careful. Damn, there I go again, giving away another trick of the trade...). Instead of walking in the dew-laden grasses, Glenn and I walked at the edge of the blackberry bush barrier alongside the top of the berm running beside the road. That way, any "giveaway" footprints we left were outside the "seeing" field of the headlights when the shooters drove into the club during the early morning hours.

Knowing the location of the club's favorite and most heavily utilized sunken duck blind from past experience, we walked out into the shooting area. Looking again with my binoculars, I spotted where the club members hid their military jeeps in a living stand of bamboo behind the sunken blind of that day's interest. Then sweeping my glasses deeper into the watered area, I located the nine- place capacity, sunken duck blind. It was a totally enclosed concrete tub large enough to accommodate nine shooters and sunken to the flooded waterline of the duck pond. There the shooters could sit in comfort remaining out of the weather and keeping dry. When the ducks flew into the shooter's decoys, the hidden from view by ducking down (no pun intended) in the sunken-pit-blind shooters would rise up and shoot the hell out of the unsuspecting flocks when they were within range. A serious killing of the unsuspecting flock would then occur in the blink of an eye and in a deadly stream of lead shot (the use of lead shot was legal in those days-today it is banned in favor of non-toxic steel shot).

Now it was our turn to hide and set up our ambush. Slowly walking along the dense line of blackberry bushes, I took out my Buck Knife. Careful to avoid cleaning out too obvious a hiding spot but making sure we could still see the action, I removed several long branches of the thorny cover. Ten minutes of like work produced a hole in the bushes large enough to hold two men who would be laying down in hiding. Finally satisfied with my little hiding place, I crawled back into the bushes for a final test. Still being a little too small to comfortably hide both Glenn and me, I cut some more limbs from the interior of the blackberry patch. Finally it was large enough for Glenn and me to look right into the nine-member battery blind without being seen by our targeted shooters or their Mexican "guards." Taking the branches from my inside cut-outs, I planned on placing them across the opening of our hiding place when we were concealed within so everything would look natural to the casual eye.

Standing out near the road and looking from that point into our hiding place, I figured it would have to do. We suspected the Mexican farmhands would soon be walking the berm's road looking for such fellows and what the two of us represented. So off the berm and out of sight we went into our blackberry hide out. Then our covering bushes were laid across the small entrance hole and the two of us were ready for action.

By pulling back into the blackberry bushes and lying still in our camouflage hunting gear, we should be able to pass muster and not be seen, I thought. When the danger from early detection by the Mexicans had passed (they left when the shooting started so they wouldn't flare off the returning birds), we could move forward to the very edge of our blackberry patch. There we could still remain out of sight and continue looking right at our suspect illegal gunners as we gathered the data needed for a subsequent court of law.

I say "illegal gunners" because the club belonged to a former California Fish and Game Commissioner who had a reputation for being an outlaw and a first-class "game hog." That reputation included many of the "friends" that chap brought to his club for their illegal shoots as well. Warden Buck Del Nero and I had caught the man once earlier trying to set up an illegally baited dove field shoot and had stopped him in his tracks. That made me an enemy of his for life as I was later to discover (he tried to have me transferred to another duty station after that little run-in). Then later, Tim Dennis (my deputy U.S. Game Management Agent) and I had caught him and his illegal bunch of attorneys and bankers in Modoc County with a hat full of illegal deer on his private Snowstorm Ranch hunting area. That little measure finally cost the political crook his position as a powerful California Fish and Game Commissioner. But my readers will have to read that story in my book, *For Love Of Wildness*, Chapter 7, "Snow Storm Mountain," to see how I put that little detail together and put the Commissioner to "bed" once and all. It is a great read and has many twists and turns before the lawless were run to ground.

Kneeling there in our hiding spot in the early morning's darkness, Glenn and I reveled in the sounds the feathered world of wildlife was making in the flooded cornfield. It was so full of ducks that I doubted you could have stuffed one more into that duck and goose "soup" in the cornfield! As I knelt there enjoying Mother Nature during one of her better days, I couldn't help thinking that what I was experiencing was a tribute to those hard working wildlife officers who had come before me... Many who had since passed over The Great Divide. Officers who were bent, stooped, broken but never bowed, all carrying the gleam of the chase of their fellow man in their eyes, until the good Lord finally "turned" out their lights...

Then bouncing crazily from the direction of the clubhouse, I saw three sets of headlights coming our way on the muddy farm road. "Quick, Glenn, hide further back in the blackberry bushes!" I said. Realizing it was "show time," Glenn carefully slid further into our blackberry patch hole to avoid tearing his chest-high waders. I soon followed. After the two of us had earlier moved up into the small opening in the mouth of the blackberry patch so we could both see the action to follow, I moved the last of the covering bushes cut from inside across in front of us to cover the opening. Now they did their "work" as we successfully hid from prying eyes.

Lying there in the cool morning's darkness, I moved my binoculars and notebook up into a ready-for-action position and then immediately froze! Quietly standing there directly in front of us in the pre-dawn dark was the figure of a human being! Damn, I thought. It was a good thing we had moved into the blackberries when we did. No more than four feet away, stood a Mexican farm laborer looking for any of us "game warden-types." Just as silently as he had arrived, he moved off into the darkness continuing his vigil for more of "our" type further down the berm's levee.

Finally the three military type jeeps carrying the shooters for the sunken blind arrived at their parking spot in the stand of bamboo behind the blind. As they did, they put to flight every duck and goose on the watered duck club area with their flashing headlights. Man, you talk about a roar of wings. The din was unbelievable! Ordinarily, one would not have driven right up to where they wanted to shoot with all their headlights flashing and the like. However, this was a very ultra-private duck club, the only one for a ways around, and beautifully loaded with water and standing corn for the critters' delight. So moving all the birds off the area for the moment was really no big deal. Because within a few moments after our gunners' arrival, the hungry flocks of previously disturbed birds began arriving back at the club announcing their presence with a host of calls and close-at-hand whistling wings. Soon the watered area was once again a host for thousands of noisy ducks and geese "discussing the day's stock market returns and the price of crowbars in Korea."

Glassing the parking area, I clearly observed nine chaps disembarking from the three jeeps. Then a long darkened string of gunners began walking out on the small levee walkway towards the sunken blind. That is, all except one chap. He stood by the parked jeeps for a moment and then began walking around the levee road towards our hiding place. It was still pretty dark so I advised Glenn of our oncoming visitor and the two of us quietly slid back slightly deeper into our blackberry bushes. Without giving it much thought, I just figured our visitor was probably nothing more than another Mexican farmhand walking the outside perimeter of the duck club looking for the likes of Glenn and me before the hunt began in earnest.

However, that was not to be! Our lone chap kept walking right towards our position like he knew we were there! Realizing he was getting closer and now walking close at hand along the line of blackberry bushes, I whispered for Glenn to move quietly even further back into the cover of our bushes. Pulling our camouflage hoods over our heads, out from the corner of my eyes I watched with increasing alarm our lad still coming our way. It was as if he was on a string leading right to our spot! Within moments, he was just feet from where we silently lay with loudly beating hearts!

Finally in the pre-dawn dark, our oncoming man stopped directly in front of our hiding spot. And I do mean directly in front of the opening of blackberry bushes behind which we quietly lay! Then turning, our lad looked back at the duck blind in which his friends were filing into with loud laughter and the flashing of flashlights as they again spooked off many ducks and geese from the shooting area.

Then the "crap," in a manner of speaking, hit the fan! Our lad took off his hunting coat and laid it not two feet from my right shoulder. Then he dropped his chest-high waders, jeans, and underpants right smack dab in front of our opening into the blackberry bushes. He was so close to Glenn that I could hear Glenn quietly trying to slide even further back into the blackberries to avoid what was coming next! Then, as if the man was not close enough to our position, he moved his "too damn close-at-hand behind" back a couple of more inches, careful to avoid the blackberry thorns. He was so close that I could have reached out and grabbed his damn hind-end if I was of a mind... Of course to do so, even what an enjoyable surprise it would have been to do, would probably have given our lad a massive heart attack.

Then I knew Glenn and yours truly were in for a long day. The man's hind-end was so close to the two of us chaps hiding in the bushes that we could hear his growling insides as he bent over! It was obvious from the noisy revolt from his suffering intestines that what he had eaten the evening before was something he should not have done. Then the rushing sounds of tremendous gas under extreme pressure foretold of even worse things to come as I struggled quietly to move even further back into the blackberries. However, that was to no avail. Both of my feet were smack dab against several blackberry bush stems and they weren't moving. And, neither was yours truly or the hind-end directly in front of my face!

Then the area not two feet from our heads blew up! The most God-awful sounds preceded a horrific telling rumbling of the man's guts. That was followed by an explosion of yesterday's food ungratefully received earlier by the man's innards. *Pleeuh!* went the most threatening sound followed by the gushing of a semi-liquid of what had to be the most evil-smelling, almost dead-like, July-heat-spoiled California gray whale guts that one ever endured from just two feet distant! In fact, my partially up raised arm was so close to his offending hind end that I could hear splattering sounds against my hunting coat!

That was followed by the man's loud verbal sounds of grateful release of pain, sounds that no one should ever endure if that fellow's great sigh of relief meant anything. By now, the semi-liquid material emanating from the chap to our front was increasing in volume and force. Then came the most God-awful smells and violent flow of warm air one ever had to endure at such close quarters as it enveloped Glenn and me like mustard gas on the Western Front during the First World War!

By now, both Glenn and I were quietly pushing back hard into the blackberries, thorn-torn boots or not! All was to no avail as those damn bushes held us captive to a very disagreeable moment in time from the "mouth of the volcano," if you get my drift (no pun intended). Damn, I was now silently dry heaving as was Glenn. On top of that, the explosion from that man's intestines had a forceful fall-out range of about three feet! That was not good if one was only two feet distant as Glenn and I were...

Then, as if Glenn and I had pissed God off something awful, the man's forceful expression of relief intensified! For the next few moments, both Glenn and I benefitted from the man's exuberance at getting rid of the dead rotten whale innards he must have eaten from the evening before. Damn, I thought, will this never end? And it didn't! Finishing with expelling the worst of it was followed with a ton of pent-up gasses and a stream of urine which ran directly into where Glenn and I were lying!

It was at that point that if I had any matches, I would have lit one and blown that chap and his evil hind-end clear across that damn duck pond! Enough was enough! I could only hope that if the fellow with the glorious hind-end shot an over limit of ducks later, it would be a big one. Because if he did, I would try to have his fine be raised to one million dollars if I could for what he made those of us hiding in the blackberry bushes endure...

Finally, the man could find no more "liquid" indignity to heap on our two hidden carcasses. With that, he gratefully stood up. When he did, that movement must have loosened some more of what he had eaten the evening before, and he quickly assumed the stance right back in front of the two of us. Once again, we suffered the indignity of having small bits of warm smelly items splashed on our hands, faces, and heads. Again, that was followed with more "gaseous perfume" and finding me wishing for an open flame of some sort, like a bolt of lightning!

Finally our chap finished his business and stood up. He commenced pulling up huge clumps of wet grasses and wiping off his last part over the fence. Then, as if he had not done enough to the two chaps still lying hidden there behind him trying not to openly gag and give away our position, he tossed the soiled grasses back into the blackberries. Blackberries, hell—the soiled grasses landed on both the heads of Glenn and yours truly. Man, I am here to tell you. If the law allowed each of us to just kill one person in our lives without fear of prosecution, that chap taking the "dump" in front of us that fine morning would be pushing up daisies today...

Finally our ordeal was over, or almost. Our chap left and rejoined his buddies back at the sunken duck blind. As for the two hidden "beautifully smelling law dogs," we were relegated to our berry patch and all the wonderful smells emanating from therein. To make matters worse, we had to crawl forward directly into the pile of sprayed poo so we could get an accurate count on the ducks killed by our nine shooters! Thank God our hunting coats were waterproof...

Fortunately, our nine lads had a field day. They shot the hell out of every flock of ducks and geese that drifted into their decoys. There was one such "party-shoot" where I counted 31 ducks dropping out of one flock from their nine unplugged shotgun barrages at one time!

Having a gut full of their lawlessness and tired of lying in another man's poo, Glenn and

I arose from our place of hiding with the goods on our shooters and made our presence known. Walking hurriedly towards our nine gunners along the levee road, both Glenn and I had a chance to assess our personal situations. Both of us had been fairly well splattered by the man's earlier violently spewed essence. Glenn had greenish-brown spots all over his face and head and so did I. Both of our arms and hands also had suspicious unnatural-looking spots dotting them that had a distinct perfume as well. However, we didn't have any time to clean up as we headed for our shooters before they hid or stomped their over limits of ducks (drove their unwanted ducks with their feet into the gooey mud in the bottom of the duck pond), or plugged their shotguns.

Arriving at the sunken shooting pit, I made our identification known. Taking a quick look at our shooters, I was disappointed that my "favorite" fish and game commissioner was not among the guilty. But there were several other less-notable Italian killers I personally knew from previous run-ins and for that I was thankful. Before all was said and done, Glenn and I had netted nine shooters with unplugged shotguns, three with no federal duck stamps, and the nine of them with taking and possessing over limits of ducks and white-fronted geese, to wit, 39 ducks and 13 geese over the daily bag limit (daily bag limits in

California in those days were eight ducks and up to six geese in the aggregate). We also garnered lots of complaints from our nine shooters about how badly the two of us smelled as we did the paperwork...

It took Glenn and me most of the rest of the day to pack out all our evidence birds of 111 ducks and 40 geese (our shooters lost all their birds because the total number comprised the gross over limit and had been taken with unplugged shotguns) and gut the same. Tossing our evidence birds across the moat surrounding the duck club several hours later, the two us stopped mid-canal and washed off as best as we could. Then changing back into our walking boots, we made several half a mile trips hauling the seized birds back to my truck. We did that because the ground was too muddy to drive the truck out to our stash of evidence birds.

We then headed to a restaurant where I bought Glenn a well-deserved meal. However, even sitting off to one side in the eatery, we both noticed that a lot of people kept looking our way as if they were smelling something unpleasant... On the other hand, maybe it was my stunning good looks and beautiful physique they were looking at, eh?

Heading home later that day, I dropped Glenn off at his trailer at the Richmond Hunting Club in Colusa so he could continue his vacation and belated duck hunting. Then I ran all my evidence birds over to Angelo Jaconetti's commercial picking facility for picking and packaging for later distribution to the needy in Colusa and Sacramento Counties.

Angelo, too, gave me a lot of dumb looks and then finally said, "Damn, Terry. Where did you get these birds? From a sewer pond?" I explained to Angelo about the incident on the duck club in the Stockton area and he nearly broke a gut laughing. That wasn't the bad part though. When I got home, my bride took one whiff of me and made me undress bare naked in the cold damn garage and go straight to the shower upon entering my home. Then, it really got bad. For the next couple of days when I met any of my sheriff's deputy lads, they all held their noses and had a good laugh at my expense. It seemed Angelo had shared my latest set of travails with my deputy sheriff friends. Piling into my waders a week later, I discovered a familiar smell. Upon closer examination, I discovered a large greenish-brown smear on the insides of my chest-high waders from my Stockton trip. I never was able to completely get that smell out from my boots, especially on a warm day when I was sweating profusely. I don't know what that chap ate to produce such a by-product, but I am still convinced it had to be grits from a dead whale. And if any of you have ever smelled a dead bloated whale lying on a beach in the hot sun, you know about what I am saying...

I have been shot at numerous times but only "dumped" on once. I think the next time such an occasion arises, if it is as bad as that one was, I would just as soon as take a bullet...

"DID YOU FALL IN, SIR?"

Eating one of my rare dinners with my family during duck season in November, my phone rang. My beautiful blue-eyed bride just looked at me from across the dinner table. She had that look that said, "You might as well as answer it. It will be for you anyway."

Grinning at her antics, I got up from the table and answered the phone. "Terry here," I said.

"The Bell Outing Duck Club has a couple of guys from a San Francisco drywall company who come up every Wednesday and are taking large over limits of ducks. The area near Blind Number 4 is baited and that is the one they always shoot," said a voice that was intentionally disguised. Then I heard a loud click as the conversation ended and the line went dead.

Having been there before when someone had called and didn't want to be identified, I hung up the phone. As I headed back to the dinner table, my mind was already trying to figure out how to "put this one together." I was not able to identify the voice, but I figured it had to be from a disgruntled duck club gamekeeper on San Jose Road near the violating club in question. Since the old Bell Outing Duck Club was located on the eastern side of San Jose Road in Section 8, the voice had to be a gamekeeper from that immediate area, to my way of thinking. A gamekeeper who had noticed numerous flocks of ducks going to the Bell Outing Duck Club instead of his own and, upon hearing all the shooting, probably deduced the area was baited. Baited means somewhere on that duck club there would be a load of food grains placed to act as a lure or attractant to any over-flying ducks in the area. It being November, the ducks and geese were somewhat gun-shy because they had been shot at for several weeks since the beginning of hunting season and were now suspicious of every decoy set they over-flew. So in order to lower the over-flying birds' caution, one had to illegally place some food near one's decoys in order to lure the gun-shy waterfowl into gunning range. And, the airborne critters were running out of feed by late winter. They had been in the Northern Sacramento Valley since August and shortly after that they were wintering in the valley by the millions. With those numbers of hungry waterfowl, it didn't take long for them to gobble up all the accessible rice grains left in the fields after the harvest.

So in order to lure the now getting hungrier waterfowl to the gun, unscrupulous shooters would "sweeten the pot" or put out convenient food (bait) for the critters. When one club did that, it caused the other nearby duck clubs' kills to drop off because all the ducks were being lured away from them to the one doing the baiting. From my past experience working in the Sacramento Valley, when that happened (less ducks on their club to kill because they were next door to a baited duck club), the duck club members would complain to their gamekeeper. He, in turn, would either follow suit with the placement of bait to increase his sports" chances of killing more ducks or he would disguise his voice and "rat out" the offending club to the local game warden or federal agent. So, I suspected that was why I got my anonymous phone call that evening.

Returning to the table, I forked some more mashed potatoes onto my plate and liberally coated them with some of my bride's delicious homemade chicken gravy. You know, the kind of thick gravy with loads of chicken drippings in it. Damn, that woman could cook, and my girth spoke plainly to that fact! Then on went a very generous amount of pepper and salt. I did all of that avoiding what I knew to be my bride's stare from across the table wanting to know, "What's on your plate now, other than mashed potatoes and gravy, Mr. Game Management Agent?"

Finally looking her way with a "I know when I am caught look," sure as God made cabbage worms, her intense stare looking at me said it all. She knew her man and figured I was off on another "damn-fool" adventure. Being always the cautious type, she just wanted an explanation as to what had just transpired and where I was off to this time and under what damn foolish and sometimes dangerous circumstances.

"That call was from an unidentified informant advising me he suspected the old Bell Outing Duck Club is using bait," I said through an "I am caught" grin and a mouthful of wonderfully tasting food. Continuing, I said, "That is the second bit of information I have had from that area on duck clubs being baited. The other one allegedly being baited is that one owned by Tennessee Ernie Ford."

"Am I supposed to guess where that duck club is or are you going to tell me?" she asked.

Damn, how I loved that woman then and even more so to this day, if that is possible. She knew I had been trained and hardened in conservation law enforcement with several years of work experience under my belt. She also knew I was a crack shot with my .44 magnum pistol that I always carried and could stop a mule with my fist and one of my right crosses if necessary. However, that still didn't stop her from worrying about her fella. Getting up from the table, I walked over to where she sat, bodily lifted her small frame up from her chair, and kissed her.

"Kiss her again, Dad," said Richard, my older son. So before Donna could say anything, I kissed her again.

"Kiss her again," said Chris, my younger son, so once again I obliged my boys.

That was when I got a swat from my bride for being such a knothead at the dinner table, much to the glee of my two small sons at seeing their rather larger dad being put on the run by a decidedly smaller but very determined mom.

Sitting back down at the table with a grin I said in a manner meant to calm my bride's concerns, "The Bell Outing Duck Club is on the northeast end of San Jose Road. I haven't had any trouble from those folks this year, but that doesn't mean they won't stray across the line now and then if given the chance and a fair opportunity at killing. They supposedly are using bait and if they are, that will also mean over limits as well, if they have their druthers. The 'voice' identified several chaps from San Francisco as the culprits and advised they are only there on Wednesdays. So this next Wednesday I will be there as well to light a fire under them if they have chosen to break the law. As far as Ford's club is concerned, it is in that same area and on my 'to-do menu'."

The next day being a non-shoot day in the Northern Sacramento Valley (most clubs only shot on Wednesdays, Saturdays, Sundays, and holidays so as not to burn out the ducks on their particular shooting areas), I scouted out the Bell Outing Duck Club. I did this by driving down the San Jose Road around three in the morning so I would not to draw any unwanted attention from the other nearby duck clubs to the fact that I was incountry. Knowing the Bell Outing Duck Club did not have any gamekeeper, I drove right into the unoccupied parking area at the clubhouse and parked. As suspected, no one was there which gave me free rein to "root around," if you will.

First I checked the area around their small boat dock. Nothing there caught my eye that was out of the ordinary. However, looking into their boats tied up at their flimsy dock sure as hell set off the alarm bells. Checking out the bottoms of the three duck club boats, I discovered fresh barley grains on the floorboards of one of them. That was always a good place to look because one using a boat to bait an area will usually inadvertently spill some grains of bait in the bottom of the boat being used so I continued looking. I located several grain sacks stored at the end of the boathouse with the same kind of grain in the bottom of the sacks that I had found in the boat. That was good enough for me, I thought, as I crawled back into my truck and drove back down San Jose Road without using any headlights to avoid detection.

Later that afternoon, I paddled my Grumman down the 2047 Canal until I arrived on the back side of the Bell Outing Duck Club. Lying on the levee bank, I got out my binoculars and took a look at all the duck blinds on the property. On one of the blinds known to me as Blind No. 4, the decoy area was alive with Northern pintail, mallards, and a pile of American wigeon. The decoy sets and the watered areas of the other blinds were basically empty of ducks.

Grabbing my binoculars, bait scoop, and a couple of plastic evidence bags for any bait recovered, Dog and I began walking across the landed area on the back side of the club. Once on the duck club proper, I walked over to Blind No. 4 and, after glassing all around to make sure no one was looking, walked out into the pond area and began dragging my bait scoop in the decoy set. (I usually made my first bait drags in the immediate area of the decoys. Many folks who use bait, as history has shown, will do so in the immediate area of the decoy set. Also, laying on the 2047 canal bank, I had spotted Blind No. 4's decoys were full of live birds. So, common sense said that was a good place to start. Plus, most decoy sets are placed in the optimum range of a shotgun's shot stream or pattern, i.e., close at hand. That was another good reason why I always started looking in the area of the decoys for bait because that is the range most shooters felt comfortable shooting at the birds. So, why not place the bait within easy gun range?).

After thirty minutes, I had found nothing in the way of bait. It was apparent that if the area had been baited, it had been cleverly done. That is, not much bait had been placed and that which was would be consumed by the time the lads shot that particular blind the following shoot day. That way the outlaw's theory was that ducks would continue coming to the baited area looking for free grits and the shooting would still be good even without any illegal evidence of bait. Also, if an officer came along and used his bait scoop suspecting a baited area, he would find none because the ducks had eaten all of it up prior to his arrival. However, I had another trick of the trade learned over the years up my sleeve. The bottom of a pond is usually muddy and gooey. But that is not always the case in many baited areas. When ducks feed in a muddy area, they will pound the muddy bottom with their bills as they pick up the bait. After a short while, the ducks will pound the mud into a semi-hard bottom. A clever officer who has worked bait before will be aware of this consistency change and will notice that the bottom is harder in the area where the bait has been placed as he shuffles his feet along the bottom of the pond. Even if there is no bait there at the time, the semi-hard bottom will be a dead giveaway to an experienced officer that bait is an issue in the immediate area.

With all the above, it quickly became pretty obvious I was pitted against a couple of pros when it came to the use of bait. But that is ok with me, I thought. The "bear" (that's me) was already in the area and win, lose or draw, I would bet he would come away with someone's miserable carcass before the day was done. After all, some days you eat the bear and some days he eats you... And before that fine day was done, Good Lord a-willin', the bear would "eat" way more than his share as I was soon to discover.

Late Tuesday around midnight, I once again drove north on the San Jose Road without using any headlights. All the duck clubs along that way were darkened as was the one of my intentions. Stopping below the Bell Outing Duck Club, I walked the last one hundred yards into the clubhouse area. It, too, was dark as the inside of a dead cow and there was only one car parked in the parking lot.

Then I quietly slipped over to the duck club's hanging facility for a look-see.

To you unwashed readers, a "hanging facility" is just that. Usually it is a screened-in facility used to hang freshly gutted ducks taken by the club's members. That way, the cool fall or winter air can freely circulate within the facility cooling out the ducks and geese, and the flies cannot get in to lay their eggs on the meat. There were no ducks hanging that evening as a result of the chaps from the one car in the parking lot not having had a shoot when they had arrived earlier. Satisfied, I hotfooted it back to my truck and got out of the area before I was discovered.

By four the next morning, I had dragged my Grumman from the 2047 Canal over to an area where I could intercept any boat and shooters hunting Blind No. 4. Then hiding my boat under my camouflage parachute so it wouldn't flare any incoming ducks to the decoys, I laid back and enjoyed my usual breakfast of Coke and a stick of hard, dry Italian salami. Dog also got a PB&J sandwich (her favorite, providing there was lots of peanut butter on it) and then we waited. Me, I watched the comings of the waterfowl into the area and Dog just snored away. However, she was busy "chasing" something as her moving feet and occasional whines spoke to a great chase in that dog's dream world.

At five in the morning, I saw a light go on in the Bell Outing Duck Club clubhouse. Then at six, I saw flashlights down by the boat dock and soon I could hear a boat's outboard motor coming my way. Sure as God creates a world of wonder for ever-seeing wildlife officer types, here came my shooters. However, instead of two shooters as reported, I had three in the boat. Those lads motored up to their blind and disembarked. First, they hid their boat under a camouflage netting and then they entered their duck blind. Moments later, I could see the "red cherries" of cigarettes glowing in the pre-dawn blackness as the telltale smell of nicotine smoke drifted faintly my way.

Then the birds my three chaps had scared from their decoys upon their arrival began filtering quietly back into the blind's decoys. Soon, more and more ducks arrived brought in by swimming ducks' ripples in the water, their feeding calls, and their remembrance of bait having been placed there for them earlier.

As shooting time approached, I could hear shotguns going off on surrounding duck clubs. However, my three chaps just stayed hidden in their blind as quiet as a mess of mice feasting on a piece of cheese. By now, their decoys harbored about one hundred ducks all looking for the elusive feed grains they had consumed a day or so earlier. Finding none, they still dove time and time again in their quest for a free breakfast. However, a barley breakfast was not to be. All of a sudden, my three chaps stood up and shot nine times into the massed ducks on the water as the birds instantly roared into the air in abject alarm!

Boy, the sounds of the three shotguns sure brought my dog Shadow out from her dreamland. Up she sat under the netting as she made ready at her master's command to "get the duck." However, that was not to be. Her master had not shot. Only the three chaps in the blind had and what a "shoot" that had been. I counted 45 dead ducks in the water or mortally wounded ones slowly circling around in the water with their heads in the water drowning because they had been so severely wounded that they couldn't even hold up their heads to avoid drowning. However after that "shoot," my "brave sportsmen" never showed themselves above the blind. They had ducked back down to reload and carefully looked all around to see if anyone had seen their deadly duck-killing "deed."

Wanting my lads to recover all their wounded and dead ducks, I just held my ground. I figured that way my lads were not only looking at being cited for taking an over limit but once the dead ducks were back in hand, for possessing an over limit as well. That also made it easier for me in a court of law and right now I was into "easy" after the crappy sportsmanship of shooting the feeding ducks on the water episode I had just witnessed.

Then I got a surprise that later turned into nothing short of wonderful. Two lads finally left their blind, went to their hidden boat, loaded up and paddling out, began picking up all 45 dead and dying ducks as rapidly as they could. Instead of returning to their duck blind like I expected, they took off motoring for the clubhouse before I could even blink! What the hell? I thought as that maneuver caught me completely by surprise. Since I had not brought my motor along because I had such a long drag and didn't figure I needed one, my two shooters had gotten clean away! But I still have one shooter in my suspect blind, and he damn sure is not getting away when the time comes to drop the hammer, I grimly thought.

Then sensing something bigger afoot, I waited. My chap in the blind never showed himself and after a short time, the ducks began slowly drifting back into his decoy set with the memory of bait still fresh in their minds. Soon the decoys began filling with hungry ducks looking for something to eat. (To my readers, see why the use of bait is illegal? There is no fair chase here, just killing. I have no problem if game is taken by fair chase. I just don't approve of cheaters or thieves who steal wildlife from the rest of us.) And with the arrival of those ducks, other ducks in the air seeing the activity on the water began flying in for a look-see as well.

Trying hard not to spook the ducks from my position, I watched my two duck hunters' final progress as they headed for the clubhouse. Soon they arrived and I could see them literally running their passel of ducks to the club's hanging facility. Then as one man hung the ducks in the hanging facility, the other kept bringing more dead ducks from their boat into the facility. Soon I could see both of the men hanging bunches of ducks in the screened facility to drain and cool out. What the hell are they doing? I asked myself. From what I could see through my binoculars, the two men were tagging and hanging the ducks in their picking facility like nothing out of the ordinary was happening. But why are they doing that? I kept asking myself.

To those of you readers who are not duck hunters, any time you leave your waterfowl in storage at a place other than your personal abode (home), they must be tagged in such a manner that they are identified by the date killed, where killed, printed name of who killed the birds, birds listed by species, and a signature of the shooter in order for them to be legally stored. That way, an officer of the law can quickly check the birds as to legality and move on. It also allows the duck hunter to store his birds and not have to carry them around with him wherever he goes. However, sometimes crooked duck clubs will have members "doctor" up the tags with false names of hunters who were not present that day and did not take any of the birds. By so doing, this method of subterfuge allows some shooters to take more than their daily bag limit allows. That is unless the officer is sharp-eyed and can untangle the tagging mystery. When the officer is successful in untangling the mystery involving tags, there usually is hell to pay because of all the intent to violate the law.

Forty minutes later, here came my two shooters back to their blind. In the meantime, my chap in the blind had not moved a hair or made a sound. It was now plain to me that he hoped to once again shoot into the masses of ducks currently looking for bait in his decoys. And I didn't have to wait long. Just as the ducks began noticing the noise of the returning outboard motor from the oncoming boat and all had their heads in the air sensing danger, my shooter rose from his blind and shot into the bunched up mass of ducks sitting on the water. That time there were five shots fired as my chap used an unplugged shotgun to "ground sluice" the birds sitting in the decoys.

Once again, the ducks fled in utter panic except for those lying still in the water or slowly swimming in circles as they drowned from their wounds. Three minutes later right on cue, my two lads in the boat arrived and motored directly into the decoys and began picking up the dead and dying ducks. It was now apparent to me that this little maneuver had been planned all along. That way by doing what they did, they had maximized their kill. Well, that wasn't the only one going to maximize his kill, I grimly thought...

That time I waited until my two chaps in the boat were on the far side of the pond chasing down cripples and opposite their escape route before I sprang my trap. Throwing back my camouflage netting, I dragged my canoe out from hiding, slid it into the duck pond, and paddled it right out into their boat channel. There I blocked any means of escape with the length of my Grumman like a big fat frog on a lily pad...

With that move in plain view, my shooter who had just killed another 23 ducks ducked back down into the blind hoping I would forget about him. Fat chance of that happening, I thought with a narrowing set of eyes. In the meantime, my two chaps picking up crippled ducks on the far side of the pond were oblivious of my blocking efforts and, of course, magnificent physical presence. That was until they had boarded all the dead and crippled ducks into their boat. Sitting there I was mentally adding up the charges soon to follow. For my three shooters when they had killed the 45 ducks, an over limit taking charge. That would be followed with a possession charge on the two who had run the over limits of ducks to the clubhouse. Then on the second shoot, my coward still hiding in the blind would be charged with taking an additional 23 ducks with an unplugged shotgun. As for the two picking up all of my shooter in the blind's ducks, another possession over limit charge was in the mill. No two ways about it, there would be three gut-shot chaps ticketed into the court system before this day's events had drifted off into the pages of history like the smell of freshly fired shotgun powder in a freshening breeze... Little did I realize just how badly gut-shot these chaps would be when all of us had returned to the clubhouse hanging facility for me to retrieve the first mess of illegal ducks somewhat later in the morning.

"Who the hell are you?" asked the man in the bow of the returning boat upon seeing my beautiful carcass sitting in the Grumman blocking their escape.

"Federal agent," I said as I held up my badge and credentials.

With those words, the man in the bow turned and angrily said something to the man running the motor. I could tell from the intense look the motorman gave me blocking their boat channel that he had been asked if he could take off and leave me behind. No such luck, I thought to myself. That is why I am blocking the only way out from this duck blind and pond. Then the lad running the motor, seeing his only avenue of escape was blocked, shut off his motor in resignation. However, his partner in the boat with him continued swearing and giving the stern man "holy hell."

With that, I paddled up to my two chaps and requested their hunting and driver's licenses. Receiving those and with my two lads in tow, I paddled over to the blind and called for the man in the blind to show himself. When he did, I identified myself and requested that he hand me his hunting and driver's licenses which he did. With all three sports' licenses in hand, I checked their shotguns, licenses, and duck stamps. All were in accordance with the laws of the land except for my chap in the blind. His shotgun, as I already knew, was still unplugged.

Then with my three chaps in tow, we slowly headed back to the clubhouse. All the way in, the one man in the bow of the boat continued to rant and rave at his two hunting partners. I heard him say that he was a distinguished member of Ducks Unlimited and that he was on the mayor's conservation commission and the like. Then his two partners caught "holy hell" once again from my furious chap with the big mouth. What the hell, I thought. The chap with the big mouth doesn't have anything good going for him and his earlier behavior either. My chap with the big mouth had shot into the flocked ducks at first light helping his partners in killing 45 of them, taking a large over limit in the process. What about that violation? I thought. However, that didn't slow down the big mouth from berating his partners all the way back to the clubhouse for exposing him to such embarrassment at being caught.

There I got another surprise. Sliding up to the boat dock, I stepped out from my Grumman canoe and tied her up to the dock. I reached down and grabbed the boat full of my two sports and big mouth, steadying it so they could safely step out. Apparently, however, I was not doing as beautiful a job as required by big mouth. Grabbing his shotgun and those of his two pals, my big mouth lunged clumsily up out of the boat, refusing my extended helping hand, swearing all the way at the world and what was in it. As he did, he caught the toe of his right hip boot on the lip of the side of his boat and plunged head first into the water at the boat dock! "Kerplush" was an understatement! It looked like someone had dropped a whale from the sky... The three

Browning shotguns he was carrying preceded him into the drink and muddy bottom of the pond by the boat slip as well! Since the water at the boat slip was only about three and a half feet deep, there was no danger in him drowning. When my big-mouthed lad went into the icy water head first, the three shotguns preceded him. In so doing, he used them as a brake for his fall.

Wrong thing to do as all three shotguns went barrel first into the soft alkali mud in the bottom of the pond. In fact, they were driven barrel first into the bottom with such force with the weight of big mouth on top of them that the barrels were completely filled with mud from chamber to the end of their barrels! Out from the water he now came sputtering and swearing even more loudly. For the forcefully stuck in the mud shotguns, that took some pulling from the other two lads to free them.

All of us were so surprised at the events that had just occurred, that we just stood there all slack jawed with a bad case of the "big eye." Then as was so typical of me, I came forth with some beautiful language perfectly applicable to the moment at hand. And brilliantly so I might add. "Did you fall in, sir?" I asked without an ounce of brains in my head. Hell, I was so surprised at what had just happened, I didn't know what else to say. Needless to say, that brought forth such a diatribe of swear words from my "swimmer" that even a sailor from an old "ship of the line" in the original Yankee navy would have blushed.

Then I got surprise number two for the day and what a surprise that would turn out to be. With big mouth's "bath" over and having nothing more to say (a good thing), I turned and headed for the hanging facility. Walking up to the hanging facility, I discovered that my two chaps who had taken the birds in earlier had tagged all the birds for temporary storage in accordance with the federal regulations. Well, sort of. They had used forged names from all the other club members not present to cover the overages of the ducks! That meant additional charges were going to be laid on my two chaps and now on the duck club itself because under federal law, the duck club was considered a person and, as such, liable under the regulations of the Migratory Bird Treaty Act.

Two hours later I had it all sorted out, the birds gutted, and seized. Loading the evidence birds into my Grumman, I asked my three now somewhat contrite lads if they had any questions regarding the upcoming Federal Court proceedings. They had none, so I paddled my way off the club and spent the next hour dragging a decidedly heavier Grumman back to the 2047 Canal. From there, the 68 ducks were taken to my friend and commercial duck picker, Angelo Jaconetti in Colusa, to be processed so they could be properly cared for and later donated to the needy.

Three weeks later, our Sacramento office secretary, Juanita Hobbs, called and advised that my three chaps from San Francisco who had shot over bait and had taken over limits in the process on the Bell Outing Duck Club, had just forfeited bail in Magistrates Court in Sacramento. Two of the lads forfeited $1,500.00, and the third lad with the unplugged gun, in addition to all the other charges, paid $1,550.00. The club was fined $250.00 for the untagged birds as required under federal law. I would say $4,800.00 for a morning's work was well worth it. Especially when my "big mouth" decided he would take a dip into the club's duck pond with three very expensive Browning shotguns. Now that I think back on that morning's events, especially when my chap had fallen in, that "Did you fall in, sir?" was an appropriate question to ask. A little stupid on my part, but regardless, "spot on," don't you think?

The next time I had a homemade chicken dinner with all the trimmings at my house, I made certain, much to the glee of my two young sons, that I kissed their mom three times as I had done during that first chicken dinner. I figured if that had worked once before and produced such a great case, I would try it again for good luck.

And if that didn't work, I at least got a couple of good "smooches" out of the deal...

AMBUSHED FROM "BEHIND"

It had been a long and hard week that winter for me in the Northern Sacramento Valley. Hard in that I had been fighting the winter rains, sticky rice mud, a bad head cold, little sleep, and the usual air head subjects killing everything within gun range, legal or not. Arriving home late one evening, I unlimbered my tired frame from my patrol truck. Walking around to the back of the truck, I lowered the tailgate and let my dog Shadow out for the evening. Walking into my garage, I grabbed a large can of Alpo dog food from the shelf and fed my dog who was wet, miserable and tired as well. Finishing her supper, she headed for her inside dog house as I washed up in the outdoor sink in my garage and took off my muddy hip boots.

Opening the backdoor into my home, I was met with a rush of warm air and the heavenly smells of my bride's great home cooking. "How did your day go, Honey?" she asked as she busied herself setting the table with my dinner (This was from a women who had taught school all day, kept my two unruly sons corralled when she got home and made me a wonderful dinner all at the same time like it was nothing. See why I am married to that little gal some fifty years later as these words are written...).

"It was alright. I caught a couple lads with over limits of geese in the Lambertville area and ran to ground five late shooters shooting an hour late on the Newhall Farms property. Other than that and getting stuck twice, the world is as fine as 'frog's hair,'" I tiredly replied.

"You need to call Buck. He has a duck club he wants to work and can't do it without your help," she advised as she put a platter of steaming hot pork chops smothered in caramelized onions down in front of my dinner plate.

Knowing my phone could ring at any time and I would once again be out the door, I sat down to my dinner without further ado. Man, pork chops, mashed potatoes with a heavily spiced pork gravy, crisp green salad with blue cheese dressing, and homemade beer buns fresh from the oven greeted my eyes. Saying a quick grace in which I invited God down for some great grits, I dove in with heartfelt relish.

Finishing my dinner with a generous helping of my bride's homemade rhubarb and strawberry pie with absolutely the world's finest crust, I finally called my friend and California Department of Fish and Game Warden, Buck Del Nero, who was assigned and stationed in the Stockton district as the resident game warden.

The phone only rang once and then the booming voice of my giant friend blistered the airwaves. "'Bout time you got off your dead ass and returned my call. That is the trouble with you goofy damn "feds." Once you become a fed, you get lazy as a cur dog and need a damn good kick in the behind to get your act in gear," he bellowed with a good natured "laugh" in the tenor of his voice.

"You cracker ass! I have been working 16-hour days and seven day weeks. In fact, I caught 35 chaps just this last week, most with over limits and late shooting. What the hell do you have to show for your feeble efforts as the Stockton warden?" I good naturedly fired right back.

Buck just roared right back with laughter saying, "I knew that would drag you out from under your rock. Just like a damn old carp. All I have to do is dangle a gob of worms on a No. 6 Eagle Claw hook in front of you or a damn good duck case in the making near the end of that Roman nose of yours, and I have you hooked."

"What do you have going, partner," I asked with more than a dollop of interest forming in my soul.

"Well, my "gob of worms" is this. I have a duck club here in the San Joaquin Delta that is getting carried away on the numbers of ducks and geese they are killing. Surprise, surprise!

Unfortunately, it is one of the political duck clubs that has been declared off-limits by our Director, G. Ray Arnett. Declared off-limits to all of us state guys because it is one I suppose in which he is invited to duck hunt on from time to time. He doesn't want to be embarrassed by us lowly badge carriers. As you know under his new policy, I can only work that duck club if a "fed" requests my assistance to do so under my Deputy U.S. Game Management Agent credentials. Otherwise, I have basically been ordered to work elsewhere and quit "hair- assing" these guys," he explained.

"You got it. I am requesting your assistance in this matter." (that was all it took to get around Arnett's foolish political order.) "Now what the hell am I assisting you on this time, as if you needed any help?" I asked, now really getting more than interested.

You see, Buck was one of my classmates from the fish and game academy when I worked for the state and one of the very best fish and game catch dogs I ever met or worked with. Hell, he sure as the dickens didn't need me when it came to catching outlaws. That is other than getting around Arnett's hair-brained political order of the day. Buck had a sixth sense that was truly God given and once he got on your trail, the only way to get him off was to shoot him. Plain and simple, the people from the State of California owe that man a huge debt of gratitude for all the wildlife outlaws he rounded up and had prosecuted. And in so doing, he made sure there was some wildlife left for their children and grandchildren to enjoy.

"I need a partner to go in with me and help pinch those rich bastards killing the hell out of my ducks and geese. Since it is one of the clubs our director occasionally shoots, I need you to go along. That way if we catch Arnett with an over limit of ducks, you will have to pinch him and take him to Federal Court. Since my local state judge down here also shoots that same duck club, I wouldn't get a fair trial if I pinched Arnett under my state credentials and he was the subject of such an investigation. That said, I need your rotten carcass, lead weight as it is, to go along with me and hold my hand," he grumbled loudly (Buck was a big old dude. He stood six feet four inches in his stocking feet, weighed in at a solid 250 pounds and all of it was as strap steel tough as they come. Yeah, I needed to hold his hand...).

"Well, since you are going to be a smart ass, I am not coming unless you have Judy" — Buck's great little wife — "cook me one of her homemade Italian dinners," I said, knowing I had my big friend over a barrel, especially since he did not trust or like any other "fed" to work with him and wouldn't ask. Plus, Judy loved cooking for big guys who were eager eaters and Buck and I fit that bill in both categories.

"Alright you big lug, you got it. But I need you here no later than tomorrow afternoon so we can get an early start the following morning. We are looking at least a 45-minute boat ride to get to this club, and that is if there is no fog. If there is fog, we are looking at a lot longer running time and a damn cold and wet ride," he continued.

"Got you covered, partner," I said. We exchanged several other pleasantries and then we hung up. Buck to further scout out the suspect duck club that evening, and me to try and get a decent night's sleep in preparation for my next adventure. And, what a "unique" adventure that one would turn out to be.

The following afternoon, I thundered into the driveway of Buck's country home on the outskirts of Stockton. Stepping out from my mud-splattered truck, I heard a shrill voice behind me saying, "Terry!"

Looking around just in time, I caught Judy, Buck's tiny little wife, as she ran happily into my arms. "Are you here to keep my old man from harm's way?" she asked with her trademark smile.

"You know me, Judy. I have to come around occasionally just to keep your old man from stepping on himself," I responded with a grin because I knew Buck could more than take care of himself. He was a strapping "horse" of a man, cat quick, and had the eyes of a golden eagle. No, Buck didn't need any help. He had other reasons for my appearance. The two of us had a chemistry that when we ran the "trails," we caught outlaws like no two other wildlife officers I have ever known or probably will ever know. And when we caught the bad guys, it was not uncommon to seize several hundred ducks and geese in the offing. No, Buck didn't need any help. He just knew we were both cut from the same bolt of rough, homespun cloth. And when together, we didn't leave much for seed, if you readers get the gist of my meaning. Besides, where else could one find 550 pounds of wildlife officers in one beautiful clump and all at one time?

That evening, Buck, true to his word, had Judy make me an Italian dinner not of this world! It was so good and rich that God and several of His friends came down and joined right in. Little did I realize that rich Italian dinner would be the downfall for one of us...

Four o'clock the next morning found Buck and yours truly standing quietly on the edge of a large and expensive duck club in the San Joaquin Delta area. It had a multi-million dollar clubhouse, and the duck club shooting area proper consisted of

500 acres of flooded, unharvested corn! And talk about a high-class outfit, it even had a telephone line (before the age of cell phones) that ran conveniently to each blind to be used under the excuse for emergencies. However, in real life, it was used frequently to warn the shooters the game wardens were in country.) A Mexican guide accompanied each blind's shooters. The Mexican guides did not shoot. They were there so the sports could shoot the guide's limit and therefore prolong their shoot. Talk about The Ritz! This was certainly about as close as one could get to The Ritz in the world of shooting waterfowl.

Every day on that flooded corn had to reside at least 25,000 ducks and 10,000 geese making it a shooter's paradise! And on our chosen day, that flooded corn had little room left for any more ducks and geese. Man, you talk about a shoot come dawn, this was one in the making. And if my experience served me well, by mid-morning we would have at least a couple of chaps who had flunked Mrs. Wilson's third grade math class when it came to counting. That was, if I didn't miss my guess and the usual killing history on that club reared its evil head.

Our plan was to walk around on the island's berm on the north side of the hunting area in the dark. From there, Buck and I would select a likely looking blind that was awash with birds. There we would head for the always present ring of blackberry bushes growing on the top of the berm surrounding the shooting area. Finding the right overlooking spot, the two of us would make sure we had a place for our two rather large carcasses into which to slide and watch undetected the antics of our shooters.

Our morning had started out well enough with a quick, unencumbered boat ride to the area and an easy walk onto the duck club proper. As was our usual method of operation, we were on site long before the duck club's shooters were out of bed and ready to go. We discovered a great spot to hide and, just like the Mexican Army at the Alamo, we were ready for whatever came our way. Well, not quite...

Predawn arrived and the two of us had crawled back into our hiding spot in the blackberries from where we had stood earlier looking on. We hadn't been there for more than five minutes when I detected the slight smell of a dead whale in the hot July sun on the beaches of Mexico! And since I never had much of a nose, you can imagine what the intensity of that mystery smell was really like. Passing off that smell as one possibly coming from the surrounding farming countryside, I let it go. Crawling deeper into the warm comfort of my chest-high waders and heavy hunting coat, I closed my eyes as I awaited the sunrise and the outlaw action that was soon to follow.

Then there was that evil smell once again!

Only this time it was even stronger! So strong in fact that my eyes flew wide open in surprise at the close at hand, absolutely rancid smell of what had to be that like dead humans on the Gettysburg Battlefield in 1863 in the hot July sun after laying two days afield...

"Buck," I said, "do you smell that? I think we crawled back into something long dead and full of stink in these damn bushes."

"Naw, I don't smell nothin,'" he quietly growled.

Thinking it might just be me and my "smeller" gone wrong, I once again nestled down into my hunting coat for the warmth it offered. Then, there it was again, and this time I was not mistaken. "Buck," I said, "did you die inside those chest-highs and then rot out in the sun somewhere? That smell has to be coming from you because I damn sure didn't pass any gas or let something crawl up inside me and die!"

Then I could hear Buck stifle a little "proud of what he had just done" chuckle.

"It is you, you bastard. Something crawled up inside you and died!" I hissed, almost gagging as I spoke as new whiffs of the "proud" gas filled the air.

Then Buck let out a quiet yet guilty laugh and moved slightly from his lying down position alongside me. Sure as God made man many times act like an idiot, when Buck moved his chest-high waders, they acted like a blacksmith's bellows. He was passing the most rancid gas I ever smelled into the confines of his chest-high waders. Then every time he moved his body inside the rubber sleeve of the waders, it pumped out the most awful, liquid like gas imaginable!

"Buck, you have to get up from here, go outside, and clean yourself out," I grumbled, half gagging once again in the process of breathing in the rancid air before speaking.

More laughter came from Buck, then he said, "All right, you wimp. I will get up and take a dump outside our hiding place." With that, he heaved his large carcass up and lumbered out from our hiding spot. However, not before once again fully perfuming our little ambush site in the blackberries. Shortly thereafter, I could hear Buck really getting after the job at hand.

Thank God, I thought. I doubt I could have lain there all morning long counting drops on our shooters while Buck was passing that kind of gas. Hell, I probably would have passed out or died in the process! I thought. Or he could have continued passing such rotten gas until he blew the two of us up after some spark had been generated by static electricity from some bird flying nearby.

Then I heard it! Our shooters were on the way

out to their nearby duck blind with Buck outside and in clear view!

"Buck," I hissed. "Get your butt back in here (no pun intended). Here they come and if they see you, our work for the day is down the tubes," I grumbled.

About that time, here came Buck all bent over pulling up his chest-highs as he ran to our hiding spot. As he did, he was just pulling up his suspenders on his chest-high waders. Plunging into our hiding spot, he just barely arrived before our shooters turned the corner on the road leading to their blind. Five seconds more and they would have spotted him running to hide!

Sliding into position, the two of us watched two shooters and their Mexican guide hustling on their flooded, graveled walkway into their duck blind as the air filled with alarmed ducks and geese. Walking out to their blind, the men settled in and soon started shooting. And what a shoot they were having! In just 22 minutes, our two shooters had 39 ducks and 18 geese down (remember, the Mexican guide only went along so his rubes could shoot his limit as well)! That was unreal, considering the limits for our two shooters was 16 ducks and 12 geese per day in total! In fact the drops were coming so fast that I could hardly keep track of who shot what and the species killed in my notebook.

Then I noticed it!

"Buck, are you passing gas once again?" I asked.

"No. Hell no! I got rid of what ailed me back there in the bushes," he said as he put more notes into his notebook on the whirl of events occurring at the duck blind in front of us.

"Damn, are you sure? I can smell those same smells and they are not only heavy and oily smelling, but nearby. What the hell did you do, crap just behind where we are hiding?" I asked my big friend in an accusing manner.

"No. I told you, I took my dump over there at the end of the berry bushes," he replied. Then he said, "But you are right. I can still smell that crap and it is strong. Let me see if I got some on my boots." He squirmed around in our hiding spot and looked at his boots.

"No, I didn't get any on my boots," he replied.

It was then I spotted the culprit creating all our lovely smells! When Buck had dropped his waders and pants to take his dump, he had not cleared his suspenders away from under his bottom. He had pooped on his suspenders! Then when I yelled at him to hurry and get back into our hiding spot before he was spotted by our shooters, he did the unimaginable. He had quickly pulled up his pants, grabbed his suspenders and jerked them up as he pulled up his waders in the same fluid movement. When he did, his beautifully but unintentionally laid dump was all over his wide suspenders. This same poo was then catapulted into his still wide-open waders. Then jerking the suspenders up over his coat had smeared what hadn't dropped outright into the bottom of his waders all over the back of his hunting jacket!

It was so bad, I began laughing into my coat to stifle any noise so our shooters would not hear me. Buck, once he realized what he had done, was beside himself. Now, his waders were full of his stinky dump and his suspenders were smearing the poo all over his clothing every time he moved! And every time he moved, he smeared even more of the dump all over his jacket. That didn't include all the "action" that was taking place inside his waders every time he moved! He was fit to be tied! Me, I just tried to avoid puking in our hiding spot over the intensely bad smell Buck was emitting and laughing at my big friend's dismay, but doing so carefully because once Buck got mad at something, he could kill a man with one punch. And, I didn't want to be that dead guy killed with one punch laying in the blackberry bushes!

Then our two shooters, using unplugged shotguns, got into a flock of mallards numbering about one hundred as they quietly sailed into their blind's decoys. Even distracted by Buck's intense "perfume," I managed counting 19 mallards dropping onto Mother Earth for their last time at the end of that singular shooting escapade by our gunning chaps in the duck blind!

"Buck," I said. "That is enough killing. Those dingbats will kill every duck coming into them now that their shotguns are unplugged. We need to 'cut their water off,'" I continued.

"Not yet," said Buck. "Because of those bastards, I am covered with "dump." If I am paying for enjoying so much of Judy's rich Italian dinner, they are going to pay as well," he grumbled right back.

"Ok," I said. "But one more flock dying like that last one and I am out of here and onto their last parts over the fence like all get out. Plus, I don't think I can last much longer in this berry patch that for some reason doesn't smell much like blackberries anymore," I said with a now starting to lose it chuckle.

About then a small flock of 17 Pacific white-fronted geese sailed into our shooters' decoys. Just as they dropped their feet to land, our two shooters jumped up and dropped nine of them deader than a box of rocks!

"That does it," I said, pushing myself to my feet in front of God and everybody. Buck followed and the two of us hustled over to our shooters' blind which was but a short distance away. For the longest time, nothing happened in their duck blind as we made our approach. Then all of a sudden, down the road leading to our blind rattled a pickup carrying two Mexican laborers obviously heading in our direction.

"Buck," I said. "Those chaps in the blind obviously saw us approaching their blind. Because they are way over their limits with 58 ducks and 27 dark geese as I count it, they have used the blind's telephone and called the clubhouse. In response, the clubhouse sent out those two poor Mexican laborers to pick up their blind's extra birds and claim them as theirs!"

"Let them. Then when they gather up some of the extra birds and try claiming them as their own, we can really raise hell and cite the whole damn bunch," said Buck.

The vehicle carrying the two poor Mexican farmhands reached the duck blind before we did. However, we now had their escape route cut off and just continued on towards the offending blind with smiles on our faces and smells in the air...

Before this day is out, there will be a couple of chaps who are going to pay and pay dearly for the error of their ways in the over limits department, I thought. There is no way they can explain away the error of their counting when it comes to killing 42 ducks and 21 dark geese over their limits.

Arriving at the blind, Buck and I identified ourselves. Our two shooters turned out to be two real estate moguls from the Los Angeles area. And as expected, the two men tried to include the Mexican farmhands for legal limits of both ducks and geese, thereby reducing their individual overages. With a wave of my hand, I shut off that hoped for avenue of escape with, "Forget it, men. The two of us have been watching the two of you killing ducks and geese since first light. No one else shot at these birds in your custody except the two of you. So let's cut the garbage of trying to blame the Mexican farm laborers and accept what the two of you have done like men."

Asking for their shotguns, hunting, and driver's licenses, Buck and I got down to the business at hand. As we wrote out our "paper" on the offenses our two chaps had committed, the two shooters and the Mexicans began acting all funny like.

Finally one of the men named Harold said, "Officers, I don't mean to be offensive, but the two of you stink like crap!"

That was all it took! I started laughing like I had just broken a gut. However, my "stinky" partner never said a word. He just continued writing out his citation but the look on his face said it all.

All he wanted to do was get our business at hand done and then get the hell out of there before the two shooters figured out what had happened. I guess Buck figured if they deduced the smell coming from the two of us was from him, his "tough guy" reputation would be somewhat besmirched among the local outlaws in the delta area... And, my big guinea friend was having none of that...

Finishing up with our part of the detail, Buck and I gathered up all the now seized ducks and geese. Staggering under the loads of those birds, we turned to leave and head for our concealed boat in the delta waters some distance away.

"Hey," said Harold. "Would you look at that," he said pointing at the back of Buck's camouflaged hunting coat.

"That is where that awful smell is coming from. Look at the back of that officer's coat. He has crap smeared all over it. And would you look at that. That crap is clear up between that big guy's shoulders. Damn, he must have tangled with a giant for the crap to be up so high on that big guy's shoulders!"

As we walked away from our two amazed shooters over the amount of dump on Buck's shoulders, it was all I could do to keep from roaring out loud in laughter! I just shook my head and kept walking with my load of seized birds. For I knew if I did anything else, my big partner just might take a "stinky" poke at me or make me walk all the way back, delta waters blocking my route home or not...

Back at the marina when we docked Buck's boat, we once again were accosted by several duck hunters who did not know who we were, wanting to know where the two of us had killed so many birds (because we were dressed like any other hunter, those chaps just assumed we were outlaws like the rest of that fraternity assembled around us). However, that adulation over our collective ability to "kill" so many birds soon dissolved. Once our admiring crowd of duck hunters got a whiff of Buck, they politely drifted back to their duck boats with a few knowing backward glances upon looking at Buck's coat of "many colors."

Back at Buck's home, I made ready to return to the Northern Sacramento Valley for the work awaiting me there. As I gutted our evidence ducks and geese, Buck stripped down and took a shower. Emerging from his back porch after his shower, I made a comment on how nicely he smelled. Only my quick reflexes saved me from receiving a whang on the head like the kick from an angry mule as Buck took a good natured swing at me.

"You ever tell anyone about my misfortune and it will be the last Italian meal I will have my wife fix for you," he grumbled. I just laughed as the two of us shook hands and I hauled my carcass back into my truck for the long ride home.

"Call me if you ever need any more "political

top cover,'" I said to my big and gruff partner. He just smiled and gave me a wave of his big hand as he filled the other one with a slightly soiled hunting coat. Then he headed over to the horse trough on his property and began washing off his coat and cleaning out his chest-high waders of some horribly smeared, evil-looking sludge...

You know, I have never told this story to anyone for fear of losing out on another one of Judy's great Italian meals. It has been 38 years now since I have seen or worked with my gentle bear sized friend. Because of the time and distance now separating us, I feel I can get away with telling this "duck club funny" on my dear friend and partner.

The last I heard was that Buck had retired and that he and Judy had moved to Mexico. In that country's time of drug related turmoil, I hope the two of them are alright. After all, that little gal Judy could sure cook. And come to think of it, I haven't had a great Italian meal like hers since that time so long ago. Dang...

WEBBED FEET AND "GRITS" ON THE "LITTLE OL' PEA PICKER'S" DUCK CLUB

Flying my Sacramento Valley duck clubs one December morning with Agent Pilot Al Weinrich, I spotted the telltale "yellow streak" signs that grains of bait leave in the water when viewed from the air.

"Al, take another swing across that duck club we just crossed over at the end of San Jose Road," I said excitedly as I pointed down at the signs of a baited area. "I received word earlier that Ford's duck club was baited but the bird hunting in that area had been so bad I just haven't taken the time to check it out in light of all the other work I have had to do," I said.

Heading out a ways so no one would be any the wiser, Al eventually turned our aircraft around and made another pass over my duck blind area of interest. Sure as my bride makes the world's best blueberry pies, there it was! Two long yellow swatches of bait dumped out on the far northwestern corner of Tennessee Ernie Ford's Duck Club located on the northwestern side of San Jose Road in Colusa County. The bait was laid out in two even rows inside the decoy set in about one foot of water in a large watered area surrounded by three duck blinds. From what I had seen, the presence of a baited area matched the mysterious phone call I had received from an unknown voice days earlier. In that "voice" over the phone, "it" had complained of the possibility of bait being on Ford's duck club and then had hung up. I did not recognize the obviously masked voice of my mystery caller, but I figured it had come from a disgruntled gamekeeper on a nearby duck club. One in which the bait had attracted "his" ducks off the club he was responsible for and onto Ford's. It always amazed me at the lack of honor among thieves... For my sharper country and western music folks, yes, this duck club was owned by the famous country and western singer, Tennessee Ernie Ford.

Streaking out from the area with the plane so we wouldn't arouse the suspicions of the rest of the San Jose Road duck clubs, I hurriedly made a crude map in my notebook on the bait's location. Landing back at the Colusa Airport sometime later, I thanked our agent pilot and headed for my truck, as he took off for other aerial details in the Sacramento Valley. Realizing that to go back to the offending duck club at this hour, in broad daylight, would only risk discovery, I switched to my Plan B because I realized the baited area would still be there when I made my "discovery" move in the dark of night. So, I just relaxed over this issue for the time being. Plus, the duck hunting had been so bad in that area that I had opted for other more pressing work details.

Firing up my Dodge patrol truck, I headed for the eastern side of my district across the Sacramento River. Heading north on River Road then easterly on Laux Road, I soon found myself looking to cross over Butte Creek into Butte County. For the last week while working that side of the Sacramento River, I had heard a series of light rifle shots just across Butte Creek in an area heavily frequented by thousands of ducks, geese, and sandhill cranes. All three times I had heard the flat shooting sounds of a light deer rifle being fired I had been tied up on other nearby cases and unable to check out the suspicious shooting in a timely fashion. Today would be different. I had usually heard such shooting around ten in the morning and figured, now that I was through with my aerial work looking for a baited area on Ford's club, I would dwell on this situation and try to solve that Sacramento Valley mystery to my satisfaction.

On the east side of Butte Creek, I had just about every kind of critter imaginable residing therein. Most of the area in question remained unharvested or was in various stages of being harvested. And on that crop rich area, there were a myriad of critters galore all hopping around trying to fill an empty gut. On those mainly unharvested farmlands were herds of deer by the hundreds, cranes by the "moving gray carpets," snow geese by the noisy "white blankets," mallards like a mess of maggots on a dead prairie buffalo, and Pacific white-fronted geese by the constantly moving brownish- tan clouds. No two ways about it. It was truly a living critters' buffet paradise.

However in the middle of all that bounty, I had

a mystery shooter whom I was convinced was up to no good. I knew my shooter was in the middle of the paradise just described because whenever he shot, the air would at once be alive with flying critters like someone had overturned a mess of bee hives. The air would be black, brown, gray, and white with every type of aerial resource flying to get away from the menacing sounds of rifle shots. It was to that "living flame like a moth" I was now drawn that cool December morning. And if I had my druthers, I would not be denied getting to the bottom of that situation on such a fine day before I returned to working my latest baited duck club...

Crossing over Butte Creek, I headed north for a known copse of trees and dense stands of brush with a few leaves still remaining for the cover they offered. Slipping my tan-colored truck off the muddy farm road and down into a small opening in the trees into the center of my suspect area, I shut off the big engine.

Grabbing a Toscani cigar from a box on my dash, I stepped out into the brisk winter air, lit my cigar, and jumped up into the back of my truck. From there, I scrambled up onto the large utility box in the back and from that high position I had a commanding view of an area holding a million game birds of every make, sort, color, and sound.

Drawing deeply on the acrid little cigar, I began glassing the area closely with my binoculars. Everywhere I looked, I could see game birds of every sort feasting on the area's unharvested rice-corn- milo-lima bean bounty. Mixed in between the great flocks of game birds were the huge, constantly undulating, blanketing flocks of blackbirds numbering in the tens of thousands. God, it was great to be alive and witnessing such a living world of wildlife at every turn in the trail! I was truly blessed that morning as I have been all the rest of my life.

Birds were constantly trading back and forth overhead, and the constant din from thousands of bills working through the seeded areas, along with the warm winter sun, began having a lulling effect on me. That was not unique to me for that time of the year, though. I had been running on about four hours of sleep per night, and it didn't take much to take the edge off my sharpness during that time of the year, especially with the warmth of a little lulling sunlight. In fact, that is one of the reasons why I smoked the strong little Italian cigars. They were so nicotine stout that if one wasn't careful they could put you on your last part over the fence in fine style. Plus, that load of nicotine they carried would have flipped open the eyes of a dead man after the first deep puff. That is, if he hadn't been dead too long...

Boom-zip went the sound of a rifle and the

crack of a long-range shot out across the flat agricultural lands. That was quickly followed by another boom and crack as a light rifle bullet sailed out across the flat farmlands into huge clouds of birds. If there was any other shooting, it was then drowned out by the hundreds of thousands of frantically beating wings lifting up from the ground and heading for safer terrain deep in the Butte Sink.

Damn, Terry. That could just be a farmer shooting out across his unharvested fields in an attempt to rid his crop of the thousands of hungry birds, quickly crossed my mind. But then, something inside my miserable carcass, along with my stirring guardian angels, told me not to lessen my vigil.

Scanning the area from where the shots had originally come, I saw nothing. Then my attention turned to a long finger of timber, brush, and an old oxbow jutting out into a huge milo field. To my way of thinking, that would also have been a good place to sneak into and shoot from without fear of detection. But still I saw nothing no matter how hard I looked with my binoculars.

Then just for a second, I thought I saw a hurrying figure dressed from head to toe in camouflage gear moving in the densely brushed old oxbow. The figure even appeared to have a greenish face! Then once again nothing as the figure "ghosted" off into the dense cover. Damn, had I seen something or not? Or, had it just been a figment of my imagination as the strong swell of nicotine had entered my veins? Hustling down off my truck and back into the cab, I ignited my patrol truck's powerful 383-cubic inch engine with the four barrel carburetor. In an instant my "Swiss watch" running engine was ready to go. Digging out from my hiding place, I zipped back down the road from where I had earlier come as I headed for another known farm road off the beaten path, but one that placed me nearer the area in question.

Turning off onto that road, I sped for the long row of trees and dense brush leading out into the edge of the oxbow. I knew of a small hiding place in those trees where I had checked many folks night time fishing for catfish in that area. A place dragged from my memory banks when I had served as a game warden during my earlier days in the valley. Then slowing, I quietly moved into the area of my hiding place in the row of trees.

Quietly rounding a bend in the muddy road, I spotted what I suspected might be hidden there! An old beat-up red Ford pickup sat quietly almost out of sight in a mess of blackberries and poison oak. Slapping on my brakes, I quickly shifted into reverse and backed down the road and out of sight from where I had just come. There I parked my truck in the middle of the small farm road which was framed by a deep ditch on one side of the road and a huge copse of cottonwoods on the other. To my way of thinking, there was no way past me except by shank's mare or over the top of my three-quarter-ton Dodge, if one chose to run with that Ford! And being a "Dodge" man, I knew the puny little Ford didn't have enough poop in it to overcome the Dodge...

Scrambling out from my truck, I grabbed my .30 M-l carbine and began quietly trotting down the muddy road towards the parked red Ford. Seeing what appeared to be a camouflaged man for just a fleeting moment earlier, it was not lost on me that he was armed with a rifle. That being the case and no matter that I was a good pistol shot, a handgun didn't compare to a long gun in an altercation. Hence my grabbing my little carbine with the banana clip. Passing the Ford, I paused and wrote down the license plate number on the inside of my hand. I did so in case I ran into someone who was not inclined towards being caught and ended up by shooting first and asking questions later, if you get my drift. If nothing else, if I came out on the short end of a bullet, the coroner would be able to see the license plate number written on the palm of my hand. Realizing its significance, he could turn it over to the local law enforcement if I was incapable of speaking for myself. The rest of that action would just be a cold tracking job... Then I felt the grill of the Ford. It was still warm signifying recent use. With that, my eyes went to the brush ahead and the muddy road below. On the road was one set of footprints heading towards the oxbow and a surrounding milo field. Hustling along but careful to keep a sharp eye peeled and using my available cover, I followed my set of tracks to the edge of the milo field. There I discovered where my chap had knelt in the mud and shot three times! Lying alongside the kneeling marks in the mud were three spent Remington .243-caliber pieces of rifle brass. Picking them up with my pen (that way I didn't smudge any fingerprints on the spent casings) and smelling them, I could tell from the fresh powder smell that they were freshly fired. Those were quickly dropped into my coat pocket as evidence.

 Realizing to try and track my chap through the endless maze in the partially flooded oxbow, especially with the abundance of quail and wood ducks who would give one away when approached, I came up with a Plan B. Secreting myself in an intercept position alongside a huge cottonwood and pile of brush near my suspect's vehicle, I dug in and waited. I figured he had to come back to his vehicle and when he did, I would have my man. For what I didn't yet know, but I was about to find out. As it turned out, I didn't have long to wait.

Twenty minutes later and all of a sudden, I realized I wasn't alone! The birds that had been singing earlier in the thicket of trees where I was hidden were now quiet as all get out. Even the little white crowned sparrows perennially scratching in and around the base of the bushes were all at once absent. Soon it became apparent as to why. Quietly entering the glen of trees where the Ford truck was beautifully hidden materialized a man clad from head to foot in camouflage gear. Additionally, his hands and face had also been painted with camouflage grease paint. My chap was short bearded and somewhat long haired, but not like a hippy. Believe me, he was no novice or hippy. Quietly backtracking into the area from behind his truck, like an Alaskan brown bear would do if he felt he was being tracked, he spotted my tire tracks. I could see my chap kneeling down, testing the muddy tire prints to see how old my tracks were. Then I saw where he realized my tracks were over the top of his which meant I had arrived after him. Finally, my chap looked all around carefully, as if looking to see if anything else was out of place. Satisfied, he "ghosted" back into the dense underbrush from whence he came. Moments later, out he came dragging three dead sandhill cranes, bird species that were very good eating but totally protected in that day and age (they can now be hunted in some states)!

Breaking into a trot, he moved to his truck quietly like a trapper of old. I was so fascinated with the man and his woods wise movements, I almost forgot why I was there. Moving silently up to his truck, he took a long look all around then opened up the driver's door. Folding his seat forward, he tossed the cranes behind the seat. Then he carefully cased his rifle and laid it out of sight on top of the cranes. Lastly, he folded the seat back as if nothing was out of the ordinary. Then grabbing a greasy rag from off the seat, he began vigorously removing all the camouflage grease paint from his face and hands.

When finished cleaning off his hands and face, he looked into his side view mirror to check out his face. That was when my chap jumped like a bug on a hot rock. In the mirror was the reflection of his semi cleaned off face and behind that quietly stood a rather large sized man with a .30 M-l carbine intently looking right at him! My lad jumped so violently that his right arm hit the side view mirror busting it off from the side of his truck!

"Morning. My name is Terry Grosz and I am a federal agent," I said, as I showed the man my badge and credentials using my left hand. That left my right hand free which was still holding the carbine at the ready as I stood away at more than an arm's length. My man's surprised eyes went from my badge, to my face, to my rifle, and then back to my face. You talk about surprised! He never knew I was even incountry, much less that close to him.

Then it was as if my man had a hand come over him erasing any sign of emotion whatsoever. Talk about weird... "Good morning back to you, officer. My name is Dale Hoffman. Can I help you?" he quietly asked, his now almost-expressionless eyes never leaving mine. By now I realized I was confronting a "cat of another color" when it came to human beings and behavior! A cat of another color with the instinct of a born killer... I have to say, that was one of the strangest encounters I ever had. Here was a chap who was as woods wise as any mountain man and yet, under surprise, was as cool as any cucumber I ever ran across. In fact, the first thought that came to my mind after looking at his emotionless eyes was that of a "gunfighter of old" waiting for me to make my move... Most unusual to say the least, I thought, as I remained still very alert.

"Mr. Hoffman," I said. "I have been watching you for some time. Behind the seat of your truck are three illegal sandhill cranes and what appears to be a pre-'64 Winchester, .243-caliber rifle with a Leopold scope. I would like you to carefully open the door of your truck, reach behind the seat, retrieve that cased rifle, and slowly hand it to me butt first. Just remember that I am aware of the dangers in asking you to do that, but I am secure in what I am doing." With those words, I shifted the carbine to an even more ready position ... just in case. "Then, I would like you to retrieve those three cranes from behind the seat as well. That done, you can proceed down the road to the east towards my patrol truck while carrying the cranes. I will carry your rifle," I advised.

For the longest time he just looked at me as if sizing me up, then finally he did as he was told. It was then I began to feel I was in the presence of a military man, or at least one with such experience. Not your usual "ground pounder," but one of our elites. When he handed me his rifle, it was butt first as I had requested and still cased. Taking the rifle in my left hand and keeping my carbine at the ready in my right hand because I still couldn't fathom what the hell I had, I casually stepped back several more feet just in case.

"Now the cranes, Mr. Hoffman, and then I need for you to head down the road in front of me until you reach a tan Dodge truck. That is my patrol truck. You can throw the cranes into the back of that truck. Also be advised, when I arrived here earlier after you had shot and went out into the field for the birds, I had your truck plate run by the Sheriff's Office. They have a Butte County Sheriff's Office unit on the way as we speak." As my readers know from some of my past readings, I had done neither. That is what one calls a "force multiplier" being used when one does not have any idea of what he has stepped into and when he might need a "backup." And in that particular instance, I still didn't have the foggiest idea as to what I had, but I knew it was unusual and "off the fence" when it came to "usual." However, when I advised Dale as to what I had done, it was as if someone had pulled his "sand" drain plug and now he was back into the real world of the rest of us chaps.

Back at my truck, I placed his rifle in my back lockbox and then commenced with the paperwork. He was standing on one side of the hood of my truck and I on the other, just as a precaution. It wasn't until then I discovered what the hell I had run across. When Dale handed me his driver's license, I noticed it was from out of state. "Do you have any other form of identification?" I asked. He slowly dug into his wallet and produced a military ID card. Come to find out after a few questions, he was a sergeant in the Green Berets!

Then out of the blue he said, "Mr. Grosz, is my commanding officer going to find out about this?"

"Why do you ask?" I questioned.

"Because it would mean I will be removed from my unit which is soon to deploy to Vietnam. I don't want them going without me," he replied. And when he spoke, I could see the emotion starting to well up in the man about being left behind from his fellow soldiers in his unit.

Then I said, "Why were you out here, Dale? Why all painted up and sneaking about breaking the law?" I asked.

"Because that is what I will be soon be doing with my unit in Vietnam. I will be my group's Scout Sniper. So I just figured I would get in some real time "sneaking around" practice while I am on leave before going overseas. By doing it the way I did, it was as close to the real thing like being in combat that I could imagine. And I had been doing well for the last three weeks until you came along," he quietly stated. Then he said, "This has been a good learning experience for me. I have never, ever done anything like this before, but figured I would hone some of my skills outside the military system and challenge the civilian system. Twice I managed to outsmart a short game warden working this area (Warden Bob Hawks). In fact both times, he came so close to me, I could have ambushed and killed him. Once I got so close to that man that I could smell the type of soap he had used that morning when he had showered. It goes without saying, this type of experience will serve me well in country once I get to Vietnam. However, I guess if this had happened to me in Vietnam, you know, you catching me and all, I would be a spent unit about now, wouldn't I? Or if nothing else, on my way to a prisoner of war camp somewhere in North Vietnam if I had survived the initial contact with the enemy. As I am sure, you know what the enemy does with snipers if they catch them alive... With those words, the rest of his sentence relative to that issue of capture drifted off into the December cool of the Northern Sacramento Valley's winter air..."

"That thought had crossed my mind," I quietly said.

"What is going to happen now?" he asked.

"Well, I was going to cite you into Federal Court in Sacramento for violating the federal Migratory Bird Treaty Act. However in light of your unique circumstances, I have changed my mind. I am going to cite you into state court instead, and that way any federal background checks run on you by the military before you go overseas shouldn't discover this legal action at that civilian level. However, I would advise you to take care of the matter or your commander will find out about today's little venture because a Bench Warrant will be issued for your arrest posthaste if you don't," I said.

Damn, I now found myself in a pickle. The man had broken the law big time in taking totally protected non-game birds with a high powered rifle. But he was a military man going off to war in a rather unforgiving situation. I guess that pretty well describes anyone going off to war, doesn't it?

Then the sun finally shone on the manure pile behind the barn as I got a hell of a good idea. I swung the boundaries of my citation into the Colusa Justice Court as a state case where I still had some clout with the judge. I later met with Judge Weyand and got the fine reduced from $500.00 to $25.00 because of the mitigating circumstances. Leaving the Colusa County Courthouse after my meeting with Judge Weyand, I met Dale coming in to pay his fine.

After waiting outside for him to finish his business with the court, Dale and I went to lunch. There he thanked me for interceding on his behalf, on not only where the ticket had been filed but what he considered a reduction in fine through my efforts as well.

It was during our lunch that Dale suddenly got introspective and then he quietly said, "Terry, if I don't come back, I will still send you something from the battlefield. I am not sure what it will be, but I know we will be fighting in conjunction with the Montagnards in the Highlands. From what I understand from those returning, it is pretty rough duty over there. But for your generosity over my foolishness and not only outsmarting me and catching me in the act but teaching me a lesson, I will remember you. Rest assured, whatever I send, it will be a remembrance for the day you caught a Green Beret doing what he did best. Even if it wasn't legal..." Then he quickly changed the mood of the moment by saying, "How is your hamburger? Mine is great!"

Dale had forfeited bail that same day and as far as I was concerned, that ended it. To my way of thinking, we were even. As you readers will soon see, not quite...

That evening, after my crane case, found me nosing around on the northwest corner of Tennessee Ernie Ford's Duck Club looking for the bait I had spotted earlier from the air. Once on the duck club it only took me about ten minutes to locate the baited area. It also helped to finally have a thousand ducks noisily feeding in the area of the bait as well! Dragging my bait scoop, I gathered up the needed evidence samples in case the issue went to court. Then I got my tail end out from the suspect area before I was discovered.

The following shoot day found me hidden in a good position from which to watch but not be seen by the shooters or the incoming ducks. As it turned out, my lads didn't shoot the area that shoot day but just brought in more sacks of bait to "sweeten up the pot." Nor did my lads shoot the area the following shoot day either. Damn, I thought, did my lads see me sneaking around or are they really baiting the area heavily so when Tennessee Ernie Ford, or "The Little Ol' Pea Picker" himself arrived, he would have one hell of a shoot? The following three shoot days were busts as well because no one showed up to shoot the area. By now I was having all kinds of concerns as to why the lads continued to bait the area and didn't even come close to shooting it. As my readers should know by now, it is ok to feed migratory game birds, but you just can't shoot over what you place out for the critters to eat or at those birds flying to or from the area. Hence, there was nothing I could do to my chaps for just baiting the area.

Then one Saturday during a driving rainstorm in the Sacramento Valley, I was sitting in my usual hiding spot on the duck club just in case someone came out to shoot the baited area. That morning, I hit pay dirt big time! Just before daylight, I observed four flashlights coming out from the duck club and begin heading towards my baited blinds. Watching with my binoculars, I counted six chaps coming my way! The air was full of whistling wings and the area that had been baited was full of every kind of puddle duck known to man. You talk about a perfect killing field! Here was one just sitting on a platter waiting to be plucked. To make matters even worse, the birds had been coming unmolested to this baited area for many days. As would be the case in that kind of situation even though being shot at in the present sense, the birds would continue to swarm into the decoys for the free "grits." And when they did, there would be a pitcher's mound sized guy sitting there with a big grin keeping an eye on things. Well, a big wet grin since I had been sitting there for over two hours getting sopping wet in the driving rain. But somehow with the flashlights coming my way, all that storm borne discomfort didn't seem to matter much now...

My six gunners moved off into "twos" and occupied the three closest at hand, baited blinds. It was then I discovered just how slick these outlaw gunners were. When it came time to shoot, only two gunners from one blind shot. Then they sat back down and when the next opportunity came to shoot, two other gunners from another blind would rise up and shoot. Then they would sit back down and the last two gunners would then take their turns. This procedure went on for over an hour during that morning's shoot. Never more than two shooters at a time and no one was using an unplugged shotgun. Their style of shooting would normally not garner any attention from any close at hand "tule creeper" game warden type. Talk about slick! These six shooters had it down pat. They were well on their ways towards shooting one hell of an over limit when they "flipped out the straw onto the playing field that broke the camel's back."

Once again showing a great deal of reserve and moxie, only two men at a time came out to retrieve their ducks. And at first they were so causal, I almost didn't catch it. When one of the lads came to a mallard or Northern pintail, the duck would be picked up in the shallow water of the pond. But when our shooters came to a less than quality duck like a shoveler, wigeon, teal or run of the mill diving duck, they were casually stepped on and pushed into the pond's soft muddy bottom! If I hadn't been carefully watching my lads as they picked up their ducks for final confirmation and identification count for my notes, I would have missed their wanton waste actions slicker than all get out!

Those wasting cracker-bottoms, I fumed. Then I watched the same process being repeated by the other two sets of shooters in the other blinds near the bait. That did it! I boiled. Crawling on my hands and knees, I moved away from my hiding place and through my covering cattails until I could cut off any runners from the duck blind nearest the trail leading to the clubhouse (By crawling away from my great hiding place, I preserved its future use if ever needed again-an old game warden trick). Then I arose out from the stinking marsh of ten thousand years of goose shit and tule roots in order to present my best Robert Redford side and John Wayne grin from the movie, *She Wore a Yellow Ribbon* (one of my favorites).

Man, you talk about setting the hair on the hind ends of my six shooters! Every one of them jumped back into their blinds and out of sight like mice after being spotted by a great horned owl. I guess they thought they could escape being seen by the "Great One" now lumbering across the duck pond in their collective directions like an Asian water buffalo. Well, a "beautiful buffalo" if I might say so myself...

Approaching the first blind, I boomed out in my best John Wayne fashion, "Morning, gents. Terry Grosz, federal agent here. Would all of you go back into the duck pond and retrieve the ducks the mess of you just stomped into the mud. And for those of you who deny such actions or can't for whatever reason find your stomped ducks, it will be a trip to the Colusa County Jail!"

Then I just stood at the first duck blind waiting for compliance. For the longest time no one moved. Then up popped their heads one by one. Following that, each blind sent out one chap to locate the ducks they had stomped into the mud. That took some doing but finally everyone arrived back at their duck blinds with their smashed and muddy, stomped "junk" ducks.

Satisfied, I then boomed out, "Why don't all of you come to this blind. Just make sure when you do, you bring all the ducks you shot this morning with you. Keep in mind when this is all said and done, I will check your blinds for any left behind ducks in this matter as well." Then turning to my two chaps in the first blind, I said, "I would like to check your hunting and driver's licenses, shotguns for plugs, federal duck stamps, and finally, all the birds you have killed this morning."

Looking at the rain soaked faces of my two immediate gunners, I was disappointed that I did not see the face of the great country singer, Tennessee Ernie Ford. By then my other four shooters were present at the first blind and I commenced checking out their licenses and gear as well. I did not recognize the "Little Ol' Pea Picker" himself in that group of faces either. However, for my own reasons, I did not return their driver's licenses at that moment.

Finishing with the routine checks, I said, "Lads, this area is baited with barley. To do that and shoot over it is a violation of state and federal hunting regulations. Anyone here care to let me know which one of you lads baited the area over this last two week period?" Those words indicating I knew when the area had been baited struck my chaps like a thunderclap.

There was a lot of looking back and forth at each other and finally one lad raised his hand and said, "I did it, officer."

"I know better than that," I quietly said. "I have been here every night this area has been baited, and I recognize three of you standing here as some of those who placed out the bait. Now, do you lads want to try again in the memory department as to who baited this club with at least six hundred pounds of barley?"

There was more eyeball searching and then all six of the men raised their hands like little kids will do in school when they needed to go to the bathroom.

"Thank you, gentlemen, for "manning up" to your guilt," I said. "Now, gentlemen, I am going out into the pond and collect some more bait samples. I want all of you to watch so you can see I am not trying to pull the wool over your eyes." Grabbing my bait scoop, I went out into the area where the barley was calf deep and made a scoop. For the most part my bait scoop came up full of barley!

Walking back to my lads, I asked with a knowing smile, "Any doubt in you folks' minds that the area is baited?" Six hanging heads indicated they had collectively seen enough.

"Where is the owner of this club?" I asked.

"Mr. Ford is the owner of this duck club and he is still back at the club. He has a touch of the flu and declined to come out this morning in the rain and all," said a Mr. Roger Davis.

"Ok, gentlemen, why don't the seven of us return back to your duck club? There once out of the rain and wind, I can issue all of you citations for taking migratory game birds over a baited area in violation of federal law," I said as the cold winter rain ran off the end of my most beautiful large Roman nose...

Twenty minutes later, we arrived back at the duck club. Once inside, the men shucked their wet gear and changed out into something dry. Then one of the men went to the bar and poured himself a stiff drink of Jack Daniels. "That looks good, Charlie. Pour about a three-fingered one for me as well, will you?" asked Roger Davis. Before it was all over, each man had one, if not two, drinks of what "Mr. Daniels" had to offer.

"Would you like one, officer?" asked Roger Davis.

"No, sir," I replied. "Any other time I would, but I am still on duty," I responded knowing full well the crap that would have hit the fan if I had taken a drink, especially in light of me writing all of them for shooting over a baited area and taking over limits as well.

About then a fairly short man (hell, most everyone is shorter than me) walked into the main club area from a series of backrooms. It was "The Little Ol' Pea Picker" himself or the great country singer, Mr. Tennessee Ernie Ford (one of my favorites).

"What is going on here, Roger?" asked Mr. Ford.

There was a long silence as all the other men looked at Roger. "We are all getting a ticket for shooting over bait and killing too many ducks," said Roger with a bright red face from embarrassment.

"Is that the case, officer?" Mr. Ford asked.

"Yes, sir, Mr. Ford. Your duck club is heavily baited and if anyone on this club tries to shoot over that area while the birds are moving to and fro in the feeding process, they will be ticketed as well. In fact, Mr. Ford, it won't be legal to shoot on your club until ten days have passed after all the bait which is currently acting as the lure and attractant is gone," I replied.

"Then you need to write these law breaking son of a bitches because they all know better," said Mr. Ford.

Turning to Roger, Mr. Ford said," I will speak to you about this, Roger, after this officer has finished and is gone!"

Then turning to me, Mr. Ford said, "You might as well as check my licenses since you are here as well, officer."

"I don't need to, Mr. Ford, because I didn't see you hunting," I replied.

"Naw, go ahead and check it anyway. I haven't been checked by you law enforcement rascals in over ten years. And since I am a taxpayer, I would like you to check my license."

Obliging Mr. Ford, I discovered he lacked a federal duck stamp! Had he been hunting, he would have gotten a ticket for that as well. Man, you talk about an embarrassed man. Mr. Ford was truly one that day after insisting I check his license. Especially after discovering he would have been in violation for not having a federal duck stamp in possession as well as shooting over a baited area, had he been hunting migratory waterfowl with the others.

It wasn't but a short time later that Mr. Ford

had a three-fingered drink of Jack Daniels after his "close call"

I never again ever had any trouble with "The Little Ol' Pea Picker's" duck club. I always found Mr. Ford to be legal and a gentleman after that run-in with some of his friends and six hundred pounds of barley. Oh well, the remaining ducks had some good eats after that, and they didn't have to worry about getting a face full of shot in the process either. As for my earlier run in with my Green Beret, like that with Mr. Ford, I quickly forgot the occasion because of other work priorities.

In 1973, I was visited at my home by a Sergeant David Adams, Green Beret, who was back from Vietnam recuperating from a serious leg wound. He had looked me up at the behest of Sgt. Dale Hoffman, the Green Beret I had earlier caught poaching sandhill cranes with a hunting rifle. During that meeting, Sgt. Adams gave me a chunk of shrapnel taken from Sgt. Hoffman's body! It was also during that meeting, Adams advised that Hoffman, his best friend, had shared his story of being caught by me as he had practiced his sniper trade in the Sacramento Valley. Dale had asked his best friend, Sgt. Adams, who was seriously wounded in battle, to look me up when he went back to California to recuperate.

Hoffman figured once Sgt. Adams was home recuperating, he could look me up and give me that piece of shrapnel. As Adams told me, the medic had just dug the piece of shrapnel out from Sgt. Hoffman's badly bleeding and torn thigh. A wound that was considered highly tissue destructive but not fatal. According to Adams, Hoffman looked at the piece of shrapnel and just laughed. Then he handed it to Sgt. Adams (who was badly wounded in that fight) to give to me in case he was unable to do so himself. A short time later, Hoffman bled out and died from an undiscovered leaking and torn femoral artery that finally ruptured! He had earlier told Adams that he had promised he would send me a souvenir and wanted to keep his word, since I had kept mine by not informing his commanding officer of his poaching incident and subsequent prosecution. I have often wondered if maybe I should have told his commanding officer so he would have been kept home and away from his "call to destiny"

   I still have that piece of shrapnel today among my collection of other historical artifacts I have gathered over the years and now the living memory that goes with it... As I see it, we all are walking between the two great eternities from the genesis of our being to the exodus of our souls. And in so doing, we all are looking for the extended hand of God... I hope Sgt. Hoffman found that extended hand of God... Thank you for your service to our country, Sergeant Hoffman...

Excerpt From Wildlife Dies Without Making a Sound, Vol. I:

CHAPTER ONE
TULE LAKE

SOUTH OF KLAMATH FALLS, Oregon, just across the California state line, lays the Tule Lake National Wildlife Refuge. It was created in 1928 in the Klamath Basin primarily as a haven for migratory waterfowl and is approximately 39,000 marshy, open, watered and landed acres in size. In the fall, this refuge acts as an important stopping off point for exhausted migratory birds traveling from their nesting grounds in Canada and the high Arctic in route to their wintering grounds in the Southern United States, Central and South America. In the early spring of the year, the refuge once again becomes an important stopping off and feeding point for migrating birds heading back north to their ancestral nesting grounds in Canada and the Arctic region.

To early man, Tule Lake and the Lower Klamath

Lake area located immediately to the west, were important hunting grounds for ducks, geese, swans, and numerous species of shorebirds; important hunting grounds because of their vast, easily accessible bounty of meat, eggs, and, in some cases, feathers. During modern times, these and the adjacent landed locations have remained important areas for migratory waterfowl, upland game, and, now, the growing of numerous varieties of agricultural seed crops. Those waste grains left behind after harvest are exactly the types of high- energy foods needed by many waterfowl species of migratory birds for continuing their long and exhausting trips to and from their nesting and wintering grounds.

It was into the Tule Lake National Wildlife Refuge complex that I was sent on a waterfowl law enforcement training assignment as a rookie California State Fish and Game Warden in the fall of 1966. Fresh out of Humboldt State College in Areata with an advanced degree in wildlife management and the law enforcement-training academy in southern California, I had just begun my career in the unique, often dangerous, and adventurous world of wildlife law enforcement as a state fish and game warden. There I began my career all bright-eyed, bushy-tailed, and soon to discover, dumber than a box of old moss covered river rocks in a creek bottom, in the "how and why" of conservation law enforcement. But that didn't deter or slow me down. Regardless of my soon to be recognized shortcomings, I still felt like I was going to show the world how it was done. But as I quickly learned, instead of showing the world how it was done, I was just as quickly shown many of life's valuable lessons in wildlife law enforcement and human behavior, including the ever-present tenants of the good, the bad, and the ugly. I rapidly came to understand that sometimes "you eat the bear and sometimes the bear eats you" when it came to living life on the wild side in the world of wildlife law enforcement, either as the "chasee" or the "chaser"...

Kissing Donna, my bride then of just three years out of a now more than 51 years of marriage, goodbye early one morning, I shoe horned my 6-foot 4-inch, 320-pound, absolutely beautiful and magnificent carcass behind the steering wheel of my dinky, one mouse powered, Mercury Comet patrol car. Hell, that species of vehicle was so small, I could have used one for each foot. I then headed north to Tule with great anticipation on my first big waterfowl task force law enforcement assignment. That assignment was to proceed to the Tule Lake National Wildlife Refuge area for the opening weekend of duck and goose season to enforce the state and federal waterfowl hunting regulations. Simple enough assignment. Shouldn't he any big deal for the world's largest and most beautiful game warden, said the spider to the fly...

Hurtling north in my mechanized roller skate-sized patrol car, I took stock. On my left breast proclaiming for the whole world to see I wore a shiny silver star, No. 220, California's newest minted game warden. Around my more than amply sized waist, I wore a black Sam Brown Gun Belt holding my handcuffs, drop pouches holding my spare cartridges, and a monster sized Smith and Wesson, Model 29, 6V£-inch .44 magnum. At that time, it was the world's most powerful commercially made handgun. After much practice, I became a crack shot with that hand cannon using full house, 240- grain loads. What more could the world's largest and most beautiful game warden want than the biggest hand cannon available? Man, if I would have puffed up any larger with all my self-importance, I would need a shoehorn and a bucket of Crisco to get my now garbage can sized head out from inside of my one mouse power propelled roller skate sized patrol car. Have any of you readers gotten the feeling from the above verbiage that I was a dyed in the wool %-ton Dodge pickup man all the way?

Hours later, I turned east off State Highway 97 onto Highway 161. There I proceeded down what is locally called "State Line Road" toward the small, historic Town of Tule Lake, California. Moments later, I was driving alongside a large watered and marshy area immediately south of the highway on the Lower Klamath National Wildlife Refuge boundary. The fall migration was fully underway and I had never seen so many water loving species of birds. The watered areas were literally alive with numerous species of ducks, geese, and every make and model of shorebird numbering in the tens of thousands. Amazed at the numbers and variety of wildlife I was seeing, I quickly realized that this house was not made with human hands. Following that revelation, I was not prepared for the next scene greeting my now large as dinner plate, rookie eyes.

As I continued driving east on the State Line Road, the south side of the highway outside the refuge boundary was literally strewn, bumper-to-bumper, with hundreds of parked vehicles because there were no restriction on the numbers of hunters in that historic area in those days. Those vehicles were scattered and parked end to end and every other which way in between under the sun. Cars, campers, house trailers, tents, and such were all strewn about apparently waiting for the much-anticipated opening day of waterfowl season. Intermixed with those hordes of the evidence of man were dozens of barking dogs and literally thousands of human beings. There had to be at least 10,000 people along that short stretch of highway awaiting the opening day of waterfowl season. Man, you talk about giving me a bad case of the "big eye." I remembered that there were only six visiting state game wardens and what few numbers of federal officers that had been scraped up assigned to control such an unruly looking mob once the waterfowl hunting season began just hours away. At that moment, in light of the hordes of humanity I was observing, I didn't feel quite so big, wonderful, and vainglorious. I was now beginning to see why Custer had better odds than our little group of officers sent there to enforce the wildlife laws of the land come the opening day of the waterfowl hunting season. Just to give you readers a slice of the real world at that time, there were only 178 United States Game Management Agents or, as they were commonly called, federal game wardens, in existence for all of the United States. And by the time you got rid of the sick, lame, and lazy, you might have had a third of that number with their boots on the ground on any given day. There goes that Custer thing again...

I headed east to the Tule Lake National Wildlife Refuge and then on to what was in those days called the state house. If I remember correctly, it was a large home owned by the State of California to house visiting wildlife personnel on assignments to that historic area. Entering, I met the other senior officers assigned to that waterfowl enforcement detail including the single resident Tule Lake game warden.

The Tule Lake fish and game warden was a tall drink of water and an older chap named Robbie Robinson. As I was soon to discover, he was a well-respected officer and a man who had a genuine smile backed by a firm handshake, which in and of itself, told me a lot about the person. To all my readers, the strength of an individual handshake is a gesture that I read a lot into and still value highly to this very day. Once all the visiting officers were gathered together, Robbie went over the court appearance dates and times, individual geographic patrol assignments, recent waterfowl regulation changes, species shooting restrictions, historical violation prone areas, and up to date information relating to the major waterfowl concentration areas. Particularly emphasized were those areas holding numerous species of diving ducks that could not legally be taken during the upcoming waterfowl season. Since we were so limited in officer numbers and Robbie expected around 30,000 hunters for the opening-day shindig, he decided we should all work individually. That way we could cover more territory and at least give the illusion of a game warden behind every bush. Somehow even being a rookie, I got the feeling that dog of a "game warden behind every bush" theory was not going to hunt. I think General Custer in 1876 had the same idea about splitting up his forces before going into battle, didn't he? How did that work out in the history books?

As was typical in those days when any of us limited numbers of game wardens had a chance to get together, there was a big feed since most game wardens are damn good cooks, eager eaters, and many drank a lot of good whiskey. That gathering of those members of the "Thin Green Line" at Tule Lake that year was historically no different. I finally broke off from the celebrating around ten in the evening, went to my room, set my alarm for four in the morning, and went to bed. Went to bed with just an inkling of what I was soon to be facing the next day in the way of new life adventures in the world of wildlife law enforcement with more than a jug full of rookie enthusiasm. Suffice to say, I spent a rather restless night.

INDIAN TOM LAKE

To be frank, I was awake before four in the morning but I waited until my alarm rang before getting up. Excited about my first major upcoming waterfowl law enforcement detail, I bailed out of bed, showered, uniformed up, and lit out. As I walked by my still deeply snoozing counterparts in the common sleeping area, hardly anyone was moving. I guess they had too much of John Barleycorn to drink the night before and were now paying the price. But I was young, immortal, in fairly good shape for a big man, and, as I had already discovered, had two guardian angels to watch over my miserable carcass. And in case you readers are wondering, yes, I had two guardian angels because I was twice as big as nearly everyone else in wildlife law enforcement in those days and, one could say, dumber than the average Yogi Bear. So now you understand my need for double angelic protection and guidance. With those forces in play, I was more than ready to "hit the decks a-running and spin the guns around" as the old Marty Robbins' song about sinking the German battleship Bismarck rattled around in my mostly empty head. So with that, out I went into the moonlit morning with a grin as wide as the mighty Mississippi River and as full of myself as that river is at flood stage during the spring runoff.

God, it felt great to be alive and a wildlife officer on a mission that was soon to turn into the passion of a lifelong vision quest. Even at that hour, I could already hear many hundreds of whistling wings moving to and fro overhead. It was almost as if the critters knew what was coming and were trying to find that special sanctuary in which to lite down and remain safe from a lethal stream of lead shot. Heading to my patrol car, I opened up the trunk, removed and slipped into a pair of cold hip boots. Then off I went to my previously assigned patrol zone, namely a fair-sized body of water named Indian Tom Lake.

Diving ducks historically favored Indian Tom Lake in those days. To all my unwashed readers out there, diving ducks can be a bear to identify especially when they are zipping along on the wing at fifty miles per hour. That goes double for similar species of diving ducks like redheads, canvasbacks, and ring-necked ducks when they are in their various stages of molts which makes all of them look like gray or brown ducks. I had been assigned that part of the Tule Lake waterfowl-hunting complex because of my recognized expertise in diving duck identification. Recognized expertise because I had B. S. and M. S. degrees in wildlife management from Humboldt State College, a nationally recognized leader in that field of study, had done my thesis on a species of maritime diving duck, and had taught waterfowl identification in college lab classes.

That year, Indian Tom Lake sported large

concentrations of diving ducks called canvasbacks. Canvasback ducks are considered a fine eating duck but, because of drought on the nesting grounds, wetland drainage on their prairie nesting habitat, and many years of commercially over-gunning the species, was now a closed hunting season critter due to its low population numbers. In other words, it was illegal to take any canvasbacks under the state and federal waterfowl hunting regulations that year in California.

Backing my patrol car up into a small sagebrush-covered draw alongside the lake, I lowered my tall dead giveaway whiplash car- to-car radio antenna and got out my camouflage parachute. Soon my patrol car was covered so no one would at first glance be any the wiser that a Tule creeper was around. Getting out a lawn chair from the backseat, I sat it up out of sight behind the patrol car, yet in a location where I could watch a wide expanse of the lake to my front and the shooters in that area once they arrived. Lastly, I ate my usual game warden breakfast consisting of hard Italian salami and a Coke®. Sugar from the Coke quickly fired up my boilers and the fat from the salami would give me a day's energy without hunger. Great game warden grits when one is young. They are not so good when one is older than dirt as I am now with clogged arteries and a more than respectable potbelly.

Finally approaching legal shooting hours, I put on my hunting coat to camouflage my uniform shirt, badge, and sidearm in order to look like any ordinary duck hunter once I began moving around. Then I grabbed an empty shotgun to further look the part. With that, I headed for a bunch of flashlights playing off the water by a nearby rocky point. As expected, the flashlights soon turned into a hunting party of three men setting out their decoys on the lake. Secreting myself out of sight in a clump of volcanic boulders and sagebrush where I still had a line of sight view of my party of hunters, I settled into the depths of my hunting coat for its warmth and comfort.

By now, I could hear people shooting twenty minutes before legal shooting time behind me in another warden's assigned area. I hoped one of my guys was close at hand to greet those early illegal shooters. Early shooting may not seem like much to my readers who are non-duck hunters, but it is not a good thing. That shooting disturbance spooks the other nearby birds off their resting areas earlier than normal and accounts for many birds being shot at, crippled or killed in the darkness before the dawn when they fly over the gunners secreted below. By its very nature, early shooting equates to many birds being lost in the darkness and terrain when killed. Additionally, it makes for higher crippling rates because of the poor light conditions in which the shots are taken. Lastly, shooting early makes bird identification almost impossible. Particularly as it relates to their sex (some ducks are protected based on the sex of the species) or because several species of diving ducks are totally protected. All in all, it is a wasteful and illegal practice. Within minutes, those waterfowl frightened by the distant early shooters began arriving at my lake by the thousands as was validated by their huge numbers of whistling wings and searching calls heard overhead in the darkness. As was typical for birds not shot at for many months because of the earlier closed season, confusion now reigned. That confusion usually translated into many birds flying low to the ground or watered areas like they normally did during the closed season when danger was not present. And now once they were low to the deck, they were within easy gunning range. Soon shots began ringing out all along the shoreline of Indian Tom Lake as I crawled into my binoculars eagerly watching the morning's events rapidly unfolding around me.

About then, seven ducks skimming just over the water slipped into my three nearby hunters' set of decoys. All three men rose in unison and emptied their shotguns into the now swimming ducks. Not a single duck rose into the air in alarm after that spate of shooting had subsided. Looking at my watch, my three shooters had shot 18 minutes before legal shooting hours. That meant later on they would be receiving citations for early shooting waterfowl in violation of state and federal laws. Then four more species of low flying ducks landed in my three hunters' decoy spread. Because of the darkness of the early hour allowed for hunting waterfowl and the speed in which they arrived, the only way I could identify those species of ducks as diving ducks was by the way they were flying with their fast wing beats. Again, my three shooters poured forth a lethal hail of lead shot (lead shot was legal in those days but is illegal today because of its toxicity if ingested as grit by feeding waterfowl). Nary a swimming duck from that little flock took to wing. By now, the air over the lake was full of flocks of confused ducks and several smaller bunches of white-fronted geese which were identified by their larger sizes, different flight patterns and unique trilling calls. Within moments, shooting around Indian Tom Lake was like that of the degree and intensity from the Union forces at General George Pickett's men as they charged the federal positions across open fields in the face of hundreds of firing cannons at Gettysburg in the summer of 1863.

Legal shooting times in the mornings for

migratory game birds is one half hour before sunrise. That regulation, based on my 32 years of field experience, is stupid and criminal. Most waterfowl hunters struggle with bird identification even when the bird is lying dead in their hands during broad daylight, much less when the bird is steaming by at forty miles per hour in poor, early morning light. Then throw into that sulfurous mix, molting diving duck species appearing to be nothing more than brown or gray ducks. Hell, numerous conservation officers of today have trouble identifying many species of ducks in the dark. By placing that species identification burden on the shoulders of a large number of uneducated sportsmen in bird identification, one must realize there will be mistakes and, in those errors, normally protected birds will be killed. So why have a shooting time that by its very nature encourages illegal taking? That shooting time regulation was a tough one for me to figure out using the common sense constant. I never shot at waterfowl one half hour before sunrise even in light of my advanced wildlife degrees, great eyes, and having taught waterfowl identification at state and federal training sessions for 27 years during the latter part of my career. It is just too difficult to correctly identify many waterfowl, especially those fast flying species of diving ducks, one half hour before sunrise. Then factor in bad weather, fog or the emotion and thrill of the hunt. These are all combinations for one hell of a legal wreck. But, I digress...

By now it was light enough for me to identify the close at hand ducks being killed around me. Checking the dead ducks floating in the water in front of my three shooters with my binoculars revealed trouble with a capital T. Every dead bird in the decoys appeared to be a totally protected species of duck called a canvasback! Not wanting my shooters to kill any more of the highly protected birds, I stepped forth to stop the action and enforce the law of the land. I slunk down to my shooters from behind. Yes, you darn disbelieving readers, a guy my size could slink with the best of them. They didn't even see me approaching until it was too late.

"Morning, Boys. How's the shooting?" I asked, trying hard to be neighborly in light of the serious numbers of canvasback problems floating deader than a car hit chicken in their decoys.

The three men whirled around in their sagebrush blind, startled by my voice, surprise appearance, and closeness. "I guess it is alright," said the tallest one, as he squinted at me in the light of the rising sun at my back to see if he recognized me.

Not wanting to lose the rest of my morning when I needed to be out and about checking other sportsmen, I cut to the chase. "Boys, I am a game warden and have been sitting right behind you since before dawn. The three of you shot early at that first group of seven ducks sliding into your decoys. You know, the ones you lads swatted on the water, killing all seven." Walking closer, I opened up the front of my hunting coat so they could see my badge. Continuing, I said, "I need you lads to empty your shotguns for me, please. When you do, be sure their barrels are pointed in a safe direction. I don't want anyone hurt with an accidental discharge. Then a couple of you need to go out and retrieve those 11 ducks floating on the water in your decoys. When that is done, I will need to check your ducks, hunting licenses, duck stamps and shotguns to make sure they are plugged in accordance with the hunting regulations."

State and federal regulations require anyone hunting migratory game birds such as waterfowl, to use a shotgun capable of holding only three shells. Many pump action or semi-automatic shotguns were manufactured to have magazines capable of holding anywhere from four to five shells, so sportsmen could also hunt endemic bird species where shotguns without plugs were allowed. However for a shotgun to be legal in most circumstances when hunting migratory game birds, they must be capable of holding only three shells that can readily be fired. Or simply put, one shell in the firing chamber and no more than two readily available rounds in the magazine. To plug most shotguns making them capable of only having two shells in the active firing position in the magazine, a wooden or plastic plug is inserted to limit the number of available rounds. That restricts the number of usable shells, hence a legally plugged shotgun as required by law.

However in today's world due to the ever expanding lesser snow goose population, one control measure used during special hunting seasons is to allow hunters the use of unplugged shotguns, coinciding with larger than normal daily bag limits, in order to control the numbers of such species. Goose populations need to be reduced because of their high numbers and collateral overcrowding on the Arctic nesting grounds with the resultant habitat destruction such crowding causes. Habitat destruction on the Arctic nesting grounds that is so expansive, its evidence can be observed from outer space. Hence the use of hunting as a wildlife management tool when it comes to controlling lesser snow goose populations through very liberal daily bag limits and the utilization of more effective killing techniques such as unplugged shotguns. But other than that, plugged shotguns are the law of the land when taking migratory game birds to add the element of fair chase and biologically control the level of species harvest.

Without another word, the men emptied their shotguns and laid them down. Then all three walked out into the shallow water retrieving their floating ducks. When they returned, I asked, "What time did legal shooting hours begin this morning?"

The lads hemmed and hawed a bit and then all three gave me different times as to when legal shooting hours started. In other words, none of them had bothered to check the legal shooting times tables that were freely distributed at every sporting goods store and U.S. Post Office in those days. I gave them the correct shooting time and then asked if they were wearing watches. That is a good game warden tactic. Anyone not wearing a watch doesn't have a legal leg to stand on when it comes to early or late shooting legal issues. Two hunters were wearing watches and one wasn't. And the two wearing watches were different from each other time wise by eight minutes from the correct time. Another good game warden tactic for all you rookie game warden readers out there. If their watches are incorrect, they have a weak legal leg to stand on when it comes to early or late shooting offenses. By doing the watch thing, many times that will show that the lads aren't really paying attention to legal shooting hours. Often that little field procedure will cut short any time related arguments later on in a court of law if that offense later rises to that legal level in a court of law.

Then I went over to the pile of ducks now lying at our feet. "Do any of you know what species of ducks we have here that you lads shot earlier and just brought to shore?"

The men quietly examined all the ducks and then identified the ducks as redheads, which was a similar looking species to a canvasback but not a closed-season or totally protected species that year.

"No, Lads, you have 11 drake and hen canvasbacks here. As you should know, that is a protected species this year since their population numbers are so low and are continuing to decline, making them a species of special concern."

Boy, you talk about instant explosions of denial. "You don't know what you are talking about. Them is all redheads, and I know my ducks. Hell, I have been hunting ducks since I was 11 with my old man, and he was a stickler on being legal," said the tallest of the three men. The other two chimed right in supporting the taller one. Not surprisingly, I now had a potential game bird identification issue in the making.

"Here, Boys, let me show you the differences," I said. With that, I gave the lads a lesson on the lakeshore about identification differences between canvasbacks and redheads. That was also followed with me giving the lads a Ducks at a Distance illustrated pamphlet showing them the differences between the two species. I also explained that I had a master's degree in wildlife management and had been a student instructor in the science of waterfowl identification while in college. I hoped that would settle down their hackles. With those revelations, their hackles finally went down somewhat. Seeing that I had made my point as well as possible, I checked their licenses and duck stamps and made sure their shotguns were legally plugged.

Not wanting to waste any more time, I issued the three men citations for early shooting and taking protected migratory game birds, To Wit, eleven canvasbacks. Thanking the lads for their cooperation, I hefted those remaining ducks not placed in the game bag of my hunting coat for easier carrying back to my patrol car, left them a seizure tag for their birds that I had seized as my evidence of the violation, and left. They each later paid $61 for their early shooting violations and $150 for jointly taking a protected species during the closed season. That was the legal process during those times since I could not identify who had shot what in the overall numbers of canvasbacks. That being the case, I was allowed to charge each shooter with the full number of illegally taken birds.

As my lake's waterfowl hunters continued shooting around me, I hustled back to my patrol car. Placing the ducks just seized in my patrol car's trunk in an ice chest for safekeeping, I hot-footed it around the lake away from of my still smarting, closed-season canvasback shooting chaps. That way, I figured no one on the other side of the lake would recognize me as a game warden or know I was out and about, especially since my recently pinched chaps hadn't had time to pull a Paul Revere. You know, telling the other hunters nearby there was a game warden in country. And once again, I could continue being effective in enforcing the waterfowl hunting regulations. The rest of that first day was a blur. By 4:00 p.m., I had written five more lads for taking closed-season canvasbacks. Into that citation mix also went several others for taking over-limits of ducks, six for killing protected shorebirds, and four for not having a federal duck stamp in their immediate possession.

Anyone 16 years or older hunting migratory waterfowl must have in his or her possession a federal duck stamp with his or her name signed across the face of the stamp in ink. The signature across the face validates that stamp and in theory, precludes one from loaning that item to another unscrupulous waterfowl hunter trying to circumvent the law. Use of another's duck stamp is a fairly common practice in today's world because of the somewhat high cost of that stamp. However, 98 percent of the proceeds from the federal duck stamp sales are used in land acquisition for waterfowl, which other animal species find beneficial as well.

With the issuance of twenty citations for a day's work on Indian Tom Lake, I "more than paid for the gas and oil" which is an old time game wardens' saying showing that one's efforts for the day more than paid for the cost of the gas and oil used during that patrol. In the process, I made sure a number of waterfowl hunters that morning figured there was a game warden behind every bush, and in the instant case, a handsome, wonderful, and beautiful one at that.

About the Author

TERRY GROSZ EARNED his bachelor's degree in 1964 and his master's in wildlife management in 1966 from Humboldt State College in California. He was a California State Fish and Game Warden, based first in Eureka and then Colusa, from 1966 to 1970. He then joined the U.S. Fish & Wildlife Service, and served in California as a U.S. Game Management Agent and Special Agent until 1974. After that, he was promoted to Senior Resident Agent and placed in charge of North and South Dakota for two years, followed by three years as Senior Special Agent in Washington, D.C., with the Endangered Species Program, Division of Law Enforcement. While in Washington, he also served as Foreign Liaison Officer.

In 1979, he became the Assistant Special Agent in Charge in Minneapolis, Minnesota. Two years later in 1981, he was promoted to Special Agent in Charge and transferred to Denver, Colorado, where he remained until his retirement in 1998.

He has earned many awards and honors during his career, including, from the U.S. Fish & Wildlife Service, the Meritorious Service Award in 1996, and Top Ten Award in 1987 as one of the top ten employees (in an agency of some 9,000). The Fish & Wildlife Foundation presented him with the Guy Bradley Award in 1989, and in 1993 he received the Conservation Achievement Award for Law Enforcement from the National Wildlife Federation.

Unity College in Maine awarded Grosz an honorary doctorate in environmental stewardship in 2001. His first book, Wildlife Wars, was published in 1999 and won the National Outdoor Book Award for Nature and Environment. He has had ten memoirs published since then—*For Love of Wildness, Defending Our Wildlife Heritage, A Sword for Mother Nature, No Safe Refuge, The Thin Green Line, Genesis of a Duck Cop, Slaughter in the Sacramento Valley, Wildlife on the Edge, Wildlife's Quiet War,* and *Wildlife Dies Without Making a Sound* (in two volumes) —and his Mountain Men Novels — *Crossed Arrows, Curse of the Spanish*

Gold, The Saga of Harlan Waugh, The Adventures of the Brothers Dent, and *The Adventures of Hatchet Jack.*

Several of Grosz's stories were broadcast as a docudrama on the Animal Planet network in 2003.

Terry Grosz lives in Colorado.

www.ingramcontent.com/pod-product-compliance
Lightning Source LLC
Chambersburg PA
CBHW031417150426
43191CB00006B/310